MUSICAL WORLDS IN YOGYAKARTA

Southeast Asia Mediated

This series considers media forms and practices, processes of mediation, and the complex evolving and intersecting media ecologies that characterize Southeast Asia whether in contemporary or historical circumstances.

Editors: Bart Barendregt (Leiden University) and Ariel Heryanto (Australian National University).

VERHANDELINGEN
VAN HET KONINKLIJK INSTITUUT
VOOR TAAL-, LAND- EN VOLKENKUNDE

281

MAX M. RICHTER

MUSICAL WORLDS
IN YOGYAKARTA

KITLV Press
Leiden
2012

Published by:
KITLV Press
Koninklijk Instituut voor Taal-, Land- en Volkenkunde
(Royal Netherlands Institute of Southeast Asian and Caribbean Studies)
P.O. Box 9515
2300 RA Leiden
The Netherlands
website: www.kitlv.nl
e-mail: kitlvpress@kitlv.nl

KITLV is an institute of the Royal Netherlands Academy of Arts and Sciences (KNAW)

KONINKLIJKE NEDERLANDSE
AKADEMIE VAN WETENSCHAPPEN

Cover: samgobin.nl

ISBN 978 90 6718 390 1

© 2012 Koninklijk Instituut voor Taal-, Land- en Volkenkunde

KITLV Press applies the Creative Commons Attribution-NonCommercial-NoDerivs 3.0 Unported License (http://creativecommons.org/licenses/by-nc-nd/3.0/) to selected books, published in or after January 2011.

thors retain ownership of the copyright for their articles, but permit anyone unrestricted use and distribution within the s of this license.

d editions manufactured in the Netherlands

Contents

ACKNOWLEDGEMENTS	vii
GLOSSARY OF SPECIAL TERMS	ix
INTRODUCTION: APPROACHING MUSICAL LIFE IN EARLY POST-SOEHARTO YOGYAKARTA	1
Musical worlds and their genres	10
Theory and concepts	21
Research methods	24
Overview	26

PART 1 MUSIC AND THE STREET

	BACKGROUND	31
	Cultural capital and its spatial variants	34
	In-group and inter-group social capital	36
1	SOSROWIJAYAN AND ITS STREET WORKERS	39
	Roadsides and alleyways	41
	Becak drivers	43
	The Sosro Bahu stand	45
	Street guides	49
	Sriwisata and the Sosro Boys	50
2	MUSICAL FORMS AND SPACES	53
	Mobile *pengamen*	54
	Street-worker *tongkrongan*	60
	Transweb	61
	Opposite Resto	64
3	MUSIC GROUPS	69
	The Sekar Wuyung group	69
	The Shower street guide band	72
	Shower at Resto and the Sosro Bahu after-party	74
	CONCLUSION	77

PART 2 HABITUS AND PHYSICALITY

BACKGROUND   83
    Habitus, gender, and socialisation   84
    Three forms of musical physicalisation   86

4 DETACHMENT ENGAGEMENT   89
    Kampung transitions   89
    From hotel gamelan to *kafe* pop   94

5 OTHER WORLDS AND SEXUALISATION   103
    Kampung *jatilan* and Kridosono metal/electronic   103
    Campursari/dangdut and *jalanan*/rock in the kampung   108
    Dangdut shows and pub rock   113

CONCLUSION   117

PART 3 STATE POWER AND MUSICAL COSMOPOLITANISM

BACKGROUND   123
    The bureaucratic field   125
    Grounded cosmopolitanism   126

6 REGIONAL PARLIAMENT   131
    Awards night *campursari*   132
    Awakening Day rock and reggae   135
    Independence Day *wayang kulit*   138

7 ARMED FORCES   143
    Campursari at an army battalion   144
    Music *jalanan* at the Air Force Academy   148

8 UNIVERSITIES   155
    The State Institute of Islamic Studies   156
    Gadjah Mada University   160
    Sunday mornings on the boulevard   161
    Hangouts, capital conversions, activities units   164
    Large-scale musical performance   167

CONCLUSION   171

CONCLUSION: *CAMPURSARI* AND *JALANAN* AT THE SULTAN'S PALACE   175

BIBLIOGRAPHY   187

INDEX   205

Acknowledgements

First and foremost I wish to thank my wife and partner, Dr. Tina Kalivas, for her love and support through the long process from planning my doctoral fieldwork to completing this monograph. Secondly I would like to thank my PhD supervisor, Professor Joel S. Kahn, for his invaluable advice and guidance, and also the School of Social Sciences at La Trobe University for the funding and collegial support given me during that time. Also from La Trobe University, Dr. Wendy Mee provided helpful co-supervision, and Dr. John Goldlust kindly proofread a late draft of the monograph. Third, countless people in Yogyakarta were friendly and shared their knowledge, experiences and ideas openly with me. Of these, I would particularly like to express my appreciation to Tyas Madhyatama Pashupati Rana, Nowo Ksvara Koesbini, and Ipeong Purwaningsih. Fourth, my PhD examiners, along with the ISEAS and KITLV reviewers, provided constructive advice on various aspects of the monograph. Dr. Bart Barendregt has been especially important in this regard. Fifth, I wish to thank the Anthropology Program at Monash University, and in particular Dr. Penny Graham, for the very important financial support and assistance with intellectual focus I received through the final stages of producing the monograph. Finally, I would like to offer a general expression of gratitude to the great many friends, family and colleagues past and present who have in one way or other helped to bring this book to fruition.

Glossary of special terms

abangan	an *aliran* social grouping, characterised by 'village sensibilities' and a syncretic or 'nominal' form of Islam (from the Arabic *aba'an*, a practicing but non-strict Muslim)
aliran	literally 'stream' or 'current', refers to the *abangan*, *priyayi* and *santri* social groupings in Java that Geertz (1960) identified based on occupational orientation and 'world outlook'
anak jalanan	street child/'street kid'
angkringan	portable tea and snack/meal stall
Astro Band	a *pengamen* group that performed regularly on Malioboro Street and elsewhere in downtown Yogyakarta
Bar Borobudur	a ranch-style pub near Sosrowijayan featuring loud live rock music
becak	two-seater tricycle pedicab
campursari	literally 'mixed essences', a musical genre that became very popular in central and east Java in the mid-1990s. *Campursari* combines gamelan ensembles with western diatonic instruments such as bass guitar, hi-tech keyboards and saxophone, and regional and national forms and instruments including *kroncong* ukuleles and *dangdut* drum.
dangdut	major Indonesian popular music genre variously associated with urban lower classes, nationalism and an Islamic ethic. Many of *dangdut*'s musical elements grew out of *melayu* ensembles, but it broadly comprises Indian *kanerva* pattern rhythms on a tabla or a *kendang* drum; flutes and keyboards played with Hindustani-flavoured lilts; and heavy-metal guitar.
dangdut Jawa	*dangdut* music with Java-specific features, these most often being song lyrics in Javanese
DPRD	Dewan Perwakilan Rakyat Daerah; Regional Parliament

| *Glossary of special terms*

electone	hi-tech programmable keyboard, also sometimes called *organ tunggal*, named after the Yamaha trademarked electronic organs of the same name
gambus	a pear-shaped lute of Arabian origin; features in Malay/Islamic orchestras often known as *orkes gambus*
habitus	concept developed by Pierre Bourdieu that conveys the idea that people's dispositions, perceptions of life chances, and habituated physical movements are products of deeply embedded social structures formed through (especially early) life experiences
Islamic Institute	State Institute of Islamic Studies (IAIN, Institut Agama Islam Negeri) in Yogyakarta; became the State Islamic University (UIN, Universitas Islam Negeri) in 2003
jalanan	of the street; having the character of the streets
jatilan	a form of trance dance popular in Java
joged	popular dance form found throughout the Indonesian/Malay world; although most often performed in couples, *joged* can also refer to solo dancers doing the two-step characteristic of the form
kafe	term for a type of nightclub that can also function as a daytime café/restaurant
kampung	neighbourhood
karawitan	general term for gamelan music that includes singing
kendang	two-headed drum that features in gamelan ensembles and *dangdut* groups
KPJM	Kelompok Penyanyi Jalanan Malioboro; Malioboro Streetside Singing Group, also important to the formation of the Malioboro Arts Community
Kridosono	sports hall and stadium that houses many large-scale musical performances
kroncong	popular music genre featuring diasporic Portuguese mandolin; Sundanese/Betawi flute runs; a distinct guitar style; a nostalgic vocal style; and lyrical themes of love, loss and the Indonesian Independence struggle
langgam Jawa	literally 'Javanese custom/style', here a musical genre closely related to *kroncong*, but which tends to feature Javanese lyrics and *slendro* pentatonic-scale patterns

lesehan	street restaurants where customers sit on straw mats on the ground
Melayu	'Malay'; in relation to music generally refers to elements or nuances characteristic of *melayu* ensembles
musical physicalisation	the manifested physical behaviours that arise around or through music
musik jalanan	street music; in Yogyakarta the term is sometimes applied to street buskers playing traditionalist genres, but more often applies to western-influenced, politically oppositional folk/rock music, with guitars being the most common instrument
Opposite Resto	a popular night-time 'hangout' for street guides and others by the Sosrowijayan Street roadside and opposite the Resto café/bar
pengamen	street busker
perek	'experimental woman', from *perempuan eksperimental*; a term for women who often have sexual encounters with (especially western) men (the less stigmatised equivalent for local-based men is 'gigolo')
Prada	a late-night *lesehan* eatery on the corner of Malioboro and Sosrowijayan streets
preman	'gangster' or 'thug' (from the Dutch *vrij man*, 'free man')
priyayi	an *aliran* social grouping featuring high-status bureaucratic/Hindu-Javanese
Purawisata	a multi-function amusement park and 'cultural arts centre'; the open-air Taman Ria venue within the complex regularly houses large-scale *dangdut* performances
qasidah	a form of Arabian-influenced lyric poetry, in Indonesia also associated with *rebana* frame drum accompaniment
Reformasi	term for the 'reform era' that gained momentum leading into President Soeharto's downfall in 1998; Reformasi and *krismon* (*krisis moneter*, financial crisis) were key terms used across Indonesian society in efforts to characterise and institute social and political change during the early-post Soeharto years
Resto	a café/bar popular with backpackers and street guides, located toward the western end of Sosrowijayan Street

| Glossary of special terms

santri	an *aliran* social grouping based on market and purest-Islamic features (Geertz 1960), more recently set in contrast to *kejawen* (Javanism) (Beatty 1999)
Sekar Wuyung	Sosrowijayan-based group whose *dangdut Jawa* music included many *campursari* songs
sekaten	refers to both a commemoration of the prophet Muhammad and a fifteenth-century gamelan set; following the Javanese calendar, each year a month-long carnival culminates in a week of formal rituals at the Sultan's Palace
Shower Band	Sosrowijayan-based musical group featuring street guides connected to the Malioboro *jalanan* scene
Sosro Bahu	name of a *becak* driver organization and their stand/'hangout' located on Sosrowijayan Street
Sultan's Palace	*kraton* in Indonesian; both home to Sultan Hamengku Buwono X (also Provincial Governor) and seen as the centrepiece of Javanese culture
Tombo Sutris	a *campursari* orchestra who played at a wide range of functions in Yogyakarta, including those connected to state power
tongkrongan	Javanese term for 'hangout' (from *nongkrong*, 'to squat')
TransWeb	an Internet café and street guide 'hangout' located by a Sosrowijayan alleyway
UGM	Universitas Gadjah Mada; Gadjah Mada University
wayang kulit	shadow puppet theatre
Yayi	the name of a 17 year old female singer who was very adept at balancing polite deference and sexualised crowd rousing in a wide range of settings and contexts

Introduction
Approaching musical life in early post-Soeharto Yogyakarta

By four o'clock the midday heat has begun to mellow. Along kampung alleyways the raucous commotion of city life gives way to the occasional sounds of playing children, splashing water, cooing pigeons. Domestic life emanates crisply out of thin walls and open windows. Some people are freshening up with a *mandi* or cooking in their kitchens; others are watching television or quietly strumming guitars by their doorsteps. The sun, by now sunk behind buildings, has given way to the calm, mild air of early dusk. Islamic calls to prayer and a church choir echo faintly across the neighbourhood; a train whistle signals the next wave of newcomers and returnees from Jakarta.

In the evening, the tranquillity of our leafy open-plan homestay is punctuated only by the fleeting rustle and murmur of a guest, family member or friend. Only 50 metres away, thousands of people are re-converging onto Malioboro Street. The food stallholders have set up along the street; customers sit on straw mats under temporary awnings to eat and chat and listen to the passing busking groups. For a time a political campaign and then a rock concert dominate the soundscape. By midnight, social life has gravitated into smaller pockets, one being the Prada eatery. Individuals and groups pull in to the roadside eatery from nightclubs and elsewhere, eat a meal or drink tea, many then staying on to chat and sing along with the Astro Band and others until the five o'clock closing time.

By this time the sky is beginning to brighten, goods transporters are up and about, and soon breakfast stallholders have set up across the street, catering to truck drivers, students, government employees. By ten o'clock all the stalls and shops along Malioboro Street are open for business, and the road, slip-lanes and footpaths are again crammed with workers, commuters and strollers.

Yogyakarta (or 'Jogja') is often described as a palatial ancient city and the cultural heart of Java. It is both a Special Region within the Republic of Indonesia and the region's capital city, and is a major centre of education, cultural tourism and religious syncretism and pluralism. The city has a vibrant arts scene and progressive student activism amidst its 'refined' (*halus*) Sultanate culture and numerous government institutions. The area has many famous attributes, including the eighth century Buddhist Borobudur and Hindu Prambanan temples, and the city's temporary role as Indonesia's national capital during the Independence era adds to its political credibility. In recent years a major earthquake and then a volcanic eruption in the region caught international attention, and at the same time signs of economic development have burgeoned across and beyond the city.

Malioboro Street is 'the centre of life for Yogyans historically, religiously, politically, economically and socially' (Berman 1994:20). With its daily transformation from shopping strip to night market to, finally, a strip of eateries, it has been called 'the world's longest permanent open-air market' (Berman 1994:20). The city merges into villages in every direction, with the region around the city including some of the most densely populated rural areas in the world (*Damage earthquake* 2006). Inner-city congestion has intensified over recent decades, with workers, students and others almost doubling the population each workday (Sasongko 2001). This is the setting for this monograph, in which I will show how musical and related activities helped to promote peace and intergroup appreciation and tolerance during a period of great social and political change. I also schematize combinations of performance setting, social relation and power dynamic that facilitated these largely peaceful interactions.

In the final years of the twentieth century, Indonesia experienced and negotiated several major changes. The Asian economic crisis that began in 1997 had a significant impact in subsequent years; and politically, President Soeharto's downfall in May 1998 signalled both the end of the New Order government's 32 year rule and the start of the Reformasi era (Aspinall 1999; Aspinall, Van Klinken and Feith 1999). In the optimism of new political freedoms and opportunities among ongoing economic crises, social relations in Indonesia were marked by both occasional horrific violence and, given the immensity of change underway, exemplary moments of cooperation.

Between April and October 2001 alone, a new mayor was instated in Yogyakarta, Indonesia's President Abdurrachman Wahid (Gus Dur) was impeached and replaced by Megawati Sukarnoputri, and the September 11 attacks in New York occurred. Large banners and roving campaigns often dominated the streetscape in political contests over public space. Meanwhile, neither completely removed from, nor wholly bound to these events, the midyear in Yogyakarta remained highly active with major rituals and festivals such as Sekaten (May), the Yogyakarta Arts Festival (June), the Yogyakarta Gamelan Festival (July), and Independence Day (August). The public, street-based nature of these political and cultural events offered rich material for sensorial ethnography and social analysis.

I undertook a study of music in Yogyakarta during the early years of Reformasi (the Reform movement). The variety of musics I had encountered on previous visits there intrigued me, and I also felt that the topic might help to reconcile theories of Javanese dominance in Indonesia with the humble living conditions of most Javanese. Given that Indonesia was undergoing its biggest changes since the mid-1960s, I wanted to capture as much detail of the current period as possible. At the least, then, the study from the outset was intended to produce a record of social and musical life in the midst of the many transitions underway in Yogyakarta.

In what follows I seek to develop a set of concepts and approaches through which to construct an account of musical influences on social relations. In Yogyakarta, as to a large extent in wider Indonesia, popular music and social relations passed through two discernible phases during the study period. First, oppositional music gained increasing momentum in the late New Order period and through to the early euphoria of Reformasi. Second, the shocking reality of inter-ethnic/religious and anti-Chinese violence, along with ongoing economic hardship, compelled several social organizations and associated musicians to promote peace as their main priority. In Yogyakarta in 1999, these were manifested in various concerts, message T-shirts and the like. When I visited in 2000, a kind of Reformasi fatigue had set in. In 2001 music remained a vital part of many people's lives; however, while it sometimes served as a direct vehicle for people to enhance their stakes in power struggles, more pervasively it helped to maintain cooperative social relations during a period of great uncertainty.

Added to the multilayered changes occurring during the early post-Soeharto period, research on social relations and culture in Java must also consider the island's long and complex history. As Clifford Geertz (1960:7) pointed out several decades ago:

> Java – which has been civilized longer than England; which over a period of more than fifteen hundred years has seen Indians, Arabs, Chinese, Portuguese and Dutch come and go; and which has today one of the world's densest populations, highest development of the arts, and most intensive agricultures – is not easily characterized under a single label or easily pictured in terms of a dominant theme.

Introduction

Archaeological evidence shows that Hindu and early gamelan instruments have been in use in central Java since at least the eighth century (Kunst 1968), and many people in Yogyakarta have assured me that *lesung* music made with rice pounders existed before that. In the turbulent years between Indonesian Independence and Soeharto's New Order, Geertz (1960) developed the Javanese/Indonesian notion of *aliran* into an important tool for conceptualising Javanese society and culture. *Aliran*, meaning literally 'stream' or 'current', refers to three broad groups based on occupational orientation and 'world outlook', these being village/syncretic *abangan*, market/purest-Islamic *santri* (further divided into reformist *moderen* and traditionalist *kolot*) and bureaucratic/Hindu-Java *priyayi*.

A number of scholars have drawn attention to the need for Geertz's *aliran* concept to more accurately define the party-political, religious and occupational differences underpinning the three groups (Kahn 1988:182-4; Newland 2000). Others have reconceptualised the three *aliran* streams, classifying the cultural orientations of Javanese into the two broad categories of *kejawen* (Javanism) and *santri* (Beatty 1999). Nonetheless, viewed historically the concept of *aliran* helped to challenge the simplistic 'traditional/modern' dualisms that dominated emerging development discourses at the time (Gomes 2007:43). Additionally, the term still resonated among the people I spoke with in Yogyakarta in 2001, albeit modified to fit current times.

Several other studies of Javanese culture and society inform the following analysis.[1] A few Javanese/Indonesian terms were central to the street life and intergroup relations I encountered. *Tongkrongan*, or 'hangout' (Echols and Shadily 1982), tended to carry the same mixed connotations as its English counterpart. Depending on speaker and context, a *tongkrongan* could be a place where layabouts laze around with nothing better to do, or a 'hip' place where real life happens. A popular *tongkrongan* site was the *angkringan*, a portable tea and snack stall. Most *angkringan* workers set their ready-stocked stalls strategically close to trading areas. By catering to basic needs, they facilitated interactions between street workers, civil servants, and others who otherwise generally remained separate, especially on and near Malioboro Street.

Other *tongkrongan* settings included *warung*, these being more permanent tea stall/shops; and *lesehan*, street restaurants featuring straw mats spread out on the ground. People would regularly gather and *ngobrol* at these hangouts. *Ngobrol* can be translated as 'chat'

---

1 Anderson 1990; Guinness 1986; Sullivan 1994; Siegel 1986; Robson 2003.

and, as with *tongkrongan*, was perceived variously as light and trivial, or as code for matters of real importance. In Part One, I attempt to problematise too straightforward a reading of these hangouts as exemplars of intergroup harmony. Nevertheless, overwhelmingly these hangouts and eateries were important sites in which amiable intergroup relations were maintained daily among diverse occupational, ethnic, and other affiliations.

Despite Yogyakarta's reputation as a 'traditional' city, several changes were occurring during the main research period. The city area was inhabited by people with a wide range of livelihoods and lifestyles, one indicator of which was the myriad uses of technology. Thousands of motorcycles crammed the roads, along with pedicabs (*becak*), horse and carts, old buses and bicycles. Garbage collectors pulled heavy carts by hand, while increasing numbers of aeroplanes flew overhead. Countless government administration offices and education institutions each featured cumbersome filing cabinets and manual typewriters. The only high technology cinema had burnt down years earlier, leaving only others built decades ago. At the same time, dozens of internet cafés and VCD libraries enjoyed high levels of business, and mobile phones numbered in their thousands (Hill and Sen 2005). It seemed clear to me that text messaging became widespread in Yogyakarta before 'modern' cities such as Melbourne.

Referring to its multi-ethnic character, several people told me Malioboro Street was the 'real mini Indonesia', unlike the fabricated 'Beautiful Indonesia in Miniature Park' (known as Taman Mini) in Jakarta. During my fieldwork, Malioboro Street was blocked to traffic by the railway line crossing its northern end, with Malioboro itself a smooth double-lane, one-way road leading southbound on a slight downhill slope. Starting from its northern end, large establishments included Hotel Garuda, the Regional Parliament and Malioboro Mall, government offices, the large, traditional Beringharjo Market, Fort Vredeburg and the Central Post Office. South again, less than two kilometres from Malioboro Mall, are the highly symbolic Sultan's Palace and its ceremonial grounds.

Malioboro Street was flanked by hundreds of stalls and shops catering to various classes, needs, and interests. Particularly from around ten am until eight pm each day, the street was chiefly characterised by the stalls cramming both sides of the pedestrian walkway under the archways. Stall items were predominantly 'commoditised culture' crafts and cheap clothing made mostly from batik off-cuts and seconds. Each morning at around nine o'clock, traders and their assistants wheeled out large trolleys from side-street depots, opened them, and set up their stalls. With a flick of the wrist, they

Becak line the slip lane on Maliboro Street

The Malioboro walkway flanked by street stalls and a brightly-lit department store

Introduction

Inside Malioboro Mall

unrolled shirts ten at a time, each previously set on coat hangers, and then swung them onto bars they had strung up and balanced between pylons. By this time, traffic had built up on the road, with the flow on to and off the main thoroughfare generally characterised by patience and courtesy. For example, motorcyclists often helped *becak* drivers across to the slip lane by bracing one foot on the *becak*'s mudguard and pushing them along.

The crowded and relatively gritty street level of Malioboro contrasted with the bright lights illuminating the evening skyline. Dazzling neons emanated from shopping malls and from department stores specialising in carpets, plastic ware, or clothing. Malioboro Mall, built in 1994, is open plan and four levels high, in many senses typical of suburban shopping malls throughout the world. But the 'Mal' was also illustrative of social relations in Yogyakarta. Hundreds of motorcycles crammed the parking bays at the main entrance, each coordinated and monitored by attendants in orange overalls. Several sellers of cigarettes and newspapers waited for incoming and outgoing customers at the bottom of the steps, as did *becak* drivers whose vehicles sat parked in the slip lane on the other side of road. The inside of the mall featured department stores and smaller specialty shops and stalls, although the main activities here were arguably not those of shoppers but rather those 'hanging out' chatting, or simply looking about, while leaning on the silver-plated rails. Many of these were students and youth, while families ambled past the shop fronts. 'Village folk' (*orang desa*) could also be seen enthralled by the novelty of hi-tech escalators and shiny surfaces.

In this light, three broad groups or classes gravitated around the Mal: the wealthy, who were able to purchase expensive coffee and goods from the various stores (see also Mundayat 2005:128-9); the middle- to lower/middle-classes, such as students and visitors from elsewhere in Indonesia, who spent little or no money at the Mal but hung out or did some of their grocery shopping there; and a section of the urban poor, who sought to carry out their trade from the entrance but rarely if ever entered the Mal proper.[2]

The highly congested and diverse setting of Malioboro Street serves as the focal point for this study. Some people regarded life here as highly agreeable and pleasant, while others saw the area as overrun with problems and stressful. Of the former, many spoke of enjoying Yogyakarta's laidback, *'santai aja'* (take it easy) lifestyle, as well as its relative affordability, with many Indonesian university graduates choosing to stay on in the city long after completing their studies. Hundreds of foreign travellers and students were drawn there by an interest in the arts and/or activism, and many rural-oriented locals spoke with great reverence of Yogyakarta's Sultan. As well as being characterised by polite 'high' culture, the region also has a reputation for inter-ethnic, -class and -religious tolerance. Exemplary in this regard was the regular socialising between shoe shiners, professors and others at tea stalls, as mentioned above. Whenever I arrived by train from Jakarta, I was struck by the air of youthful vitality around Malioboro Street. Talking with passersby on the street, I often felt that, as with the popular saying about New York, Yogyakarta had as many interesting life stories as it did people.

At the same time, tension and conflict were by no means absent from Yogyakarta in the early post-Soeharto years. The movement of pedestrians along Malioboro Street was severely hampered, forcing many to take the slip lane only to then experience repeated near misses by bicycles, *becak* and horse and carts, especially those travelling northbound against the legal flow rather than take the impractically long route via Joyonegaran Street or through narrow residential alleyways. Many people treated crossing Malioboro as an adventure, but the absence of traffic lights and zebra crossings made this an even more perilous task. The recent economic cri-

---

2 On shopping malls and social differentiation in Southeast Asia, see Young 1999; Van Leeuwen 2011; on Yogyakarta specifically, see Wibawanta 1998.

sis had played a role in exacerbating the strained conditions on Malioboro Street, but there were other factors involved. In the mid-1970s, a long-time resident told me, Malioboro became the site of battles among *becak* drivers, resulting in the deaths of a number of ethnic Batak drivers from North Sumatra. He added that something similar could well happen again.

Another source of resentment stemmed from the early 1980s, when the then Sultan gave away Malioboro pavement spaces to petty traders. Yogyakartans, for the most part being irresolute in business matters, did not take up the offer. However, other groups did, in particular 'immigrants' from the island of Madura off the northeast coast of Java. Nowadays, the argument ran, these same groups were selling the spaces back to long-term residents at exorbitant prices, causing tensions and arguments over trading rights. Finally, resentment on Malioboro Street towards Malioboro Mall's profiteering managers was such that it would only take someone to walk down the main street with a megaphone calling for street traders to mobilise against this injustice, and within an hour, it was said, the mall would be ablaze.

Social tensions and conflict also extended beyond Malioboro Street. Longstanding hierarchies continued to be exercised through subtle but effective language use and physical gestures. Although prior to September 11 and the Bali Bombings, militant wings of organizations such as Laskar Jihad were certainly active in Indonesia. Political campaigns by the Gerakan Pemuda Ka'bah (GPK, Ka'bah Youth Movement) and others sometimes menaced the streets. Finally, nature and 'human error' sometimes combined to inflict suffering in Yogyakarta. Transport accidents and power blackouts were commonplace, and the more recent earthquake and volcanic eruption caused indescribable trauma and devastation.

In the heavily congested Malioboro Street area of Yogyakarta in 2001, the friendly and tranquil interweaved with the exclusivist and occasionally violent. Relatively wealthy, footloose visitors could easily romanticise the quality of life there, particularly given the jovial bearing of many materially poor locals. On the other hand, while focusing on the numerous social problems in and around the city reveals underlying issues and realities that such a view ignores or avoids, much commentary on Indonesia concentrates only on problems and conflict. This view is blind to signs of contentment, pleasure or acts of goodwill and cooperation, and also the roles that these can play in progressive politics. During the eight months in which I spent most waking hours in the crowded Malioboro area, gestures of kindness were always evident. In light of the heightened political, economic and inter-ethnic tensions of

| *Introduction*

the time, the incidence of public conflict was remarkably low. As I will seek to demonstrate, musical practices played an active role in facilitating these relatively peaceful social relations.

MUSICAL WORLDS AND THEIR GENRES

The following chapters present an ethnographic account of a number of musics and social situations in Yogyakarta.³ Amidst the explosion of musical diversity across much of early post-Soeharto Indonesia (Barendregt and Van Zanten 2002), in Yogyakarta gamelan ensembles, Islamic choirs and punk bands could all perform at the same event. Single acts combined classical (gamelan), folk (*rakyat*) and western pop instrumentation and playing styles. The ethnic-Chinese *barongsai* lion dance re-emerged in street parades and began to influence other musical performance styles. Islamic a-cappella groups, known as *nasyid*, were gaining popularity.

This monograph takes these hybridized musical realities as a primary focus, rather than any single genre, subculture or artist. Arguably, analysing a broad range of public performances and genres can produce different understandings of social and musical groups and connections to those possible through a singularly focussed study. To that end, this study begins and concludes with the street workers I conversed with on a daily basis, and who subsequently became central to the research.

I seek to minimise a reliance on high/popular, traditional/modern and other established classifications of cultural practice. Instead I analyse music by considering the variables of event theme, physical setting, social context and behaviours, and musical genre. The setting, function and content of musical events tell us a great deal about the social and political factors that underpin them, and furthermore allow for the incorporation of all of the musical phenomena involved. In turn, musical dimensions affect and are affected by participants and their social relations. While opinions vary as to the academic and political significance of these kinds of interplays, most important for my current aims are the studies of

3 In relation to contrasts and commonalities of popular music trends such as these across wider Indonesia, a prominent Indonesian musician told me that the country has four main centres, each with their own characteristics: 1. East Java has those who praise and commemorate nationalism and its heroes, such as Gombloh and Leo Kriste; 2. in Yogyakarta musicians tend to focus on social concerns through mixing poetic lyrics with traditional musical forms; 3. Bandung leads in national and international fashion and trends; and 4. Jakarta, despite being home of *kroncong* and *dangdut*, is 'the big toilet'.

music and social relations that identify social and cultural contestation but then go on to examine how music also helps to bridge social divisions.[4]

Relatively objective musical genre characteristics and subjective pronouncements of taste intersect and combine in particular contexts to form musical identities. The clusters of these mutually constitutive variables are what I wish to call 'musical worlds'. I borrow the term 'musical worlds' from Ruth Finnegan's ethnography (1989) of music making in an English town, which she in turn derives from Howard Becker's *Art worlds* (1982). Approaching musical practices through the concept of 'worlds' is arguably less problematic than through a notion of 'culture'. Joel Kahn (1995) and others have pointed out how scholars too often seek to separate examples of 'culture' from their socio-historical contexts. By contrast, it may be said that people move in and between socially-situated musical worlds, rather than simply belonging to one or another culture.

A focus on musical worlds also calls attention to the often overlooked regularity of musical events, and highlights the extra-musical organizational work involved in planning and carrying out these events. The term 'worlds' in this context emphasises the 'local social contexts of arts production' (DeNora 2000:4). This in turn prevents the analysis from being restricted to 'the "reading" of works or styles' (DeNora 2000:1), and facilitates the identification of signs of local-level cooperative relations in the works that are produced (Howard Becker 1982). As Tia DeNora (2000:5) points out, studies of 'art worlds' in this sense parallel the studies of scientific laboratories that reveal the social production of scientific 'facts' (Latour and Woolgar 1979). More generally, the idea of musical worlds can be seen as a variant of new heuristic uses of terms such as 'scene' (Williams 2006; Straw 1991) and 'gathering' (Simpson 2000), also keeping the 'text' of the music itself firmly in the picture.

Analysing the social production of events informs rather than replaces the music itself, which is approached here through the concept of genre. Arguments abound over what constitute particular musical genres (Indonesian *jenis*).[5] The framework for the current study has been influenced by Finnegan, who categorises 'musical worlds' by genres such as classical, folk, brass bands, and pop and rock, and discusses the organizational aspects of performance settings such as clubs, pubs, and schools. Musical genres

---

4   Eyerman and Jamison 1998; Martin 1999; Epstein 2000; Wong 1995; Wallach 2008.
5   Yampolsky 2001; Frith 1987; Pachet, Roy and Cazaly 2000; Zorn 1999.

Introduction

are not clearly demarcated categories that exist in a power vacuum. Instead, they involve articulations of taste that serve to mark social boundaries (Bourdieu 1984). At the same time, the pleasures that people draw from music cannot be reduced entirely to contests for status. I would argue that a credible study of the roles of music in peaceful and tolerant intergroup relations requires that attention be paid to both contestations over social boundaries and the relatively straightforward enjoyment derived from musical practices.

As will be addressed later on, this monograph touches on musical genres ranging from indigenist *jatilan* and Islamic *gambus* to western-style pop and metal. However, of foremost importance are the genres of *campursari* and *jalanan*. In my field experience, *campursari* and *jalanan* often featured in discussions and events around the inner-city streets, and can therefore be seen as pervasive musical identities in Yogyakarta. In order to gain an understanding of *campursari* and *jalanan*, however, it is firstly necessary to consider the genres of gamelan, *langgam Jawa*, *kroncong* and *dangdut*.

The first of these, gamelan (from gamel, or 'hammer; to beat'), refers to world-famous percussion ensembles found predominantly in Bali and Java, and in combination with singing is termed *karawitan*. Gamelan ensembles vary greatly in size, but generally consist of several kinds of 'metal slab instruments and [tuned] knobbed gongs' (Sutton 2009:232), and in central Java often include *suling* (flute), *rebab* (Muslim spike fiddle) and *pesinden* (female singers). Most ensembles are tuned broadly to either the 'slendro' or 'pelog' tonal systems (Lindsay 1992). This reflects a richness of musical variety in Indonesia, but also a constraint on individual villagers who might wish to collaborate musically with someone from another village. The development of *campursari* has been one means of standardising gamelan tunings, in turn both facilitating new intergroup syntheses and causing concern over cultural homogenisation (Mrázek 1999:49).

Langgam Jawa means Javanese custom or style (Echols and Shadily 1982) and, unlike gamelan, has received little scholarly attention. Generally, *langgam Jawa* is played by a soloist or in small groups, usually with pentatonic scale patterns. A major related musical genre is *kroncong* (Judith Becker 1975; Harmunah 1987; Kartomi 1998), the name being onomatopoeic of the strumming of the *cak* and *cuk* (higher and lower pitched three-string ukuleles). *Kroncong* can be seen as a variant of what Steven Feld (2003:235) terms 'Pan-Pacific acoustic string band popular music', but more broadly draws on five centuries of East/West interactions and influences from western Java, the former Portuguese empire, eastern Indonesia and Hawai'i. As is the case with many forms of popular music, *kroncong* grew out of the cultural expressions of the urban poor to become an emblem of national pride (Manuel 1988). Among its most recognisable features are diasporic Portuguese mandolin, Sundanese/Betawi flute runs, a distinct guitar style, a nostalgic vocal style, and lyrical themes of love, loss and the Indonesian Independence struggle. Additionally, in Yogyakarta *kroncong* instruments and songs are often blended with *langgam Jawa* melodies and scales, and both of these are variously played on the street and included in *campursari* orchestras.[6]

Dangdut is variously associated with urban lower classes, nationalism, and an Islamic ethic.[7] *Dangdut* arguably vies with *kroncong* as the nation's internationally best known musical genre after gamelan. Many musical elements of *dangdut* grew out of *orkes melayu* ensembles, but broadly comprise Indian kanerva pattern rhythms; a tabla or a *kendang* drum (and the onomatopoeic 'ndang dut' sound of the rhythm); flutes and keyboards played with Hindustani-flavoured lilts, particularly as heard in Hindi film music; and heavy metal guitar.

Examining the many twists and turns of *dangdut* in the public perception is beyond the scope of this monograph, but a couple of comments are necessary. Firstly, many Indonesians have referred to *dangdut*, generally derogatorily, as 'musik kampungan', meaning roughly 'hick music', in an attempt to distance themselves from the urban lower classes. On Malioboro Street, most moving cigarette and sweets traders became physically engaged each time a street group performed *dangdut* music, whereas middle-class people made a point of disparaging the genre. Yet *dangdut* was also enjoyed by an increasingly broad spectrum of Indonesian society (Perlman 1999:3), even if only in certain circumstances.

Second, many female *dangdut* singers performed with overt and at times controversial eroticism. Ceres Pioquinto (1995) has discussed this in relation to Sekaten in Surakarta, and as I witnessed in 2001, organizers of Yogyakarta's Sekaten Night Fair banned *dangdut* music, costumes, and dance styles, only for some music groups to slip sexual display back into the proceedings through *dangdut* music and mannerisms. *Dangdut* in these ways has given rise to heated public debate over Islam, gender politics, and the state. Female superstar Inul Daratista became the focal point of these

---

6   Philip Yampolsky (cited in Mrázek 1999:47-8) asserts that *langgam Jawa* has come to mean any *kroncong* music sung in Javanese. My interpretation here is based primarily on discussions in Yogyakarta in 2001.
7   Frederick 1982; Simatupang 1996; Lockard 1998. For an in-depth study of *dangdut* combining historical, ethnographic and musicological approaches, see Weintraub 2010.

| Introduction

debates across and beyond Indonesia (Heryanto 2008), and subsequent debates over a proposed anti-pornography bill brought new factors into issues of public sexuality.

Gamelan, *kroncong, langgam Jawa* and *dangdut* all feature in this study, especially in relation to *campursari* and *jalanan*. *Campursari*, or 'mixed essences', combines gamelan ensembles with western diatonic instruments such as bass guitar, hi-tech keyboards and saxophone, and regional and national forms and instruments including *kroncong* ukuleles and *dangdut* drum (see also Mrázek 1999; Supanggah 2003; Perlman 1999). *Campursari* took central Java by storm after the release of Manthous' first album in 1994. Manthous, who was later debilitated by a stroke and passed away in early 2012, talked about his life and explained many aspects of *campursari* to me when I stayed at his Gunung Kidul studio for a week in 2001. In addition to the largely Javanese and Indonesian aspects of his musical life, Manthous had performed in Japan several times in the early 1990s, where he met and befriended Chaka Khan, Tina Arena and others. He enjoyed a wide array of musical styles, including those of jazz musicians such as Chick Corea, but said that his number one musical idol was David Foster of the band Chicago.

Manthous in his Gunung Kidul recording studio

Manthous' Campur Sari Gunung Kidul (CSGK) orchestra

Campursari orchestra at a kampung Independence Day event

Introduction

Manthous contended that, while several people had experimented with gamelan and western diatonic scales (compare Supanggah 2003:1-3), he was the first to do so successfully. He also explained that a *campursari* composer remixed existing melodies, often drawing strongly on *kroncong*, *dangdut* and other genres. He suggested that as far back as the 1930s *langgam Jawa* lyrics contained love themes, and that *kroncong* lyrics celebrated the beauty of flowers and of love. These were 'the seniors' of *campursari*, he said, but *campursari* also added humour. By 2001, according to Manthous, there were around 400 *campursari* orchestras in the region. In the same period, I noticed that many people less familiar with the *campursari* genre used the term as a catchword to denote the combining of any otherwise largely discrete genres. While the experts generally associated *campursari* with the numerous orchestras in the region, the label was nonetheless complicated by the fact that many *campursari* songs were slightly modified versions of earlier *langgam Jawa* and related folk tunes. Quite often, enthusiasts called such a song *campursari* even if it was played on solo guitar.

Of particular significance to this study, it is difficult to exaggerate the levels of enthusiasm for all things *campursari* exhibited by the *becak* drivers I encountered in Yogyakarta. By contrast, urban-based tourist street guides and university students generally had little time for *campursari*, instead favouring more westernised popular music and, in some cases, *wayang kulit* (Javanese shadow puppets). I take up this divergence of musical tastes in the following chapters. A variation on this divergence was the occasional elderly street worker who lamented that *campursari* was promoting boisterous audience participation, and then harked back to days when audiences apparently sat still and watched the wayang while listening to the gamelan ensemble. These examples provide clear evidence of links between musical taste and social groupings. More ambiguously, *campursari* gave rise to interesting tensions and accommodations with *dangdut* at kampung events, particularly when increasing *dangdut*-isation signalled a shift into more sexualised lead performance and audience participation.

Finally, *musik jalanan* (street music) was, according to many of its affiliates, any music played on the street that was relatively free from rules and regulations. In practice however, many people did not apply the term *jalanan* to the *campursari* subgenres that buskers often played on the streets. Instead, in their usage the term referred to the urban-oriented, western-influenced and often politically oppositional folk/rock developed by Iwan Fals, Sawung Jabo, the Kelompok Penyanyi Jalanan (Streetside Singing Group) and

Introduction

others. *Jalanan* music can therefore be conceptualised along a spectrum, as follows.

At one end, borrowing from Craig Lockard (1998), is what I would call folk/rock. In particular, figures such as Iwan Fals had long raised the profile of the politically oppositional guitar-playing balladeer, such that this form and style of playing became very popular through the 1980s and 1990s (see also Baulch 2007). But so-called 'photocopy' cover versions of songs such as Pink Floyd's 'Another brick in the wall' could also be considered *musik jalanan* if played on the street. In this study, it is the street guides, and to some extent university students, who identified with, played, sang and listened to various strands of folk/rock, in contrast to other street workers such as *becak* drivers, who expressed little interest in it. At the other end of the spectrum, the *musik jalanan* term was occasionally applied to music of the street buskers, much of which was *kroncong, langgam Jawa, karawitan* and related genres constitutive of *campursari*.

A number of *musik jalanan* groups on Malioboro Street drew on yet other musical elements and cultural influences. Members of the Malioboro Arts Community were not openly disparaging of the *kroncong-* and *langgam-*playing buskers, but they rarely played these musics themselves. Although they sometimes played heavy metal or rock classics, the music that enjoyed greatest prominence in this circle constituted a distinct category. Like *campursari* players, many *jalanan* performers combined 'Javanese', 'western' and other elements and associations, but they did so in markedly different ways. Guitars were more prominent, for example, yet some of the scales,

Folk/rock-influenced *jalanan*; roaming buskers (*pengamen*) (1988)

Iwan Fals fans

KPJM (Kelompok Penyanyi Jalanan Malioboro)

rhythms, instruments and/or lyrical themes employed were consciously Javanese and/or Indonesian.[8]

There were also street groups such as Jagongan, who played in the Islamic *qasidah* format that usually involves singing in Arabic to the accompaniment of a *gambus* orchestra but here drew on Indonesian language and 'Javanised' percussion. Finally, the *jalanan* performer most popular among street children and guides – but less so among *becak* drivers – was Pak Sujud Sutrisno, a wandering *kendang* (drum) player who had been singing humorous and topical lyrics since the mid-1960s (Body 1982).

Jalanan, as with 'street' in English, is an adjective applied not only to music but also to homeless people, especially children and youth (*anak jalanan*; street child). The numbers of homeless children in urban Java rose sharply after the onset of the economic crisis in 1997 (*Street children* 2005). Street music legend Sawung Jabo told me that people on the street in Yogyakarta freely shared their knowledge and possessions. Owning a guitar was a privilege beyond the reach of many people, he added, but 'open house, open mind' attitudes meant that music was a unifying and mutually supportive activity. The term *musik jalanan* generally applied to the politically conscious musics that arose from these street-based social groups. Like *campursari*, the term was used around Malioboro Street with such frequency that it could be said to signify a subcultural identity. My main respondent explained the rise of *musik jalanan* as follows:

> In the early 1980s, the formation of a group named the Streetside Singing Group (KPJ) shifted the *jalanan* term away from applying solely to the homeless. KPJ first arose in Jakarta, inspired by the pop novel series *Ali Topan anak jalanan*. Ali Topan was a young man from a broken home. Although his parents were very wealthy, he chose life on the street with stallholders, street vendors and buskers. He was very heroic, defended the weak, and sometimes when weary would lean against his trail bike on the roadside just to play harmonica with the few street musicians around at the time.
>
> KPJM (KPJ Malioboro) formed in Yogyakarta some years later, and is credited with having formed a creative umbrella organization for friends on the street who needed an escape from family stress and other problems. For these people, socialising together on the street built a strong sense of unity. Sometimes they made

---

8 Some of the senior proponents of these Java-inflected variants of *musik jalanan* were former members of the Bengkel theatre group (Curtis 1997). See also M. Dwi Marianto 2001.

their own rules, which many people valued highly. These were the roots of gangsterism (*premanisme*), but fortunately KPJM had something positive: the public performance of music. Even now, the wider community still consider the street arts as second rate – this is because of the prevailing image that street life is rough. People on the street are often determined to do almost anything, without fear of consequences!

KPJM are able to resolve most intergroup problems that arise around the arts on Malioboro. Our organization was initially considered a nightmare to society. However, step by step KPJM's good work of helping people to share each other's burdens and cares, and of helping those around them struck by difficulties, these efforts gradually increased the community's sympathies. Nowadays many groups readily queue up to become part of KPJM. Because of this, KPJM has formed a more flexible umbrella organization, one able to harness community energies toward the street arts. This is the Malioboro Arts Community, which to this day is still running strong.

Musik jalanan was therefore derived as much from a quest for public solidarity as from sympathy for, or expression by, the homeless. The Pajeksan area near Malioboro Street was the Malioboro Arts Community's main base. Here the Community and friends and associates socialised and organized musical events and welfare activities, often in cooperation with Humana (Girli) and other organizations (Berman 1994). Malioboro Arts Community members such as Tyas, Kenyeot and Jasmati, who were central to the organization of many of the performances to be discussed, held formal roles such as 'coordination', 'research and development' and 'culture'. It is these members, and a number of their associates, that I sometimes refer to generically as 'street-arts leaders'. By contrast, other figures such as Yanto and Visnu were friends with some of the Malioboro Arts Community leaders, but they were influential in politicised manifestations of the largely separate world of *campursari*.

Musical genres can never be determined solely by objective criteria, even with the use of digital-precision measurements (Pachet, Roy and Cazaly 2000). In the case of Indonesia, Geertz (1960:304) noted that 'many Mojokerto people refer to all popular songs as "*krontjongs*"'. I also noticed a similar tendency around Indonesian Independence Day in Yogyakarta, indicating that the naming of a genre sometimes had more to do with the broader social and political context than its specific musical elements. At the same time, while the musical dimensions and lyrical themes of mainstream *dangdut* had not shifted significantly over the recent decades, by many accounts the status of being associated with it certainly had. In other words, in the Independence period each year, many people expanded the term *kroncong* to draw numerous musics into the history of the nationalist struggle; on the other hand, while arguably the concert and recorded versions of most *dangdut* music remained relatively static over the course of two decades, the class base of its followers shifted.

In addition to these shifting and ambiguous articulations of musical taste and social affiliation, more often than not the music itself was a combination of recognisable parts of the various genres. To cite a few examples, *dangdut* songs were performed street style, pop songs in the *dangdut* style, *kroncong* songs played as *karawitan*. These various forms were some combination of conscious style decision, response to audience requests, and other factors such as instrument availability and shared repertoire. In the following chapters I refer to these cases and to published works on popular music in Indonesia, and use Bourdieu and alternative perspectives I have devised as a means to better understand the roles of music in peaceful social relations in early post-Soeharto Yogyakarta.

THEORY AND CONCEPTS

This monograph draws on social identity issues and concepts modified from those of French sociologist Pierre Bourdieu, and seeks to critically engage these with specifically Javanese/Indonesian and musical ones. A number of social scientists have formulated understandings of identification and social identity, each of which in varying ways helps to locate living social interactions within the power structures that influence them. Henri Tajfel and John Turner (1979) for example have theorized group formation and conflict in social-psychological terms, and Anthony Giddens' structuration theory (1984), somewhat like Bourdieu's *habitus*, seeks to conceptualise ways in which social structures and rules both govern and are influenced by human actions. In this study, I discuss social identity by relating three of Bourdieu's key concepts to interplays between spatially defined cultural spheres, musical genres and social relations such as class, gender and nation.

Loïc Wacquant notes that researchers using Bourdieu's work have tended to concentrate on the concept or work associated with their own discipline, and as a result often misread his

Introduction

wider logic (Bourdieu and Wacquant 1992:4-5). In response to this, I engage with his concepts of capital, *habitus* and fields in a 'traditional city'. As will be further discussed, Bourdieu sees capital as a source of power and domination that includes but is not restricted to its economic dimensions; *habitus* as a means to identify connections between social structure and habituated behaviour; and fields as the arenas where struggles over particular stakes (or capital) take place. These concepts, as mobilised by Bourdieu, provide helpful tools for understanding musical identities. They focus attention on seemingly disparate phenomena such as everyday social strategising, bodily movements and socially embedded power structures.

However, in order to conceptualise how music helps to promote intergroup appreciation and tolerance in the midst of power struggles and contestation, for a number of reasons I have felt it necessary to modify Bourdieu's theories. Firstly, while his work serves to dispel romantic notions of the peaceful benevolence of phenomena such as music and of intergroup relations in countries such as Indonesia, it fails to adequately capture the simple acts of cooperation that also coexist with or challenge relations of domination. Second, Bourdieu's approach does not adequately allow for the debates that centre on cultural globalisation, popular culture, cosmopolitanism and hybridity, each of which encourage greater attention to cross-cultural interaction and domination than allowed by Bourdieu.[9] Inda and Rosaldo (2002) highlight how cultural imperialism proponents tend to see consumers as passive; globalisation as simply culture flows from 'the West' to 'the rest'; and they neglect culture flows that circumnavigate the West. And discussions of hybridity can challenge essentialist categories on both sides of the cultural imperialism debate (Bhabha 1994; Nederveen Pieterse 2004). While Bourdieu remains useful for maintaining focus on the often-disguised power dimensions that influence social life, his concepts are arguably of limited use in light of such post-colonial and anthropology of globalisation arguments.

Third, while Craig Calhoun (2002) points out that Bourdieu's writing style presents special difficulties for English readers, it remains the case that most of his writing is especially dense and his means of drawing on particular individuals and situations stilted.[10] At the other extreme, the texts of adventurers, travellers, pilgrims, artists and reporters are in many cases lively and widely accessible,

9 Palumbo-Liu and Gumbrecht 1997; Couldry 2004; Craig and King 2002.
10 Notable exceptions to this include Bourdieu 1977:97-109, 1979, 1998; Bourdieu and Wacquant 1992:62-260.

but on ethical or epistemological grounds have long troubled anthropologists and social theorists (MacClancy and McDonough 1996). Sitting somewhere in the middle, ethnographic narrative as a mode of representation can arguably provide a relatively accessible and appealing means of discussing academic ideas. Several examples in the areas of urban, Indonesian and/or musical youth cultures provide useful models in this regard.[11]

Finally, while Bourdieu has been instrumental in bringing 'the body' into social science research, developments in sensorial ethnography provide additional scope for conceptualising contest and cooperation. This is a matter I explore in relation to *habitus* in Part Two. As David Howes (1990) notes, debates over the status and credibility of ethnographic knowledge have been premised on the shift from Geertz's 'culture as texts' (for example, 1973:412-53) to the 'interplay of voices' as exemplified by James Clifford and George Marcus (1986) and many post-colonial theorists. As far back as 1990, Howes argued that this shift from 'text-centred' to 'speech-centred' anthropology remained fixed within a 'verbocentric' framework, thus reinforcing anthropologists' engagements with literary conventions while downplaying 'bodily modes of knowing, and the place of the body in the mind' (Howes 1990:3-4). Related research on hearing is especially relevant for the current study (Bull and Back 2003; Erlmann 2004).

The modified and/or alternative concepts I seek to develop in the following chapters are intended to problematise the reduction of all social interaction to contests over capital, which is a tendency of Bourdieu's approach. These alternative concepts are: inter-group social capital, which includes the community resources generated through social activities that facilitate cooperation between groups; musical physicalisation, this being the physical movements that arise through music and their influences on gender relations; and grounded cosmopolitanism, an openness to cultural difference reinforced by both a sense of place and a resistance to bureaucratic forces. I use these alternative concepts to better allow for human motivation that includes, but is not restricted to, quests for gain in arenas of contestation. At the same time, I have taken Bourdieu as integral to the process of producing depictions of social and musical life in Yogyakarta that incorporate tension and harmony, out of which a richer understanding of social relations and identity in Indonesia might be reached.

11 Zorbaugh 1929; Whyte 1943; Geertz 1960; Cowan 1990; Murray 1991; Diehl 2002; Meintjes 2003; Nayak 2003.

| *Introduction*

RESEARCH METHODS

On a visit to Yogyakarta in mid-2000 I made and renewed social contacts and attended as many performances as I could. During this period I established most of the relationships that were to guide my research the following year. A chain of people, from linguist Laine Berman to her tattooist partner and on to the founder of an education centre for street children, led me to leaders of the Malioboro Arts Community and music groups such as KPJM, Kubro Glow, and Tombo Sutris. In particular, Tyas was to become both a close friend and a vital source of local insight and contacts. Separate to the Malioboro community, Indonesian scholar Umar Muslim suggested I visit Sanggar Olah Seni Indonesia music school, where I subsequently took guitar lessons over several months with a son of the late nationalist composer Koesbini. University contacts at Gadjah Mada and elsewhere were also important in terms of learning about musical performances and sharing experiences and ideas.

During the main fieldwork period, from April to October 2001, I talked about music with hundreds of people, mostly in Indonesian. These discussions took place incidentally at tea stalls and elsewhere, and through interviews with band managers, musicians, radio announcers and others. I also gathered written literature from universities, newspaper and government offices, and around the street, and bought or was given cassettes from shops and stalls. Through the assistance of the Malioboro Arts Community and other bodies and individuals, I also met and spent time with prominent musicians such as Sawung Jabo, Manthous and Iwan Fals, along with their lesser-known colleagues Untung Basuki, Amien Kamil and Bram Makahekum.

While discussion about music was important to the research, more generally I sought to keep an ear attuned to the sounds of daily life and the music of street buskers. More central still were the dozens of musical events that I attended. These took place in a range of settings and with various themes, often with several acts at each. I learned of events through inquiring, being informed or chancing across sound or signage, and then observed musical acts and audience characteristics, recorded samples, talked with people and gathered paraphernalia.

In a small 'manbag' I carried a notebook, basic camera, wallet and room key (but not a hand phone), and also a minidisc recorder on which I recorded around a thousand minutes on hundreds of tracks. In each case I held the small microphone high into the air,

Introduction

both to maximise sound quality and for the ethical reason of not wishing to record secretly. Back in my room, I wrote my notes and recollections in prose form onto a laptop and edited and logged the recordings. The recordings helped me to analyse sonic dimensions of events and settings. I also participated as a musician in group rehearsals and performances, and gave and received music lessons of varying formality.

I resided in a comfortable homestay in the inner-city Sosrowijayan kampung, a highly concentrated and culturally diverse but quiet neighbourhood next to Malioboro Street. Most of the tourist street guides and *becak* drivers that I came to know were based here, as were many restaurant workers, domestic tourists, and others. Often after retiring for the night in Sosrowijayan, only to wake up a few hours later, I took the short walk to the nearby Prada eatery. This produced late-night musical data, and involved me in the 'stay up all night' (*begadang*) lifestyle of musicians and others. I had a bicycle, and generally travelled beyond the inner city on the back of fellow music enthusiasts' motorcycles. In mid-2005, I returned to Yogyakarta for a couple of weeks, and have visited a number of times since then. This has enabled me to revisit and reflect on many of the people, places and events that were central to the fieldwork in 2000-2001.

In practically all cases during the field research, music proved to be an agreeable topic of conversation or activity, and to my knowledge rarely became a source of displeasure or delicate cultural sensitivity among respondents and participants. As I discuss further in relation to particular cases, the presence of a westerner undoubtedly exerted an influence on some performances. However, residing in a backpacker area and focusing on guitars and a range of popular musics also enabled me to blend into the general landscape.[12] In addition, being a musician meant that I could both observe and participate in musical events as performer, teacher, student, and audience member. Participating in musical activities around the city streets seemed to facilitate the kind of common ground and experience that might have been difficult if the focus was, for example, religion and politics, or even traditional theatre.

In the process of mapping out and attempting to schematize all of the recordings and field notes, patterns began to form in terms of correlations between where events took place, who was involved, the stated and actual themes dominating proceedings, the genres

---

12 'The performance and reception of guitar music exemplifies the interplay between local and global cultures' (Dawe and Bennett 2001:2).

| *Introduction*

that featured and when, and so on. At the same time, Bourdieu's central ideas, while at first difficult to penetrate, proved a most useful way to relate the empirical material to wider issues and debates. As mentioned above, the modified versions of capital, *habitus* and fields in turn emerged from a felt need to understand Indonesian social relations through a framework that addresses questions of power and domination and at the same time identifies pleasure and goodwill.

OVERVIEW

The mode of presentation in this book combines what Emerson, Fretz, and Shaw (1995) term analytic arguments and thematic narratives. I introduce and conclude the three parts with analytical arguments (at times with vignettes from the field), while in the chapters I present the various cases through thematic narratives. The musical performances I discuss begin with impromptu, informal, non-stage music making, and then move through to planned, large-scale events that involved numerous performers, audiences, organizers and sponsors. Part One focuses on neighbourhood relations and informal performances, particularly among street guides and *becak* drivers, while Parts Two and Three focus on larger-scale performances, most of which were open to the public, and analyse their organizational and thematic aspects.[13] The settings for the large-scale music performances range from neighbourhoods and commercial venues to the state institutions of the regional parliament, military institutions, universities and the Sultan's Palace. Event themes range from routine evening entertainment, to birthdays and circumcision rituals, through to those of national commemoration or regional religious significance. In this framework, discussion of musical performances moves broadly from street-level sociality to cultural representations and the institutions of power.

The analysis begins with the musical tastes and practices of two occupational groups: firstly, *becak* drivers and *campursari* music; and second, street guides and *musik jalanan*. I then investigate a wide range of music performances in the context of all of the above

---

13 A number of musical events that I documented during the research are not included in this study, as I was not able to fit them into the analytical model I developed. These include the Yogyakarta Gamelan Festival, the launching of Java Tattoo Club, and (to be discussed elsewhere) several events at the Sultan's Palace.

variables, and in the Conclusion return to variations on these two groups, this time through music performances at the Sultan's Palace. I begin the study with a discussion of how each group orientated themselves around and acted on ideas of the local, regional, national and global. I return to this at the end, and confirm the sense that the groups indeed diverged in significant respects. Both supported, identified with, and had expertise on the region, Yogyakarta, as exemplified by their attendance at, and commentary on, events at the Sultan's Palace. However, the groups most closely identified with what might be called 'self-sustaining regionalism' and 'grounded cosmopolitanism' respectively. These characteristics can to some extent be seen as variants of traditionalism and modernism, but my more central aim is to explain the two groups' divergent yet peaceful coexistence through the interplay of the main variables discussed in the conclusion: the Sultan's Palace, the bureaucratic field, and grounded cosmopolitanism.

In the table below, the three parts are represented in rows, with two sets of variables in columns. The first of these variables is the performance setting; the second set combines aspects of identity and power with musical and social dimensions characterised by pleasure, cooperation, and appreciation that emerged amidst, or even in opposition to, prevailing hierarchies and relations of domination. I identify correlations between, on the one hand, these setting/context and power/identity variables, and on the other the musical genres and social groups that weaved horizontally through them.

	Setting(s)	Aspect of identity	Power dimension (Bourdieu)	Other dimension
Part One >	Street	Class / Status	Capital	Inter-group Social capital (Cooperation)
Part Two >	Commercial Venue / Neighbourhood	Gender	Habitus	Physicalisation (Pleasure / Agency)
Part Three >	State institutions	Nation	Bureaucratic field	Grounded Cosmopolitanism (Intercultural appreciation)

Table 1. Overview of the book

| *Introduction*

In Part One, I focus on the musical tastes and practices of street-based workers, and analyse how these influence connections and boundaries among and between the workers. Bourdieu's concept of social capital is modified in order to identify in- and inter-group social capital and spatial variants of cultural capital that underpin the everyday roles of music in nonviolent cooperation. In Part Two, I analyse physical manifestations at musical events in neighbourhoods and commercial venues, and discuss how these reflect and influence gender and class differentiations in these settings. Here Bourdieu's concept of the *habitus* helps to identify the influential role of patriarchal social structures on habituated physical movements, but this is also problematised in light of the ways in which gender and other social boundaries are negotiated and contested in situations of intensified musical physicality. In Part Three, I discuss music performances at state institutions, engage Bourdieu's concept of the bureaucratic field with that of grounded cosmopolitanism, and through these seek to demonstrate how much of the populace was both caught up in political forces and continued to interact with openness and goodwill. Through this framework, I attempt to construct a model that identifies and schematizes links between music, social identity and power in the maintenance of peaceful intergroup relations in Yogyakarta, Indonesia.

PART 1

Music and the street

Background

On Saturday night in Yogyakarta, the fourth of August 2001, the full moon cast iridescence through the city lights. Thousands of Indonesians, cashed up after their monthly payday, were further cramming the bustling city centre. Preparations for Independence Day added to the fanfare. Megawati had replaced Gus Dur as Indonesian President, after a drawn out and often heated showdown between leaders and supporters alike. On the streets of Yogyakarta, hundreds of red flags were posted along roadsides and across the front of buildings, while the Islamic parties' green flags had, for the time being, all but disappeared.

In the Sosrowijayan kampung near Malioboro Street, the Shower Band had just finished their first public performance at Resto café/bar. Most of the band's dozen members worked as tourist street guides, and resided close by the popular backpacker-patronised Resto. An air of jubilation surrounded the Shower Band musicians, most of whom, with several others, drank and talked at their hang-out across the street from the bar. Gradually they clustered into smaller groups: a few settled on the makeshift benches; some made their way home; and half a dozen, carrying three guitars and small bags, headed eastbound toward Malioboro Street.

At the Sosro Bahu *becak* driver stand, the musician-guides met with a drifter who carried and played his trumpet wherever he went. The bench inside the stand, usually occupied by *becak* drivers, was now transformed into a venue for a drinking and music-making party for street guides and a few of their friends. The young guides, already quite merry, settled in and began to strum and sing along together. Soon some of them were slouching back comfortably in the relatively luxurious, padded roadside seating; others standing and singing at the tops of their lungs.

Significantly, Sosro Bahu *becak* drivers returning to their stand from their evening's rounds neither joined in the gathering nor expressed any discomfort toward the guides. Instead, they walked their *becak* along the nearby alleyway and to the rear section of the Yogya Tours office. By 2am, the stand was awash in alcohol-soaked reverie as a soaring rendition of the Bee Gees' 'I started a joke', accompanied by the few remaining guides, echoed faintly throughout the neighbourhood.

On the streets of Indonesia's cities, three years after the downfall of President Soeharto, confidence in Reformasi (the Reform movement) was under strain due to harsh economic realities, interethnic conflicts, and continuing political fluidity. Much international media and academic research have focussed on violence in this period, reinforcing negative representations of social relations in Indonesia. Nonetheless, street brawls and political campaigning did occasionally menace sections of Yogyakarta. Much confusion surrounded the myriad party-political, religious, and ethnic tensions. And Stein Kristiansen (2003:131) argues that over this period '[violent youth] groups are locally-based, and violent episodes and fights occur occasionally over regional and border disputes when one group enters the other's territory of economic and ideological dominance'.

In the context of frequent territorial and other tensions and disputations, it is equally important to gain an understanding of how everyday actors manage non-violence (Kahn 2003:409). John Pemberton (1994) points to the (now former) Soeharto government's obsession with the appearance of social order, and many contemporary studies focus explicitly on the subject of violence in Indonesia (for example, Zurbuchen 2005; Coppel 2006). While the importance of such studies is beyond question, we can also expect to draw lessons from the peaceful acts of cooperation and coexistence that characterise daily life among millions of Indonesians. Joel Kahn (2003:408) alerts us to the importance of this with reference to Immanuel Kant's cosmopolitanism:

> '[C]oalition in a cosmopolitan society' may arise [in large part] from human individuals and groups who already 'exist successively side by side', who cannot avoid 'constantly offending one another' and yet who recognise also that they 'cannot do without associating peacefully'.

In this light, I wish to argue that there is a need to better understand how the gathering of street guides described above did not result in conflict, despite their apparent intrusion into the territory of *becak* drivers. In Part One, I explore the roles of music and capital conversion in the maintenance of conflict avoidance between these work groups.

Street guides as a group had more power around the neighbourhood than did the *becak* drivers, which in part explains the guides' ability to make themselves at home in the stand. However, many street workers entered Sosrowijayan as outsiders and had to earn acceptance among the neighbourhood business dealers. A *becak* driver, Pak Harno, had begun working in the area over the recent months. He was instrumental in establishing the drivers' Sosro Bahu stand. On the evening in question, however, he quietly parked elsewhere rather than join the gathering. For Ari, by contrast, a young street guide and also a newcomer, merrymaking at the stand was a boost to his standing.

The *becak* drivers and street guides were overwhelmingly male, Javanese, lower-class Muslims. While Javanese are renowned for disguising social tension (Mulder 1996:117-23; Keeler 1987), over time it became clear to me that interactions at snack stalls were all-but never acrimonious. Nonetheless, the two work groups did remain largely separate from each other. In part, their divergent lifestyles can be explained by reference to the three *aliran* explored by Geertz (1960), as well as its more recent critiques. Most *becak* drivers for example had a penchant for the 'village' life, aligning them with the *abangan* stream. However, as Lynda Newland (2000) contends, *abangan* is nowadays a demeaning term with which few villagers identify. Moreover, the street guides, younger and more urban oriented, fitted into all three *aliran*, in that they were generally lower class (*abangan*), Hindu-Java/Muslim (*priyayi*) and Muslim petty entrepreneurs (*santri*). Andrew Beatty (1999:28-9) shows how more recent studies largely replace Geertz's three cultural variants with a dichotomy between pious *santri* Muslims and *kejawen* ('Javanism'), the latter subsuming both *priyayi* 'high culture' and *abangan* 'native peasant tradition'. Both *becak* drivers and street guides in different ways identified with *kejawen*.

While the analysis of religion in Java provides particular insights into Javanese society and culture, my central concern is to relate the divergent musical tastes and practices of *becak* drivers and street guides to various conceptions of capital in an environment of intense global traffic and economic imbalance. The *becak* drivers' music of choice was *campursari*, the genre combining Javanese gamelan with other instruments such as *kroncong* ukulele, *dangdut* drum and electronic keyboard. In contrast, street guides preferred western-influenced folk/rock or *musik jalanan* generally played on the guitar and the practice of which extended into style statements such as reggae t-shirts, body piercing and sculptured haircuts. While people's musical tastes often change over time, and according to context, this divergence between the street guides and *becak* drivers was a sign of marked social division in downtown Yogyakarta, one I encountered repeatedly in casual conversations and impromptu music making.

Becak drivers displayed little knowledge of or interest in the western and Indonesian rock music played by street guides, while most guides were not familiar with the *campursari* songs that *becak* drivers enjoyed. This difference of musical taste was also manifest in attendance at, support for, and involvement in public musical entertainment, as I will show in later chapters. Concepts of class and status provide a useful starting point for seeking to better understand these groups and their tastes. Notions of class have come under heavy scrutiny, not least because urban/industrial working populations are no longer easily divisible into capitalists and proletariats, due in particular to the growth of middle classes and an increasingly dispersed ownership of the means of production (for example, via shareholdings) (Lash and Urry 1987). Nonetheless, for the current study I maintain a link between class and status, thereby enabling identification of some of the processes that connect notions of prestige to economic factors. More specifically, in Part One I explore ways in which the two street worker groups' social relations and capital conversion strategies influenced and were affected by their differing musical tastes. In so doing I will formulate and apply concepts of cultural and social capital.

CULTURAL CAPITAL AND ITS SPATIAL VARIANTS

Cultural theorists such as Adorno and Horkheimer (1999) have drawn attention to the ways through which cultural products enter the market, and Jacques Attali (1985) argues that music as a cultural form anticipates, rather than merely reflects social change. It is in the context of these kinds of culture debates that Bourdieu's *Distinction* (1984) has proved to be a landmark study. Culture, which in Bourdieu's formulation means being conversant in matters of aesthetic refinement, is a crucial site for struggles both between and within classes. The key point is that aesthetic appreciation, far from being separate from its social and historical context, is mobilised by dominant classes as cultural capital, and can in turn be converted into economic capital.

As David Palumbo-Liu (1997) remarks, 'for Bourdieu, pronouncing culture is an act of articulating positionality. Culture is eminently commodified and conspicuously consumed, viewed for its exchange value'. Adapting Bourdieu's concept of cultural capital to the current case, it can be argued that the musical tastes and practices of street workers involved projections, orientations, associations, sensibilities and, in particular, knowledge. These are all forms of cultural capital, which in turn can be converted into monetary gain. However, unlike the forms of 'statist capital' I discuss later, cultural capital among street workers was what Bourdieu (1977:187) terms 'scholastically uncertified', meaning that, without officially sanctioned recognition, such capital was 'constantly required to prove itself' (Bourdieu 1986:248).

I want to suggest here that music can be categorised as cultural capital based on how participants relate it to different spatial areas. Drawing on the distinctions made by Nayak (2003; Richter 2004) among localist, survivalist, and globalist subcultural tendencies, the Sosrowijayan street workers' practices can be analysed according to what I term 'regional', 'national', and 'global' variants. These refer to different domains of affiliation (identity) and knowledge (and, potentially, power). For example, regionalism (in its sub-national sense) is synonymous with Javanism, or more specifically the ideals of communal village life. *Becak* drivers often espoused these ideals with reference to *campursari* music. Most street guides on the other hand, apart from being multilingual, played globalist (especially western) popular and rock music, even when critical of what they saw as western individualism and obsession with material progress. Nationalist music making potentially drew *becak* drivers and street guides together. However, as I will further discuss, the workers' musical preferences in the realm of nationalist music most often remained divided into *dangdut* and *jalanan* respectively.

In relation to work practices, street guides' social connections with certain kampung actors granted them greater local-level power than that available to the drivers. As a result, many guides were able to draw on and build up globalist cultural capital and, through local connections, convert this into money. As I will show, the capital at the *becak* drivers' disposal was, by contrast, more diffusely regionalist. An examination of various forms of capital can therefore help to explain the dominance of the street guides over the *becak* drivers. However, to the extent that agency is recognised in these street-level actors, capital analysis is less readily able to explain why or how the two groups were also able to coexist relatively peacefully, such as was the case at the *becak* drivers' stand. In this light, Bourdieu's concepts need to be modified to allow for simple acts of cooperation. I will seek to do this by means of a concept of social capital.

IN-GROUP AND INTER-GROUP SOCIAL CAPITAL

There are in the literature two rather different uses of the term social capital. The first emphasises the 'capital' gathering strategies of social networking and the uneven distribution of the various capitals involved. Bourdieu (1986), for example, argues that possession of social capital is another means of dominance. According to Bourdieu (1986:249):

> [A] network of relationships is the product of investment strategies [,] consciously or unconsciously aimed at establishing or reproducing social relationships that are directly usable [;] i.e., at transforming contingent relations [...] into [...] durable obligations objectively felt.

Individuals and groups transform social capital into power by converting it into economic capital. For example, parents may utilise their networks of connections to ensure that their children go to good schools, and the children in turn are subsequently able to secure large incomes (Calhoun 2002:262-4).

On the other hand, a communitarian reading of social capital stresses the 'social' as a community-based alternative to economism. Here, social capital is most often viewed as a benevolent community-building resource, with indicators of its existence including social trust, informal cooperation and voluntary involvement in social groups (Putnam 2000). In this sense, social capital is generated between people, as expressed in the notion that 'relationships and networks are forms of capital to the extent that they constitute a resource' (Field 2003:1). Given these readings, I contend that understanding the peaceful roles of music in the street workers' daily lives requires an appreciation of the ways that social capital can sometimes be an instrument of power, at others a community resource, and yet others a combination of the two.

In other words, a focus on the economy of practices, with economy understood as a 'system governed by the laws of interested calculation, competition, or exploitation' (Bourdieu 1977:172) is valuable, even essential. At the same time, it cannot hope to encapsulate the entirety of social and musical life. Particularly in the case of lower-class street workers, it is not helpful to interpret every act of resource accumulation as evidence of calculative strategies for personal gain. As John Field (2003:17) notes, such an orientation toward social capital cannot account for 'affect'. I therefore adopt Bourdieu's theory only to the extent that each possessor of capital has the 'potentiality' of an act of power (Bourdieu and Wacquant 1992:145). At the same time, communitarian readings of social capital have come under increasing scrutiny for their lack of attention to the divisive effects of social networking, and for government attempts to promote a communitarian view while actually 'shor[ing] up the individualist assumptions on which neo-liberal economics is based' (Scanlon 2004:6).

The following chapters seek to carry the tension between these understandings and uses of the concept of social capital, and in this way account for cooperation around music and social relations in the midst of contestation. Building on the work of Bourdieu (1986), Marshall Sahlins (1972) and Robert Putnam (2000), the terms I have devised for this task are 'in-group' and 'inter-group' social capital. By in-group social capital, I mean social resources that are mobilised by and for the benefit of a discrete group. The effects of such mobilisations can be read in at least two ways. Such 'immaterial' exchanges may be tied up with economic interests, exacerbating social inequality; alternatively, in-group social capital may be part of a relatively healthy collective identity, necessary to intergroup tolerance. Inter-group social capital is different, but can also be read in two ways. It may be a community-generating social resource built on networking and cooperation across groups that are otherwise largely separate. On the other hand, interaction between groups may result in collusion between leaders of formerly separate groups at the expense of their former constituents, and thereby exacerbate inequalities (Cleaver 2005).

In simple terms, it may be said that economic capital refers to 'what you have, in monetary terms', while cultural capital is 'what you know, especially in the realm of the arts', and social capital 'who you know'. As I will seek to demonstrate, regionalist and globalist music making built in-group social capital at the *becak* driver and street guides' respective hangouts. Inter-group social capital on the other hand arose around music evoking the nation and/or a kind of trans/international regionalism, meaning music associated with a region that is neither Java nor what is commonly understood as the West (such as Batak or Latin America). It also became manifest more readily when encounters occurred in relatively neutral social domains.

1

Sosrowijayan and its street workers

In Yogyakarta's Sosrowijayan neighbourhood, 'village-like' kampung conventions intermingle with urban dynamism. Sosrowijayan is bordered by Marlioboro Street to the east and the city's central railway station to the north (see Map to Part One). It accommodates the majority of Yogyakarta's 'sloppily dressed western tourists' (Mulder 1996:180) and merges into the Flower Market (Pasar Kembang) red-light district. The nearby areas of Pajeksan and Dagen indicate the earlier courtly roles of prosecutors and woodworkers respectively (John Sullivan 1992:23); and the Flower Market's former name of Balokan (timber yard) is well known. By contrast, the history of Sosrowijayan rarely receives much attention, in everyday conversation and scholarly research alike.[1] The neighbourhood was a single administrative district up to the time of Japanese occupation (1942-1945), but was subsequently divided in two. In 2001 the eastern tourist-oriented half consisted of ten neighbourhood units (Arta 2002).

Despite the renown of Sosrowijayan (or 'Sosro'), a surprisingly large number of Yogyakarta residents I spoke with knew little or nothing of the area. Some who were familiar nonetheless did not know their way around its many back alleys behind Malioboro Street, and many described the area as 'grubby' or 'shabby'. One man further commented that many mischievous people frequented the area. When pressed to be more specific, he described the eastern, Malioboro end as 'an international kampung' in a fairly neutral tone, and then denigrated the western end inhabited by a plethora of commercial sex workers who, as Patrick Guinness (1986:89-90) notes, had been in operation since before 1975 (see also Mujiyano 1985).

Economic disparities between locals and foreigners underpinned the high financial stakes for local business. A sense of the differing levels of economy is evident in the average prices of commercially purchased meals in 2001:

---

1 Studies by Norma Sullivan (1994) and John Sullivan (1992) are relevant here.

Setting	Average price of a meal	
	Rp	US$
High-class hotel	50,000	5.00
Backpacker café in Sosrowijayan	12,000	1.20
Roadside eatery in the city, incl. Sosrowijayan	2,500	25c
Eatery in a surrounding village	600	6c

Table 3. Average price of meals by sector, 2001

Meals were at least 400% more expensive in Sosrowijayan than in surrounding villages. Economic imbalances between foreigners and locals were even more striking, particularly after the onset of the economic crisis. But the social groups operating in these economic arenas to some degree blurred and overlapped. Locals from various class backgrounds and some foreigners ate snacks or drank tea at roadside eateries. In these cases prices were considerable for those locals who usually operated in village economies, and extremely affordable for foreigners. At the same time, many street guides engaged in social or economic activities with foreigners regularly ate at the latter's expense in backpacker cafés and even high-class hotels.

While 'long-term budget travellers' (Riley 1988:313), students, development workers and business people all contributed to Sosrowijayan's economic imbalances, collectively they also underpinned the extensive local/foreigner social and cultural interaction that characterised the area. In the realm of popular music, Sosrowijayan's international dimension exercised considerable influence among and between workers, residents and visitors on the street. Understandings of Sosrowijayan's popular history generally centred on the 1970s. This was the beginning of the neighbourhood's mainstream incorporation into the 'hippy trail', and a period associated with international popular and rock music trends such as reggae and British heavy metal. Older residents and former street guides also mentioned Indonesian pop groups that had been popular and influential in Sosrowijayan since the 1970s, such as Koes Plus and D'Lloyd.[2]

However, street guides and their associates most often spoke of and played music from the mid-1980s 'Jakarta Spring' period of cultural liberalisation (Lockard 1998:105-13). *Jalanan* figure Sawung Jabo suggested to me that such songs were a vehicle for the expression of anger or resistance during the Soeharto years, but

---

2 See Lockard 1998:4-5. On developments in theatre in the mid/late 1970s Yogyakarta, see Hatley 2008:13-38; on music in Indonesia more broadly, see Piper and Jabo 1987.

were nowadays mostly a source of fun. Sosrowijayan-based street guides generally considered pop groups of the Reformasi period to be for middle class and largely depoliticised youth, although there were exceptions, such as Padi, RiF, Boomerang, and newer songs by Slank. Many teenagers enjoyed Padi, Dewa and Sheila on 7, as well as international artists such as Ronan Keating.

For *becak* drivers in Sosrowijayan, the presence of foreigners was a greater influence on business than cultural practice, even though given the opportunity most drivers were keen to promote *campursari*. In general, the presence of foreigners in Sosrowijayan has increased both business competition and intercultural exchange. Due to these differing social interactions, street guides held certain advantages over *becak* drivers in their access to economic and globalist cultural capital, as well as conversions between them.

ROADSIDES AND ALLEYWAYS

Tourism workers situate themselves around the places that supply both daily needs and occasional activities, including food, accommodation, telecommunications, transportation and tours. These settings double as 'hangouts', which in 2001 could be classified according to their 'roadside' or 'alleyway' location. This roadside/alleyway classification of hangouts needs to be distinguished from residential-based socio-spatial formulations that use similar terminology. Guinness (1986:vii) has identified residential-based kampung and the more affluent and influential 'streetside' society bordering a Yogyakarta kampung 'beside a wooded river', just as Howard Dick (1990) distinguishes between modest kampung housing and larger houses located on main roads. Alison Murray (1991) analyses divisions between 'crowded off-street alleys' and the 'streetside' in her Jakarta-based case study, and Dahles (2001) differentiates Yogyakarta's kampung and the more formal 'streetside' tourist industries.

Based on my own observations, much of Sosrowijayan displayed these kampung/streetside divisions. However, many buildings deep in the eastern 'international' kampung were solid and attractive, in part a result of their well-established commercial outlets and desirable tranquillity. Most importantly, social life around the street inverted the above division. Hangouts along the alleyways were in a sense more refined, in that activities and actions there tended to comply with kampung conventions of cleanliness and quiet. In contrast, those located near the wealthy, more privatised family homes and commercial outlets on main roads were grittier and the social and spatial boundaries less clear.

Musical worlds in Yogyakarta

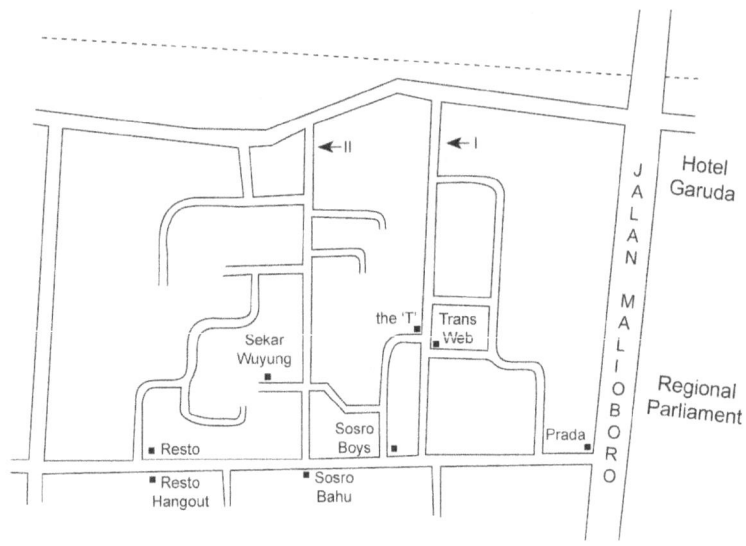

Map to Part One: Prominent street guide and *becak* driver hangouts in Sosrowijayan, 2001

The areas marked on the Map to Part One show where public interactions involving street guides and/or *becak* drivers often took place. The alleyway hangout that will feature at length is a pedestrian 'T' intersection on Gang One, bordered by the Woodpecker restaurant and, especially significant here, the TransWeb internet café. A string of batik art, craft and book shops, guesthouses, eateries and private dwellings led south into Sosrowijayan Street and north to 'Flower Market' Street. Newcomers wishing to work as street guides in Sosrowijayan often began in the narrow alleys between Malioboro Street and Gang One, earning credibility as commission agents by bringing tourists from Malioboro into one of the so-called 'exhibitions' of batik artworks. Gang Two was quieter than Gang One but also had a series of tourist outlets. The smaller alleyways westbound off Gang Two featured residential houses, sex work outposts and a few guesthouses. As will be further explored, Sekar Wuyung's guesthouse and *campursari* rehearsal space was located toward Sosrowijayan's west end, as was the Shower Band's rehearsal space.

The well-maintained Gang Two also housed community life independent of tourism and sex work. Numerous houses, a community meeting hall, and the main local mosque were located here,

1 Sosrowijayan and its street workers

as was a dusty commons area where children played soccer and people raised homing pigeons and held community events such as funerals, Islamic rituals, and national commemorations. The Sosro Bahu *becak* driver stand sat opposite the end of Gang Two on Sosrowijayan Street, with the longstanding street guides' Sriwisata travel office located back toward Malioboro Street (marked 'Sosro Boys'). To the west along Sosrowijayan Street, the relatively new Resto restaurant, very popular with backpackers and others, was usually open 24 hours a day; and the roadside across the street became a major hangout for street guides and their associates. Finally, the Prada eatery on the corner of Sosrowijayan and Malioboro streets was generally open from evening until daylight.

Workers thronged the streets of downtown Yogyakarta, many of whom held multiple occupations. Trinket stallholders, transporters and moving food traders merged with department store, restaurant, and government workers shopping and/or making their way to or from work. Geertz (1960) and Guinness (1986:48-68) have formulated comprehensive maps of urban work groups in Java, and the 'Indonesia Citizen Biodata' form current during my research contained 23 work categories. Here I focus on the two largest mobile, street-oriented, occupational groups that dominated the street outwards from Sosrowijayan: *becak* drivers and street guides.

BECAK DRIVERS

Becak is usually translated as 'pedicab', but it is more vividly described as a two-seater tricycle taxi that looks like a 'big painted rocking chair on wheels' (Van Gemert, Van Genugten and Dahles 1999:98). *Becak* have been contentious in Indonesia for decades. Seen as remnants of the past, impediments to development, and 'inhuman' in the physical demands they make on the drivers, they have long been banned from major city centres. However, they also provide employment and fares are widely affordable. In places such as Yogyakarta, *becak* are seen as integral to 'authentic' tourism (Van Gemert, Van Genugten and Dahles 1999:98-9). In 2000-2001, *becak* drivers remained a prominent feature of Yogyakarta's streets, with several dozen plying Sosrowijayan Street and occupying strategic roadside locations. Most of the Sosrowijayan-based drivers fitted what Van Gemert's team have termed the 'top location [,] tourist transporter' category (1999:99-100, 109), but their success and strategies varied, as did people's perceptions regarding their social status. A young secretary cautioned me to stay away from them, describing them as lower class, crude, and untrustworthy. By contrast, my homestay manager corrected my use of the term *tukang becak* and suggested that the less class-bound *pengemudi* (driver) was more in keeping with Reformasi.[3]

Becak drivers are renowned, especially among tourists, for their persistence in seeking and then exploiting fare opportunities (Van Gemert, Van Genugten and Dahles 1999:97). In my experience however, most drivers went to great lengths to avoid suggesting a fee. And, while Niels Mulder (1996:118) notes that expressions such as 'Whatever you think is right' actually disguise very real expectations, my sense was that most drivers were not interested in purely economic gain. The drivers' fares averaged around Rp 700-1,000 per kilometre, and daily incomes appeared to range from Rp 5,000 ($US50c) to Rp 20,000 ($US2), although this estimation was difficult to substantiate. Every fare, being the result of negotiations between driver and customer, varied depending on the weather, terrain covered, and perceived wealth of the customer. Additionally, business was inconsistent, such that on some days a driver would barely land a single job, while on others he might secure half a dozen or more. Drivers often helped each other to avoid such extremes by sharing their clients, thus reflecting the benevolent form of in-group social capital under discussion here.

Two-thirds of the 30 drivers who were to join the Sosro Bahu Association resided in a village, often *becak* driving in the city for five days at a time and tending rice fields and/or animals at other times. Many of the drivers behaved quite bashfully around Sosrowijayan, yet just as regularly they laughed and joked uninhibitedly. Few spoke English, but many kept abreast of national and international news, contrary to the claim that they 'live in their own small world' (Van Gemert, Van Genugten and Dahles 1999:110). These men tended to know the whereabouts of various establishments better than anyone else did. Some of them 'dressed down' for their city work while maintaining fine rural dwellings, while many others were physically drawn and clearly undernourished. In addition to the difficulties of interpreting power relations in cross-cultural context (Errington 1990:58), this range of characteristics makes it difficult to gauge the *becak* drivers' capital conversion strategies in Sosrowijayan. Toward this end, I will trace the establishment of a drivers' stand and then analyse their musical tastes and practices.

3   A *tukang* is traditionally a 'skilled labourer or craftsman' (Echols and Shadily 1989), but in 2001 the term evidently carried connotations more akin to being a 'coolie'.

THE SOSRO BAHU STAND

In mid-2000, a loose consortium of *becak* drivers and local business owners erected a simple bench, comprising three wooden planks each around ten feet long, under a hibiscus tree and opposite the southern entrance to Gang Two. The small patch of land by the roadside continued to serve as a shaded parking bay for *becak* drivers, but now it also offered a place to sit, talk, drink and eat and, particularly in the midday heat, sleep. While Van Gemert's team (1999:108) write of a large 'Jalan Sosrowijayan' *becak* driver organization, the only other *becak* driver organizations I detected on Sosrowijayan Street operated toward the west end, and these had no clearly delineated socialising area and did not seem to gather much business. By contrast, the new consortium near Gang Two managed to establish a base that, being near a commercial pedestrian thoroughfare and close to Malioboro Street, was strategically located to catch potential customers.

Just prior to the establishment of the *becak* drivers' stand, a man named Pak Zaf relocated his telephone exchange from Sosrowijayan's west end to larger premises on the corner of Gang Two. A few of the *becak* drivers, already acquainted with Pak Zaf and his two associates, now acted on this new opportunity for practical cooperation. A couple of the drivers began sweeping out the telephone exchange and emptying the rubbish bins, and in return Pak Zaf often returned from his driving expeditions with small treats for them. With the involvement of the owner of a nearby souvenir shop and of Pak Jaya, co-owner of the adjacent Yogya Tours, a bench was installed, the first part of the Sosro Bahu stand.

Becak drivers and street guides offer different services – local transportation and cultural tourism advice – but both compete for the tourist dollar. The *becak* drivers now began to increase their entrepreneurial skills. In the lengthy quiet periods they would rest and talk, at times spreading their conversations across the street to the front of the telephone exchange. These business owners were important to the rural-based drivers, who lacked the economic, social, and cultural advantages of most street guides. Most of the street guides from the nearby Sriwisata ticket office, and a few hotel managers for whom they acted as commission agents, mixed nearby but rarely at the *becak* drivers' stand, at least in the early months. Street guides, *becak* drivers and others often bought food and drinks at a centrally located food stall run by an elderly couple, but they generally carried their purchases back to their separate hangouts.

Becak drivers at Sosro Bahu, 2001

Becak driver at Sosro Bahu, 2009

When I returned in April 2001, the drivers had installed a corrugated-iron ceiling, providing additional shelter from rain and the midday sun, and a radio and a small wooden box were fixed to the rear wall. Among our regular conversations, which most often related to their much cherished *campursari* music, a couple of the drivers urged me to come along to the inaugural meeting of the Sosro Bahu Association, also explaining that 'Sosro Bahu' relates to Arjuna, one of the Pendawa brothers from the ancient Mahabharata epic originally from India. The meeting began at nine-thirty pm in the customer area of Yogya Tours near the stand. Aside from a confectionary retailer sponsor, the Yogya Tours manager Pak Jaya, and me, all 30 men present were Sosro Bahu drivers. In stark contrast to their dusty street personages, most drivers now sported long pants, fresh shirts and carefully combed hair. Similarly, while by day they were variously jocular or deferent, in the meeting behind closed doors a more earnest air came to the fore.

Pak Jaya began proceedings with the counting of the monies, collected as follows. Each of the 30 members contributed Rp 8,000; a member sorted and added up the cash drivers had placed in the small box usually mounted and locked at the stand (Rp 100 per fare exceeding Rp 2,000); and another collected money from the confectionary retailer and other donors. In total the group amassed Rp 470,000 (US$47). Rp 220,000 was set aside for family emergencies (*sosial*); Rp 150,000 for the *arisan* lottery to be drawn later in the meeting with three equal winners;[4] and Rp 100,000 for refreshments and other organizational items such as pens and glasses.

It can be argued that the Rp 8,000 entrance fee was an economic barrier to membership (Van Gemert, Van Genugten and Dahles 1999:111). At the same time, the social support component (Van Gemert, Van Genugten and Dahles 1999:108) was clearly an economic benefit of in-group social capital, and the lottery added to the conviviality of proceedings. With the monies sorted, Pak Jaya formally reconvened the meeting, soon stating that sticking together had become particularly important since the onset of the economic crisis. He then urged members raise any issues now, rather than airing them quietly in small groups after the meeting. Eventually one driver mentioned that jealousies could arise around the trust system attached to fare contributions; another voiced similar concerns over allocations of social support monies, all of which was noted. The meeting broke up by midnight on an optimistic note.

The Sosro Bahu group subsequently held meetings every 35 days in accordance with the Javanese calendar. At another meet-

4 *Arisan* are 'rotating credit groups run as lotteries' (Murray 1991:69).

ing I attended in early August, Pak Jaya and two other sponsors were now honorary members, while from among the drivers there was a head, a spokesperson, and a secretary. During the meeting, the group carried a motion that members should work to collect extra *sosial* for a driver whose wife had just had another baby. Issues around toilet regulations and the feasibility of bathing at Yogya Tours were also discussed, matters of some importance given that drivers would often spend the night there. Significantly, one member brought up the possibility of a *campursari* or *congdut* (*kroncong/dangdut*) performance as part of Sosrowijayan's upcoming Independence Day celebrations, also suggesting that they could use a band to promote Sosro Bahu. In the previous year, the Sosrowijayan kampung had celebrated Independence Day on Sosrowijayan Street with a rock group followed by a *dangdut* group, much to the delight of hundreds of spectators from many occupations and lifestyles. In 2001, by contrast, celebrations were to be small, patriotic, and not very popular.

As had been finalised at the August meeting, early the following morning a half dozen members held a small religious service, then carried out a working bee on the stand. With the added financial assistance of Pak Zaf, a few of the *becak* drivers restructured the bench, then padded it and covered the padding in vinyl upholstery of a brilliant blue, while a couple of others painted the ceiling and inside walls in white. By afternoon, the drivers had completed the restructure and facelift of the stand. The opening incident, in which street guides occupied the stand musically, was to occur there a couple of days later.

The formalisation of Sosro Bahu served to build in-group solidarity among the drivers. They gained financial security and were able to 'be themselves' and influence decisions in meetings. Sosro Bahu also fostered relations with representatives of other groups or work sectors, initially between a small number of drivers and Pak Zaf, and then with the involvement of local sponsors. However, it also committed the drivers to the Sosrowijayan area, and their increased dependence on tourism did not necessarily empower them (Van Gemert, Van Genugten and Dahles 1999:110). Additionally, the plan of Sosro Bahu members to affiliate themselves with a local *campursari* performance never came to pass. Had it done so, this would have enhanced their legitimacy in the kampung and hence their potential access to the tourist dollar. Its failure to take place may reflect a lack of intergroup connection between them and the Sosrowijayan-based Sekar Wuyung *campursari* group (discussed below). However, it may also have been due to the active intergroup rivalry of others in the kampung. A number of long-term Sosrowijayan-based *becak* drivers derided Sosro Bahu, and on being pushed as to why would only mutter that they were untrustworthy with money. For reasons already mentioned, street guides too may have wished to curb the expansion of Sosro Bahu's standing in the kampung.

STREET GUIDES

Up and down Malioboro Street and into Sosrowijayan, street guides generally sustained themselves as commission agents for tourist services, with some seeking sexual, romantic and/or business involvement with western women in the process. The Sosrowijayan-based guides were adept at negotiating in a number of languages, and many even had an uncanny knack for identifying westerners' nationalities based solely on their walking styles and general bearing. Several of the guides were also connected with hotel owner/managers, themselves former street guides. As with the case of the *becak* drivers, guides' actual incomes were difficult to measure. Dahles (2001:137) suggests that in the mid-1990s a relatively successful guide could make Rp 15-20,000 per day in commissions from tourist agencies to which he had brought customers. On top of these commissions, guides could enter distinctly higher levels of the economy than the *becak* drivers could. One popular means was to tell a newly arrived foreigner that a rare art exhibition was currently underway, which within an hour could lead both parties to a batik art shop and the foreigner paying a thousand per cent mark-up for a standard work. Establishing friendships with foreigners often led the latter to pay for guides' meals and drinks in backpacker restaurants, which in some cases led to successful export business enterprises. A good example was Toto, who rose from being a guide to an agent earning US$120 per month, an income level unimaginable for *becak* drivers.

At the same time, many of the guides lived very humbly and without anything like the *becak* drivers' ability to fall back on village residency. Their incomes depended on the goodwill or gullibility of tourists, many of whom referred to guides as 'hustlers' and treated them with suspicion. Such inconsistency of income could be intense for younger or probationary guides who were former street children. In addition, many people regarded the Sosrowijayan guides with either quirky amusement or quiet resentment, reflecting the reputation for laziness and even dishonesty that they had to endure. Moreover, the musical tastes of the vast majority of Javanese outside relatively westernised Sosrowijayan had more in common with *becak* drivers than with street guides. *Campursari* retained an important connection with gamelan and other regionalist forms, whereas many Javanese adults likened (particularly electric) guitars to children's toys. For both *becak* drivers and street guides, then, a measure of social capital helped to smooth over rough patches in business and social exchange.

Defining street guides as a distinct group requires some clarification. Most guides are urban practitioners of 'occupational multiplicity', a term used by commentators on Indonesia to refer to the numerous productive activities that individuals are forced to manage (for example, White 1976). Dahles (2001:177) writes of guides that, of the hundreds of 'young men offering their services to passing tourists [, many] are students, shop assistants, hotel personnel, taxi drivers, and office clerks, even civil servants and teachers with more or less permanent jobs'. Additionally, given that most street guides combined international sales techniques and Javanese indirectness into extremely good acting skills, and the fact that many of them sincerely wished to converse more than gain business, it was difficult to gauge the degree to which a young man's approach constituted 'guiding'.

Often twice a day I drank ginger tea while 'hanging out' with a number of guides at the *angkringan* next to their Sriwisata ticket office. Conversational topics and conventions here differed starkly from those in formal Indonesian settings, where parties usually exchange extensive biographical detail in a matter of moments. Instead, our familiarity grew through humour and innuendo, often involving Jakarta-derived street slang known as *prokem* (Murray 1991; Slone 2003). Personal knowledge of each other barely extended beyond nicknames, even after a number of months (Willis 1978). In order to identify some of the street guides' capital generation and conversion processes, below I focus on the Sriwisata organization and related groups, and then in following chapters analyse their music-making practices.

SRIWISATA AND THE SOSRO BOYS

The street guides' Sriwisata ticket office was, unlike the *becak* drivers' Sosro Bahu stand, a longstanding and formal business outlet, but both had virtually all-male membership of around 40 members, and the *raison d'être* in both cases was tourism business. However, identifying street guides within the Sriwisata organization requires consideration of a large, loose-knit group of individuals around Sosrowijayan known as the 'Sosro Boys' (*anak sosro*). The Sosro Boys were in some senses a 'gang', although the term also often described anyone with 'roots' in the kampung. By attaining membership in Sriwisata, a street guide earned the in-group status and security of being associated with the Sosro Boys. And Sosro Boys, Sriwisata members and street guides were all far more likely to identify with urban-oriented *musik jalanan* and its subcultural sensibilities than the *campursari* world of *becak* drivers.

Sriwisata resembled Sosro Bahu in that many of its members often spent time out of town. However, whereas *becak* drivers returned to their villages on a regular basis, many guides' business and social commitments took them on long journeys at short notice. In mid-2001 for example, Ari took three months off to return to his aging parents' home in Bandung; MJ, a 'gigolo' (male equivalent of the '*perek*' discussed later), travelled to Sumatra with a Dutch woman for six weeks; and a lower ranking member of the group returned to Sosrowijayan after a long absence, now with a young family. Flexible commitments and the sharing of tasks among small groups helped to accommodate these extra-Sriwisata priorities, and also to maintain the smooth functioning of the group. Despite the fluidity of membership and roles, Sriwisata members held monthly meetings in the local meeting hall. The organization was established in 1991, after nearly two decades of a loose group regularly approaching and socialising with international visitors to the area, and in 2001 it was still running well.

Chandra and Cil were important connections between the Sosro Boys and the Sriwisata group, both socially and financially. Both often took part in Sosro Boy excesses, such as Sriwisata's tenth birthday party in which around 20 members ended up swinging their shirts above their heads and falling over each other on the Bar Borobudur dance floor. However, Chandra and Cil were also entrepreneurial in initiating projects and developing their professional business skills. One evening outside the Sriwisata office, they sat perched forward facing each other and with unusual seriousness discussed local planning. Unlike any of the *becak* drivers, Cil had just completed a two-day tourism course at the government offices midway along Malioboro Street, and was now exploring ways for Sriwisata to expand their business operations. Their most pressing project, he said, was to open a large café/music venue in Sosrowijayan, as 'not unfriendly' competition to the successful Resto. Chandra added that securing finance was not a problem, but the choice of venue had yet to be finalised. As the discussion began to unwind, Cil chuckled and remarked that their ventures always did well, because the success of any business in the area depended on their support. This comment was an indirect reference to the fact that some forms of social capital relied on the threat of physical force (Bourdieu 1994).

In these ways, street guides were often able to draw on local connections. They also exercised 'global' skills in a number of languages, identifiable as cultural capital, to converse with and win over business. By contrast, the *becak* drivers' strengths were more diffusely regional/sub-national in terms of both connections in the kampung and with potential foreign clients. In many ways, the two groups coexisted more than cooperated or openly competed. However, there was also subtle inter-group competition between them over securing tourist commissions. Also at the in-group level certain issues sometimes brought cooperation into tension. In the case of the drivers this was evident in fare contributions and allocations of group funds, and for the guides through efforts to gain acceptance through business success.

2

Musical forms and spaces

The 'acoustic panorama of the Indonesian city' (Colombijn 2007:269) is both distinctive and under-theorized. In Yogyakarta's Sosrowijayan, music and the broader 'soundscape' (Shafer 1977) were integral to the roadside/alleyway division outlined in the previous chapter. These in turn influenced and were influenced by social relations such as those between street guides and *becak* drivers. Greater Sosrowijayan is hemmed in by three noisy, busy roads, and Sosrowijayan Street itself, which in 2001 was sleepier but nonetheless accommodated waves of motorised transport ranging from motorcycles to trucks and buses. To enter the alleyways off any street, however, within metres the street sounds gave way to a soundscape of kampung activities. Varying with some consistency over the course of each day, sounds included chatter, faint echoes of children playing, murmurs and scuffing shoes of passers-by, devotional sounds from mosques and churches, soap operas on television, melancholy ballads and talkback on radio, guitars and singing, the clinking of cooking utensils and whoosh of gas cookers, trickles of running water, cooing pigeons, and the 'tok tok', 'puk puk puk' and other signals of passing traders (Nakagawa 2000:133-4). The neighbourhood aural environment resulted from a combination of thin walls and open windows, in turn deriving from climatic compatibility and economic scarcity, as well as locally enforced noise regulations such as bans on riding motorised vehicles, and on making undue noise after hours, especially after midnight.

This chapter explores the two main spaces and forms of public music making that regularly took place on the roadsides and alleyways in Sosrowijayan: that of mobile buskers (*pengamen*) and that at hangouts. Self and cultural expression played a role in both kinds of music making, but they differed in terms of social affiliations, musical genres, and also in their relation to monetary exchange. Moving buskers sought cash directly, while those playing music at hangouts did not, although as outlined earlier such locations also served as bases for seeking business. Below I seek to demonstrate how these forms of music making generated and converted various forms of capital, drawing particularly on examples of musical genres that can be plotted broadly along a sub-national/regionalist to globalist axis. The analysis thereby posits links between musical genres and social capital among *becak* drivers and street guides, and seeks to articulate the roles of these in conflict avoidance in situations such as that at the start of Part One, in which street guides musically colonised a *becak* drivers' hangout.

MOBILE *PENGAMEN*

Java has a long history of travelling performers (Body 1982; Cohen 2006), whose forms have ranged from large theatre troupes (Hatley 2008:22-4; Foulcher 2004) to 'street tough' *kroncong* soloists known variously as *buaya* (crocodile) and *jago* (rooster) (Judith Becker 1975). Urban itinerant musicians are socially and financially marginalised yet, paradoxically, are central to the development of many musical forms that powerful politicians subsequently laud as national treasures (Manuel 1988:18). The Indonesian term for busker, *pengamen*, translates as 'singing beggar'; indeed, like beggars (*pengemis*), most *pengamen* in Yogyakarta are poor in economic terms. Unlike beggars however, many elicit some respect, a reflection of their greater cultural capital. In turn, *pengamen* generate situations that either reinforce or help to transcend boundaries between *becak* drivers, street guides, and other people on the streets.

In 2001, music making on Yogyakarta's streets and other public spaces projected both court/village and urban/street associations. On the one side, many Javanese street musicians played instruments and forms from, or resembling those of, courtly gamelan orchestras (Lockard 1998:58). As discussed earlier, *karawitan, langgam, kroncong* and to a degree *dangdut* all underpin much of what constitutes *campursari* music. On the other side, many people meant by *musik jalanan* the generally western-influenced folk/ rock music such as that of national superstar Iwan Fals. While the inner-city *anak jalanan* term tended to engender sympathy or derision (Solvang 2002), *musik jalanan* generally carried 'street cred' and pop culture iconography to the point of being a subculture. These court/village and urban/street musics projected regionalist and globalist cultural affiliations respectively, which in turn map broadly onto the *becak* driver/tourist guide street-worker division.

My previous encounters with music making around Yogyakarta's streets were a prime reason for choosing this research site. By 2000 however, streetside music making seemed to have waned. I discussed this matter with Mas Gunanto, a local anthropologist who had researched *anak jalanan* around Malioboro in the 1970s. Gunanto concurred, suggesting that before the 1997 economic crisis *pengamen* were concentrated in Malioboro, with a different group passing through Sosrowijayan every ten minutes. More recently, he pointed out, most *pengamen* played on trains, buses and at busy intersections. I too had noticed the explosion of *pengamen* on public transport and amid the din of traffic intersections. This exacerbated competition for already scarce resources. Many of the new buskers in these locations merely held an instrument and pretended to play it, although a student informed me that this 'dummy playing' was now declining because the public had begun refusing to reward such advances.

While some *pengamen* in Yogyakarta did not actually play at all, others gave spectacular performances of topical songs, as well as more comforting and familiar traditional ones. On Malioboro Street too there was still a considerable variety of *pengamen*, including street children who played in the evenings near the Tourist Information Centre (Solvang 2002), and generally older, itinerant musicians in Beringharjo Market. These *pengamen* trends reflected the sharp rises in urban unemployment and drops in domestic and international tourism at the time. The decreased activity and diversity of musical activity around the inner city was somewhat disheartening; but as described below, this situation at least enabled me to distinguish between the regular and the occasional *pengamen* around Sosrowijayan.

One regular group consisted of an elderly man and two to three middle-aged women, all dressed in traditional Yogyanese style. They played regionalist *karawitan* (gamelan music with singing), including the well-known nationalist *kroncong* melody 'Bengawan Solo' (Solo River) accompanied on a zither (*celumpung*) and, at times, *kendang* drum. A husband and wife team recently arrived from East Java, aged 30 and 36 respectively, performed *langgam* and *campursari* music. They both sang while he played the zither, and on some evenings he played the same songs as a solo guitarist. Most days the elderly Bu Yani sang *langgam* and *campursari* while shaking her tambourine, despite restaurant and eatery staff often admonishing her for repeatedly returning to the same site and customers. Both Bu Surati and Pak Wasirun were *kroncong* solo guitarists of long standing in the area whose playing around tables and stalls occasionally gave rise to requests and etiquette-laden bowing.

All of these *pengamen* tried their luck at backpacker cafés, the domain of tourist guides, yet their music had more in common with the tastes of *becak* drivers. As a result, their endeavours to attain economic gain through regionalist cultural projections were rarely successful. Furthermore, foreigners generally favoured the more purist forms of gamelan in their palatial settings, and western pop music, with the relatively hybridized forms of the *pengamen* falling between the two.

A couple of *pengamen* acts passing through Sosrowijayan received a more positive response. A young, lower-class woman sang 'Hati yang luka' (A wounded heart; see Yampolsky 1989) in the *kroncong*-style thrumbing of her mandolin at the Resto entrance one afternoon. As her friend stood breastfeeding her baby in the background, the performer won the approval of the street-savvy Indonesian women there for the novelty of her rendition. On another occasion, a 40 year old Sumatran man named Girang played his beaten-up guitar that had recently fallen from a train, with his baritone voice and delicate plucking style producing soulful cover versions of nostalgic ballads from the early 1970s such as 'Gubahanku' (My composition). In both these cases, the players' unusual renditions of nationalist music bridged regional and national associations into greater social interaction than the other players mentioned above.

In their musical and dress presentations, all of these *pengamen* manifested what I am calling a regionalist identity, but they varied in terms of the types and levels of capital with which they operated. The *karawitan* musicians played songs favoured by *becak* drivers, and they sometimes mingled quietly at food stalls. These interactions, while not based directly on music, seemed to encourage mutual support (including economic support). I noticed on visiting the East Java duo's residence that they owned a colour television and an antique display. When playing in Sosrowijayan however, they usually perched on the dusty ground of roadside café entrances, which suggests that local residents and eatery staff did not pay them much respect. The young woman at Resto briefly interacted with other women there, although the attention she received clearly made her uncomfortable.

Finally, the itinerant *pop nostalgia* musician mentioned that fellow *pengamen* often valued the new ideas he brought with him. This exemplifies musical collaboration among buskers at the in-group occupational level, but also across groups in terms of ethnicity, gender and other identity markers. It also demonstrates that, while *pengamen* sought economic return, such practices at this level of the economy did not necessarily lead to inter-group tensions and exploitation. Here Girang mentioned *congrock* (*kroncong* and rock), a new hybrid enjoying increasing popularity at the Simpang Lima Plaza in Semarang that was only beginning to gain currency in Yogyakarta.

In contrast to the above cases, two *pengamen* groups had a direct influence on social and musical interaction between *pengamen*, *becak* drivers and street guides in Sosrowijayan. The first was a five-man group who sang and played two acoustic guitars, piccolo flute, bottle-top percussion, and *dangdut* drum. On a typical evening the group would enter from Sosrowijayan's west end and stop in at the relatively high-class Bladok restaurant, and then try the locally patronised *warung* across the road. They then moved on to the Resto entrance before carrying their gear eastward and into Gang Two, continue through to the T on Gang One, then take either the north or south route, stopping at one or two more places before continuing along Malioboro Street.

The group's Javanese-inflected *dangdut* with guitar-based *kroncong* nuances received a mixed reception in Sosrowijayan. One evening at the Resto entrance, their *dangdut* song was not enthusiastically received. Despite the group's commanding presence, the restaurant staff did not readily dim the stereo, which at this point was playing Sundanese *musik degung* popular with international visitors. Lacking support from the guides and Resto staff, the group moved on. Their mediocre reception was also due in part to the group's song choice, which had little cultural cachet with staff, guides, and customers.

A different situation arose when the group played at the *becak* drivers' stand on the evening of Indonesian Independence Day and a couple of weeks after the incident. A few of the Sosro Bahu members sang along with the group. Especially during 'Prahu layar' (Sailboat), a traditional Javanese song by Narto Sabdo currently popular with *campursari* orchestras, the audience became so enthusiastic that some of the drivers danced on the road. With this combination of national Independence celebrations (not evident anywhere else nearby), rice wine (most *becak* drivers very rarely drank alcohol), and a *dangdut* busking group playing familiar regional *campursari* tunes, the *becak* drivers were transformed from their normal Sosrowijayan composures into singing and dancing performers. The *dangdut* combo, for their part, sang with great joy.

In this case, then, the transmutability of *dangdut Jawa* and *campursari* helped to facilitate interaction between a *pengamen* group and *becak* drivers, who sang along together, exchanged stories and built a sense of solidarity. Regional music and a national theme encouraged a sense of cooperation and trust between the two groups, and did not involve monetary exchange. Passing street guides in the meanwhile neither joined in nor seemed intimidated by the gathering.

The second, and more influential, *pengamen* group featuring regularly in Sosrowijayan's public spaces was the Astro Band. Astro Band's extraordinarily large repertoire ranged from *campursari*, new and old Indonesian pop and regional favourites, to the Beatles and Latin American songs, some of which they experimented with by blending regional, national, and global musical elements. One song request folder they carried contained the Indonesia categories of 'pop hits', 'nostalgia', *kroncong*, *daerah* (regional) and *kebangsaan* (national). Their second folder contained categories such as 'Bowie – England', 'Eagles – Amerika Serikat' and 'Italy'. The Astro Band comprised a core of six men in their early 20s, some of who had come from Surabaya to live in Yogyakarta over the past few years. Their core instruments were double bass, folk guitars, banjo, and two conga drums with a thin chain strapped to them that could be gently tapped and sharply swivelled. Most members sang harmonies and at different times took the lead vocal position. Numerous others also joined in, including fellow street workers such as portrait artists but also holidaymakers and domestic and international students.

Astro Band playing at Malioboro *lesehan*, 2001

2 Musical forms and spaces

Astro Band playing at Malioboro *lesehan*, 2009

The Astro Band worked along Malioboro Street and elsewhere every evening, except to attend prayers twice a week. They generally began around seven pm by playing to the *lesehan* outside Hotel Garuda, where they received anywhere between Rp 500 per song and, on rare occasions such as when a Japanese party hired them on the spot for a whole evening, Rp 300,000 (US$30). From around midnight until between two and five am, the group usually settled at the Prada eatery on the corner of Sosrowijayan and Malioboro Streets, interspersing their playing with sitting back and sipping tea while chatting and engaging in creative wordplays, known as *plesetan* (Heryanto 1996:102-3). Unlike the *dangdut Jawa* group's performance at Sosro Bahu, financial gain clearly remained on Astro Band's agenda. Nonetheless, their combination of music making and hanging about at Prada both built their own experience and knowledge, and at times facilitated interaction between ethnicities, nationalities and, to an extent, class groups. This was especially evident given that many of the participants would otherwise rarely sing together, converse and exchange ideas and information.

While the Astro Band interacted quite freely on the corner of Malioboro Street, their relations with most Sosrowijayan-based workers were more measured. To my knowledge, they never mixed with the Sosro Bahu drivers, although in the early morning hours they sometimes chatted with other *becak* drivers at another *lesehan* on Malioboro Street. However, the band sometimes played in the Sosrowijayan alleyways. One evening they broke into song at the entrance to Woodpecker by the T. The music caused quite an impact in this sleepy area, with all band members singing the choruses to their rendition of a popular Latin American song. By the third verse, many of the clientele and staff at the Woodpecker applauded, some placing a few notes (between Rp 500 and 3,000) in the cup that the banjo player circulated while the others continued playing. Although they moved on, their presence served to enliven the area, as was evident when staff at a neighbouring café turned off the talkback radio show and put on a Deep Purple cassette. More generally, while well aware of the Sosro Boys' strong territorial claims to the area, Astro members sometimes befriended street guides via such musical exchanges, with guides highly valuing their storehouse of repertoire and playing techniques. As I will further discuss, musical exchanges also helped other 'outsiders' to enter the social world of the guides and, by extension, the Sosro Boys.

Of the *pengamen* music that featured around Sosrowijayan in 2001, the *campursari* genre was best able to combine regionalist gamelan-related zithers and *langgam* scales with nationalist *kroncong* guitar styles and *dangdut* rhythms and songs. To some extent, this provided common ground for the tastes of *pengamen* and *becak* drivers. By contrast, *pengamen* who played globalist popular music received some endorsement from street guides and café staff, although such musicians were generally mindful of encroaching onto the guides' territory. In all of these examples, *pengamen* performed in a context of economic transaction.

STREET-WORKER *TONGKRONGAN*

Music at street-worker hangouts (*tongkrongan*) tended to differ from that of the mobile *pengamen* in a number of ways. Most often, hangout music making around Sosrowijayan was performed by younger men connected to the street-guide business; and guitars were by far the most common instruments. As mentioned, the kinds and levels of participation in music making in these settings were also not as clearly premised on economic exchange. Features of this music making were prominent at the TransWeb Internet café in Gang One and opposite the Resto restaurant/bar on Sosrowijayan Street, which in turn reflected some of the roadside/alleyway distinctions outlined earlier. To set the context for discussion of these street-guide dominated sites, here I briefly return to the Sosro Bahu stand in the light of *tongkrongan* music making.

Literally all of the Sosro Bahu drivers I met were intimately familiar with *campursari* lyrics and song structures. Music at their stand usually served as soothing background to the harsh conditions of the drivers' urban toil, with *campursari* in particular invoking their fondness for the villages where they typically resided. Usually one or two would quietly sing to a *campursari* song playing on the radio, either from memory, or with the aid of small lyric booklets. By contrast, one late afternoon around a dozen drivers broke into song, with one using his *becak* seat as a drum, the only instrument in use. Everybody sang 'Sewu kuto' (A thousand towns), a popular *campur-*

2 Musical forms and spaces

sari song of the time. Most of those present became highly animated, singing with great vigour and stepping rhythmically in and out of *joged* dancing. The atmosphere quietened down as quickly as it had erupted, and it was only in the villages and at the Sultan's Palace that I was again to see the *campursari* world of the *becak* driver come to life.

TRANSWEB

TransWeb Internet café was located by the T intersection connecting Gang One to a narrow westbound lane. Being close to the Gang One but well away from motorised traffic, TransWeb was part of the aurally sensitive and 'refined' (*halus*) alleyway environment. The nearby T was a semi-public zone where neighbouring shop and restaurant staff, their friends and petty tourist goods traders regularly mingled. Particularly in the late afternoon and early evenings, workers would variously survey for potential clients, chat, and recline to rest against the cool walls. Inclusion at the T *tongkrongan* seemed to rest as much on one's means of livelihood as whether or not one was of Yogya origin (Guinness 1986:128-68).

Life is quieter in the kampung

But *becak* drivers did not stop in at the T, if for no other reason than that the size of their vehicles prevented it. And the TransWeb staff and their friends socialised close to but actually separate from the T. Guitar playing and singing often emanated from TransWeb, adding to the T's soundscape of background component stereos, hospitality work and general chatter. The internet café's interior had low light and cool but slightly stale air caused by the combination of small fans and constant smoking. There were six small semi-open booths against the three walls, each facing the centre of the room, while more general socialising took place at the service desk, around a low table in the centre of the room, outside on a long park bench between the front window and the gangway, and on the entrance steps themselves.

Pablo, Syari and Chandra ran TransWeb in overlapping shifts. Each had an influence on the people entering their space. Syari was a young woman new to Yogyakarta, and made many friends from outside the city. Pablo and Chandra by contrast were street guides and Sriwisata members with close affiliations with the Sosro Boys. Added to this, Pablo was also a musician and a 'gigolo', meaning a young Indonesian man having intimate relations with a number of older foreign women. Most of the regular visitors to TransWeb were heavily involved in popular music and were at least part-time street guides. There was also a sex worker (or, as will be discussed later, more accurately a *perek*) known as Doris. Most clientele at TransWeb were young overseas travellers or students. Many of these were newcomers to Yogyakarta, with the convenient location and friendly service as yet preventing their knowledge of TransWeb's relatively high fees. But long-time friends and partners also visited the café regularly.

TransWeb fostered a loose subgroup joining Sosrowijayan insiders and outsiders through popular music and backpacker tourism. The combination of staff, friends and clientele affected social interactions there, as well as the music played. Staff kept the stereo volume below conversation level, and most often played CDs of the Red Hot Chilli Peppers, Moby, Lenny Kravitz, and Eric Clapton. Music making usually involved Pablo's classical guitar, a good quality Japanese-made Yamaha he bought for Rp 200,000 from a tourist in 1998 and kept permanently in the corner of the café. During quiet periods, Pablo would play a blues scale along to an Eric Clapton CD. At other times, Andi would sit on the café veranda and, either on his own or with a young, western woman sitting quietly next to him, sing the Red Hot Chilli Peppers' 'Under the bridge' with a pained expression and draping back his long sweeping hair. On some early evenings, two or three people playing guitars would spread across the bench and onto the steps. At these times, the participants often sang 70s and 80s western pop songs such as 'Crazy little thing called love', 'Patience' and 'No woman, no cry', as well as 'Wonderwall' by Britpop group Oasis.

Music making sometimes helped to establish social networks and, in turn, economic gain for street-based workers by linking newcomer guides with Sriwisata members. Andar of Surabaya was a prime example of such capital generation and conversion. Like Ari, a Yogya outsider who, in the incident that opened Part One, negotiated Sosro Boy insider status at the Sosro Bahu *becak* driver stand, Andar's familiarity with national and international songs and playing styles quickly led to his involvement in street guide social life. His body piercings, mop-top hairstyle, and general pop-star persona complemented his unusually good guitar playing, according him great esteem among his new peers. Problems with his Jakarta-based funk band had delayed their album recording project, and so he decided to spend some time in Yogyakarta where, he said, life was easier and more affordable.

Andar's involvement in music making at TransWeb provided an entrée to the status of Sosro Boy, and therefore access to economic opportunity. For example, one quiet afternoon when I visited TransWeb, Andar was playing Pablo's guitar on the steps while Agus and Ari sat on the nearby bench, and Pablo sat with us, except to duck inside to take care of business. Andar returned us to an earlier conversation on guitars, and at their suggestion I brought mine over. Now with two guitars, the opportunity arose for Andar to exchange some of his musical knowledge with the other guides. Their playing and singing became markedly more upbeat and excited as two tall and scantily dressed blonde Scandinavian women entered the T and stood there for a time. Later, without any western women nearby, they played songs of the Bandung-based band Dewa such as 'Aku di sini untukmu' (I am here for you). Andar showed Agus the accompanying chords, and by the end of the song, they were able to play it together. Andar also played original compositions and improvisations, including tasteful jazz and mood chords, none of which he could name. Later the young men ran through several Doors' songs, with the older female staff inside the Woodpecker restaurant across the way chuckling at their youthfulness.

Music making at TransWeb could incorporate young, urban-oriented newcomers such as Andar. Andar's musical prowess and pop-star style markers, more than his multilingual ability, led to him being included in social occasions such as a Sriwisata birthday party and a large-scale rock performance. Andar thereby utilised his nationalist and globalist musical skills to mix freely in the relatively high economic circles of backpacker cafés. By contrast, music making at TransWeb did not generate any common ground or joint projects with the regular buskers or with the Sosro Bahu *becak* drivers. Music making at TransWeb, then, generally took place between late afternoon and early evening, often in the context of interactions between Indonesian street guides/gigolo and non-Indonesian women.

The guides' musical interludes at TransWeb did not impose sonically onto the T, and socially too they remained largely separate from their immediate surrounds. The songs the guides played at TransWeb contained many western pop features. Some of the lyrics identified them with the nation, but never with regionalist Javanese lyrics and musical forms. This combination of cultural associations enabled newcomers such as Andar to deploy their globalist musical skills in order to win (or help others to win) the affections of western women, who would then more readily part with some of their money. And as long as the newcomers shared their earnings, this conversion facilitated their acceptance by the local Sosro Boys and enhanced their social acceptance in the kampung.

OPPOSITE RESTO

The other major music-making hangout involving street guides was what I refer to here as 'Opposite Resto'. Most of those who socialised at TransWeb also frequented Opposite Resto, and the strategic locations of both hangouts served to maximise guides' prospects of meeting foreigners, especially women travellers, although clearly sexual and monetary favours were not their sole interest. But Opposite Resto also differed from TransWeb in that it only came to life at night and, like the Sosro Bahu stand, was situated on Sosrowijayan Street.

People gathered at moveable benches by a dimly lit cigarette stall directly opposite Resto cafe/bar, and on the ground around five metres to the east, while by day the locale was no more than a closed stall and a patch of dirt on the roadside.[1] Being on a road

---

[1] By 2009 a 'Circle K' convenience store had been installed here. The extended steps at the storefront, known as *pantai* (beach), became Sosrowijayan's most crowded night-time gathering place.

2 Musical forms and spaces

A 'base camp' some 20 metres to the east of the Opposite Resto *tongkrongan*, where members of the sometimes-militant Gerakan Pemuda Ka'bah (GPK, Ka'bah Youth Movement) gathered

and distant from residents, and therefore not subject to kampung regulations, Opposite Resto had few noise restrictions in terms of both music making and the motorcycles, trucks, and buses that encroached into participants' physical and aural space. Again in contrast to TransWeb, alcohol consumption was popular, participant numbers could reach 30 or more, and music making here sometimes extended into acoustic jam sessions with whole groups singing out choruses.

People at most *tongkrongan*, in particular the *angkringan* tea stalls, seemed to welcome or at most be indifferent to the arrival of an outsider (Murray 1991:59). In contrast, Opposite Resto lacked a clear spatial boundary, and its primary function, unlike that of drinking tea or eating a snack, often shifted. There was a greater tendency towards volatility there, in part due to its strategic position allowing the guides to catch business prospects entering, leaving or merely passing Resto. Any guardedness displayed toward outsiders may seem accountable by the illicit activities taking place there, if not for the fact that prominent signage for, and sale of, homebrew alcohol were on display for a time. Music making was a regular feature, but so too accounts of recent violence circulated quite openly, perhaps in turn influenced by its location near a political 'base camp' where militant street campaigners gathered.

One evening I joined a small group at Opposite Resto. Six of us sat on the ground exchanging songs while passing round three guitars and two large water bottles filled with 'Sunrise' (beer, vodka, and Kratindaeng energy drink). As we sat and drank, playing music took precedence over talking. Edi swayed back and forth as others played the blues. Ari suggested and then sang the U2 song 'With or without you' with passionate conviction; the entire song is a repetition of four basic chords, so we accompanied him with ease. We also played and sang national-language *jalanan* songs by Iwan Fals, Sawung Jabo and others, ranging from lighter relationship themes, such as 'Kumenanti seorang kekasih' (Waiting for a lover), to the anti-New Order classics 'Bento' and 'Bongkar' (Tear it down). Newcomer Andar in each case added colourful embellishments on guitar, again enhancing his cultural capital. On this occasion however, just as Andar and I had begun to exchange Javanese *langgam* scales, a former guide named Han suddenly stood and, turning to the sky, screamed 'Fuck off!' while throwing his motorbike helmet crashing across the road. Unlike the younger, more optimistic Sosro Boys, Han's bitter cross-cultural relationship experiences both alienated him from, and made him aggressively protective of, Javanese language and music. Significantly however, Han never behaved aggressively in the kampung environment of TransWeb.

A similar incident occurred on another evening inside Resto itself. Han and Studs were slouching back on dining chairs and quietly playing older protest songs such as Pink Floyd's 'Another brick in the wall' and the Doors' 'People are strange', and then Swami's 'Bongkar'. A young American man approached and asked if they knew any Didi Kempoet or Sheila on 7. His familiarity with these Javanese musicians, *campursari* and pop stars respectively, at first generated laughter and apparent acceptance among the guides. Then Han suddenly shouted 'Yha Sheila, fuck you!' at which point the young American quietly withdrew. Han and a few others sometimes showed signs of excessive *shabu shabu* methamphetamine consumption, including glazed eyes and a trembling, sweat-drenched body. His exclamations were by no means typical of the street guides, although I did hear of an episode at Opposite Resto one night when a French student was beaten up after making a joke in Javanese.

Drug use, oppositional music, and occasional abrasiveness characterised the Opposite Resto *tongkrongan*. But it was also more likely to be a place for spontaneous humour and creative expression. One evening as I approached the stall there to buy a cigarette, the atmosphere was tense and unpredictable. Of the 20 or so people there, most were drinking, and four men and a woman sitting by the stall were engaged in creative *plesetan*. One of the men, looking worn down by long bouts of deep thinking, sat with his face turned to the moon and, rare at Sosrowijayan *tongkrongan*, sang a lyrically and musically spontaneous song, in this case about the futility of seeking to pin down the meaning of life. The Opposite Resto hangout on this evening was characterised by a kind of blunt directness and honesty; participants were neither keen to please nor testy with those around them.

The final Opposite Resto example involved Han, a rough diamond known as Stan, and one of my main respondents, Tyas. As we sat to a drink, two young gigolo/guides also joined in from busking in Prawirotaman, Yogyakarta's other, quieter and more middle-level backpacker area. With songs played on two guitars and drinks flowing, Stan and others urged the few westerners passing by to join the 'full moon party'. A German with dreadlocks and a quiet Austrian couple joined the gathering, and a few other street guides stopped by for a drink and chat before wandering on. Musical renditions included lyrical alterations directed at tourists. Han bellowed out the Eagles' 'Hotel California' with the line 'this could be heaven or this could be Holland [hell]'; while another, perhaps in sympathy with Han, sang Bob Marley's 'I shot the tourist [sheriff]'.

Later however, they played songs by Indonesian musicians. Tyas accompanied on Ebiet G. Ade's 'Nyanyian rindu' (Song of longing) in a calypso style, with the guides singing the choruses in parody of Ebiet's intensely self-exploratory vocal style. At another point, he played a Spanish-style modal lead break to the evergreen protest song 'Bongkar', to which Studs accompanied with shouts of 'Ole!' I found it quite striking that Tyas' musical proficiency on this occasion helped to steer the increasingly intoxicated participants away from potential antagonism and into outbursts of musical expression. His nationalist and globalist musical skills enabled him, firstly, to express sympathy with Han, and then to ensure that Han did not indulge in any tendency towards physical aggression.

A number of similarities and contrasts characterised music making at Sosrowijayan's main *tongkrongan*.[2] Sosro Bahu members possessed a vast knowledge of *campursari* music, or what might be called (sub-national) regionalist cultural capital. However, the environment was not compatible for making music: despite lyrics harking to a simpler village life, it is paradoxical that playing regionalist *campursari* in its full glory required gamelan instru-

---

2 Jeremy Wallach's discussion (2008:140-62) of street-based workers and music at a *tongkrongan* in South Jakarta illustrates the generally greater level of inter-ethnic interaction that features on Jakarta's streets.

ments, keyboards and a supply of electricity. Therefore, *campursari* at the stand soothed and to an extent bonded the *becak* drivers, but they did not convert any in-group solidarity that this generated into economic gain or extended social influence.

While the main function of *campursari* for Sosro Bahu drivers was to invoke other places and times within the region, TransWeb regulars sometimes used music making with national and international inflections to enhance their social status. Street guides and their friends in my experience never played the regionalist genres enjoyed by the *becak* drivers and regularly performed by *pengamen*. At Opposite Resto, many participants consumed alcohol, and the music involved angst and political protest to a greater extent than was the case at TransWeb. Older guides, some of whom risked marginalisation while others were regarded as success stories, influenced this. The example of Tyas' influence on the volatile Han demonstrates how music can promote peaceful social interaction in this context.

Becak drivers shared with the majority of itinerant *pengamen* passing through the kampung a taste for regionalist *campursari* music. While this provided some common ground among them, street guides by contrast mobilised their ability for globalist music making to enter the economic realm of backpackers. More specifically, both TransWeb and Opposite Resto had in common the guitar playing of male street guides; in both cases music played a central role in drawing in relatively wealthy foreigners, from whom the street guides could exchange their cultural for economic capital.[3] The next chapter locates these informal musical interactions in the context of the formation, agendas and activities of two musical groups based in Sosrowijayan, both of whom carried versions of these genres and cultural associations into the realm of organized public performance.

---

3 Interestingly, by 2010 several mid-range hotels had been established along the south side of Sosrowijayan Street. These were in the main patronised by middle-class Indonesians from outside of Yogyakarta, including families and business and government groups. This provided new avenues for business among *becak* drivers, but less so for street guides.

3

Music groups

Many musical performances that project across public space are socially inclusive. But as Martin Stokes (1994:9) reminds us, so too can the crashing sound of one group be a deliberate ploy to enforce the boundaries between groups. Such inclusive and exclusive ploys and their effects also featured at Sosrowijayan-based musical groups' rehearsals and public performances. One example of this in the kampung was the long-running *kroncong* group, which rehearsed most Saturday evenings in the Old Woodpecker restaurant at the north end of Gang One. Friends and relatives often sat in, sometimes taking the lead singer role, all of which helped to elevate the atmosphere from that of a formal rehearsal to a music-oriented social gathering. During my research however, passing *pengamen* in Sosrowijayan did not join the Old Woodpecker gatherings, even though they shared the repertoire. Furthermore, *becak* drivers and street guides seldom if ever participated in these sessions. By contrast, a couple of groups I was introduced to shared more in common with *becak* drivers and street guides respectively, and thereby warrant attention here. These were the Sekar Wuyung and Shower Bands.

THE SEKAR WUYUNG GROUP

I first saw Sekar Wuyung perform outside the Sultan's Palace, and later came to know them in Sosrowijayan. They rehearsed on Thursdays and Sundays from two until five-thirty pm at Pak Wawan's under-patronised guesthouse along an alleyway between Gang Two and the red-light area. There were 15 members, including the singers, most of whom were in their mid-30s or older. Reflecting the influence of context on intersections between taste and genre outlined earlier, the term they applied to their repertoire alternated between *campursari* and *dangdut Jawa*. The group's founder and manager owned two hotels in the area, and was attempting to buy and incorporate a set of gamelan instruments. Given that Sosrowijayan no longer had a gamelan set, this was a particularly popular prospect among regionalists. In the meanwhile the instruments, all played by men, included the keyboard and the tabla-style drums typical of a *dangdut* group (Sedyawati 1998:128; Weintraub 2010), and Udin on mandolin (*cuk*) added a *kroncong* sound. All songs were sung with Javanese lyrics and, with the exception of the manager and a member's daughter in primary school, all singers were the wives of the instrumentalists. The singers generally determined the choice of songs, as was the case with most groups that aimed to perform a more traditional entertainment function.

Sekar Wuyung's regular practice sessions involved the surrounding kampung in various ways. Rather than closing off their rehearsal space, they placed the large public-address speakers at the guesthouse entrance, thereby booming the sound out across the neighbourhood. The musicians squeezed around the open spaces inside the guesthouse proper, while the singers sat in the guest room at the front and, when singing, alternately faced the band and looked out onto the alleyway. Young sex workers at a nearby rooming house, along with a few children and older women up and down the alleyway, sat outdoors during the rehearsals, mostly on the steps of their premises.

Some of the Sekar Wuyung musicians had grown up outside Java and married Yogyanese women, including 'Murni' from Europe, Wawan from Bali, and Visnu from Sumatra. Playing in Sekar Wuyung seemed to 'Jogjafy' the musicians, both in the music they played and in how they projected themselves publicly. But not everyone in the neighbourhood could become a member; for example, a street-hardened sex worker with a large tattoo on her right arm told me she once tried to join the band but was refused. Nonetheless, for those in the band at least, the rehearsals were social as much as they were musical occasions. During the midsession break, which lasted for at least half an hour, members would chat over tea and snacks, with topics of conversation gradually gravitating toward band matters such as song details and upcoming or potential performance engagements.

At the first rehearsal in which I participated, a number of the musicians apologised that they had only been playing together for the past six months. Indeed, as I was to learn, a number of their acquaintances thought the group, most notably the singers, needed considerable work. The group nonetheless took their music very seriously. As time went on they posted their organizational structure on the guesthouse wall, including details of management costs and the individual roles of different members. Discussions of strategy and musical direction sometimes became passionate. Among the musicians, there were moments of disagreement and general bickering, usually over song structures. On one occasion when only a few of us had gathered because the others were attending a funeral, two of the members discussed possible English translations of 'Sewu kuto', and then tried out my electronic tuner on their instruments. In both cases, these tasks switched from being light-hearted explorations into competitions involving personal pride.

The group struck me as reminiscent of the American alternative country scene. Musicians and audiences alike were mostly in the 30+ age bracket, were lower/middle class, and often sang of a loss of and longing for a rural life they may not have themselves experienced. Unlike alternative country however, Sekar Wuyung's music also evoked the supernatural and other more distinctly Javanese phenomena that *becak* drivers engaged through *campursari* music, particularly in songs such as 'Kuda lumping'. As well as providing entertainment in the kampung, Sekar Wuyung constituted an important social network for its members. Additionally, their participation in larger-scale events contributed to the general appreciation of the arts for which Yogyakarta is renowned. Over time, moreover, Sekar Wuyung improved musically, in turn increasing participants' sense of pleasure and achievement. Each week Pak Visnu meticulously added the lyrics and chords of new songs to the binders, and the news of each new gig brought a wave of excitement to the sessions.

Sekar Wuyung functioned as community entertainment, and provided its members with potential opportunities to embark on projects with others in the kampung. In these ways, Sekar Wuyung provided important in-group social cohesion for members, and created possibilities for joining forces across groups. However, no such collaboration was to occur between Sekar Wuyung and the Sosro Bahu *becak* drivers. Particularly through individuals such as Udin, being both band member and friend of some of the drivers, Sekar Wuyung might have been of considerable interest and value to the Sosro Bahu group. Despite Sekar Wuyung and Sosro Bahu's common regionalist musical interests and sensibilities, and their physical proximity to each other, the lack of connections between them prevented such an outcome. The following case contrasts with this in terms of the social influence of music making, and leads us back to the street guides' music party at the Sosro Bahu stand that opened Part One.

| *Musical worlds in Yogyakarta*

THE SHOWER STREET GUIDE BAND

Unlike Sekar Wuyung, the Shower Band was comprised of street guides connected to the *jalanan* scene, and they played American popular and folk songs at commercial venues. Their formalisation began on 2 August 2001, a bustling evening in downtown Yogyakarta. I was on my way from a 'New World of Islam' concert to a Sosro Bahu meeting when the street-guide leader Jolong called me over to inform me of the group's practice session scheduled for the next day. The group also planned to perform at Resto, he said, adding that there would be an 'all acoustic' line-up of up to 11 members. He also explained that they were not in it for the money but rather for communication and harmony.

The following afternoon I sought out the band's practice session at Bu Haji's boarding house. After being lost for some time in the bleaker alleyways of Sosrowijayan's west end, I finally heard the band echoing across the rooftops and followed the sound to their space. Over a dozen Sosrowijayan tourist workers lived in the large boarding house. The band was playing on the small balcony up a narrow set of stairs above the third floor, with a refreshing sunlit skyscape and, in the gaps between other roofs and hanging clothes, views to the street below. Twenty young men, including some of the younger Sosrowijayan-based guides with either *gondrong* shoulder length or Britpop hairstyles, were crammed into the small space. Jolong, Imam Rasta and a few others stood along the side, while the players formed a circle sitting on chairs and ledges or squatting. There were four acoustic guitar players, a double bass player, three percussionists, and Joni, provider of many of the instruments, who with his violin helped to give the overall sound a polished and professional touch.

The session had a festive atmosphere. Participants laughed and smoked Dji Sam Soe brand cigarettes constantly. They also drank local wine and *beram hitam* (black rice/tapioca alcoholic drink) mixed with two large bottles of beer which, as usual, they passed around by the glass. All the same, the men were embarking on a group project, the outcome of which depended on the cooperation of all involved. They played songs while referring to a few books of handwritten lyrics, most often a thoroughly used and collapsing scrapbook with '70an' (seventies) written on the cover. This book contained around 60 songs, most of which were American popular/folk songs from the 1960s and 70s that, over the years, participants had played in the streetside *jalanan* format. Each page consisted of an artistically written title and the complete lyrics of

3 Music groups

Shower Band rehearsal

a song. However, none of them had the accompanying chords, and similarly the players did not draw on cassettes for reference. Instead, they would settle on matters of musical structure by going through a song, partly from memory and partly with practice.

Here was a good example of how musical group formation linked musical genre and social identity, in turn building the more benevolent variant of in-group social capital by nonverbal means. A young percussionist repeatedly sped up the tempo of a ballad, to the point where other members had to pull him into line, which they did sensitively. Many song endings were initially loose and unresolved; however, rather than a leader dictating the structure and thereby hampering each participant's sense of contribution, the group as a whole sought to resolve such structural issues in practice. While at times this called for repetitions of final verses, intros and so on, when the song finally fell together a real sense of accomplishment ran through the group. There were also no pre-arranged rules determining vocal participation. Many participants took the role of lead singer at different times, with several others joining in on the choruses.

This group of street guides showed substantial initiative, thus challenging the perception of the wider public and tourists alike that they were lazy no-hopers. In terms of aesthetics it could be argued that they merely replicated worn-out old songs, but on another level the group had consolidated a number of harmonious renditions within a few hours. Additionally, in performance their 'rolling' philosophy, this being the constant rotation of singers and instrumentalists, was clearly building community, at least within the specific locale. The rehearsal session broke up as evening approached. Jolong reminded them that they were scheduled to play at Resto the following evening, and that this was a trial to be taken seriously.

SHOWER AT RESTO AND THE SOSRO BAHU AFTER-PARTY

The Shower Band's plan to perform at Resto had a history that requires some explanation. According to local legend Pa'En and others, in Sosrowijayan in the early 1970s hippies would lay down straw mats outside the Old Woodpecker and play guitars, sing and freely smoke 'ganja'. According to an older traveller I met, ganja was freely available at street stalls in Yogyakarta in 1969. It was outlawed in 1976, and in the mid-1980s reggae singer Masanies became renowned for being the first Indonesian jailed for marijuana possession. Over recent years, many musical activities around Sosrowijayan had become associated with the Sosro Boys, alcohol and heavier drugs such as methamphetamine *shabu-shabu* and heroin. Because of this atmosphere, a nationally renowned protest singer once remarked to me that he no longer plays there, as the concerts always end up in brawls.

The prospect of hosting live music at Resto had been in the pipeline since late 2000. For some years, most live western style entertainment in the Sosrowijayan area took place at Bar Borobudur. However, the professionalism of the bar's management had steadily declined, with payments to musicians dropping drastically and equipment left to deteriorate. A band's popularity was nonetheless integral to the social and financial success of an evening. Some of the Sosro Boys got involved in jam sessions (known as 'dabbles') at the bar. This was particularly the case for TransWeb regulars, who were skilled at playing cover versions from a wide variety of popular genres, and also at joining in with various combinations of players and instruments. Given the general paucity of venues however, Resto's decision to house live music was significant, not least because it brought to the fore the dynamics between Sosro Boys' social capital and Resto management's economic capital.

Resto's first performers, the Dayak Etniks, debuted in July 2001. According to a street guide, this was because the Shower Band was not yet ready. Dayak Etniks was a perplexing name, all the more so given that the restaurant management hung a banner with huge, bold letters on the roadside entranceway. Dayak, a term used to describe the majority indigenous groups in Central Kalimantan (Thung, Lan, Maunati and Kedit 2004), had become sensitive because of the horrific clashes between Dayaks and settlers from the island of Madura off East Java. Many Madurese also worked in roadside occupations around Malioboro Street. As such, the use of this band name at Resto seems to have been a conscious attempt to evoke the exotic for tourists, at the same time sending a warning to the industrious Madurese nearby.

All of the Dayak Etniks members lived near the Indonesian Arts Institute and were studying or had previously studied ethnomusicology there. Each had ties with Kalimantan, ranging from periodically returning for further field studies to having relatives there but being born and raised in Jakarta. As planned, on the day of the first Shower Band performance I played music with the Dayak Etniks at their 'culture house', this being a common area set aside for rehearsal, prayer and discussion, located near the Institute. At seven pm the five of us carried our instruments into town on three motorcycles.

Resto was a large house converted into an open-plan British colonial style restaurant/bar with a lemon-coloured interior and featuring several batik artworks. It seated around 50 people comfortably. As on previous occasions, on this Saturday night the Dayak Etniks played from eight until nine o'clock, which the audience seemed to enjoy. The Dayak Etniks left soon after, a couple going back to the Institute and others to their usual *tongkrongan* near the southern square of the Kraton. Meanwhile the moment had arrived for the Shower Band's first performance.

Whereas the Dayak Etniks sat on the floor against the back wall of the small stage, the Shower Band set up two rows of stools and were soon playing their first song, an extended version of 'Blowin' in the wind'. The sound was pleasant, its volume not overpowering conversations among the customers. Multiple percussion and guitars, along with the double bass, provided a cushion of sound on which one and at times, half a dozen or more vocalists could sing. As planned at rehearsal the previous day, the second song was a Latin American favourite, followed by 'Leaving on a jet plane', 'El Condor Pasa', 'Country roads', then 'Alusia', a popular Sumatran Batak song and then another Latin American song. They then repeated some of the songs they had played earlier.

Resto's six to eight-thirty pm dinner period was always the busiest, and so by nine-fifteen pm, after the Dayak Etniks and when the Shower Band were about to begin, the number of clients had dropped. However, quite a few who would otherwise have left stayed on, and others arrived later. The band members and their immediate friends occupied the large rear section corner table tucked around out of street view. One member would periodically smuggle in vodka and Kratindaeng energy drink, but they also bought beers and snacks at the counter. About half of the other 20 customers at the restaurant were Shower Band associates, sitting down briefly to chat before heading back to their own tables. Most of the others were women, including two groups of European backpacker/students and a group of four Indonesian Islamic University psychology students.

The group's music had an infectious effect, with applause increasing by the song. The levels of alcohol consumption undoubtedly also added to the general air of celebration and, increasingly, rowdiness. The group was scheduled to finish by ten o'clock but ran over time. Upon finishing they soon packed up, this being the moment at which I began Part One. This was when the band members gathered at Opposite Resto, with some then going on to the Sosro Bahu stand to sing and drink until the morning hours, all without the involvement or obvious resentment of the Sosro Bahu *becak* drivers.

Conclusion

I began Part One with a description of street guides making themselves at home in a *becak* drivers' roadside hangout. I then proposed that identifying capital in its various guises helps to gain an understanding of the roles of music making in the maintenance of peaceful inter-group relations social relations in Yogyakarta, with those among and between the *becak* drivers and street guides in Sosrowijayan being a case in point. I noted that Bourdieu had formulated an important way of understanding domination beyond purely economic measures, through social and cultural capital. I also suggested that a communitarian reading of social capital ensures that Bourdieu's focus on power and inequality does not reduce all social interaction to these dimensions. I then described and examined musical discussions and practices as a means to better understand interplays between economic capital, regionalist, nationalist and globalist cultural capital, and in-group and inter-group social capital in the daily lives of the workers.

Considering the musical dimensions in more detail, it needs to be remembered that the music of the street guides' *jalanan*-inflected Shower Band did not include *campursari*, beloved of *becak* drivers and most rural dwellers working in the city. Consequently there was a lack of interaction between the guides and *becak* drivers on the night of their first gig. The guides' drunken music making at the drivers' stand did not perform a unifying role, but rather reinforced boundaries between the two groups. At the same time, despite the economic disparities brought by tourism, Sosrowijayan-based music making in the main did not lead to tension and conflict. This is a point worth reflecting on. Where musical tastes and sensibilities did not meet, as was most notably the case between *campursari* and rock-influenced *jalanan*, the separate identities these maintained did not lead to open conflict.

As I will discuss further in the chapters that follow, conflicts around inter-political, inter-neighbourhood, inter-ethnic and inter-religious divisions were a considerable concern to people in the midst of great social and political change during the early post-Soeharto years, as was the potential for tension between street-based occupational groups generally. Given this context, the relatively peaceful coexistence of street guides and *becak* drivers is a matter of some importance. It is therefore reasonable to conclude that music not only reflected conflict avoidance, but also played an active role in it.

Globalist *jalanan* and regionalist *campursari* music making were forms of cultural capital that served to reinforce social capital at the in-group level. Newcomers could contribute to in-group solidarity, and established workers maintain it, by sharing musical skills or income-generating abilities. The street guide Andar exemplified this in musical circles. The Sosro Boys quickly accepted him due to his musical prowess and his ability to attract relatively wealthy western women. He also facilitated the entrée of other outsiders to street-guide circles, especially through musical exchanges at the semi-commercial Prada and TransWeb kampung hangouts, but less so at the roadside settings of Sosro Bahu and Opposite Resto.

Among the *becak* drivers, Pak Parno advanced quickly from newcomer to authority figure within the Sosro Bahu group, thus demonstrating the importance of business skills among *becak* drivers. The relationship between music, occupation and economic capital was not clear-cut in the case of the *becak* drivers. *Campursari* at most helped to foster the acceptance of newcomer *becak* drivers by providing a pleasant focal point of conversation or quiet listening. In contrast to this, newcomer street guides could derive direct economic benefit and social prestige from firstly, drawing on their musical skills, and then sharing their profits with established street guides. And these guides could benefit from succeeding in business and sharing their profits with the established guides. In other words, street guides converted globalist music making into economic capital in the kampung, whereas for *becak* drivers income earning and cultural activities remained separate from each other.

While globalist *jalanan* and regionalist *campursari* did not facilitate interaction across the street guide and *becak* driver groups, those who played Indonesian national musical genres were more able to do so. This was sometimes evident among mobile *pengamen* combos. The *dangdut Jawa* busking group shared common musical tastes with, and to some extent befriended *becak* drivers at their Sosro Bahu stand. Similarly, the Astro Band met street guides in the context of nationalist and globalist music making at the Prada eatery. Most often, establishing social relations across groups required a well-placed actor, or a favourable situation, such as a meeting in neutral cultural space.

Related to this, busking and public performances provided opportunities for inter-group social interaction when they involved the mixing of groups and genres. In Table 2 below, occupation and musical genre are plotted in relation to spatial forms of capital and in-group and inter-group interactions and separations.

Conclusion

Occupation	Musical genre	CAPITAL		
		Cultural	Economic	Social
Becak driver	*Campursari*	Region (to nation)	Regional	In-Group
Busker (*Pengamen*)	*Karawitan* *Kroncong*	Regional		Inter-Group
	Dangdut	National		
Music group	International folk	International		
	National rock	National		
Street guide	*Jalanan*	Global (to nation)	Local and global	In-Group

Table 2. Occupation, musical genre, and capital in Sosrowijayan

Based on the material presented in Part One, I suggest that musical group formation and performance in Sosrowijayan provided street workers with an important social and expressive outlet. Musical activities did not eliminate conflict and unify all social groups, but they did give people alternatives to joining and promoting local and party political militia groups (Kristiansen 2003).

Reggae band in Sosrowijayan, 2005

The changes I witnessed among these groups and locations over subsequent years demonstrate how the *becak* drivers' stand and surrounding areas – sites of contestation between street guides and *becak* drivers around which this book has so far revolved – continued to harbour complex social interactions among the work groups. The musical preferences of each group had not shifted significantly, and it remains difficult to determine whether the takeover of the *becak* drivers' stand by the street guides was a case of maintaining barriers between groups, therefore stemming possible violence, or a flagrant abuse of one group's power over another, thereby exacerbating tensions between the groups. This difficulty supports my central thesis that in Sosrowijayan competition and cooperation coexists and needs to be conceptualised within the same framework, and that musical analysis provides a means of identifying ways in which social groups manage to coexist peacefully in times of political and economic conflict. In Part Two, I build on this discussion by comparing gendered and related aspects of identity that were manifested at musical events in kampung and commercial-venue settings.

PART 2

Habitus and physicality

Background

For some years now I have often heard Yogyakarta's Sosrowijayan neighbourhood described as either a 'typically conservative kampung' or a 'tourist ruined commercial zone'. In Part One I sought to problematise this division by examining music making and capital conversions among *becak* drivers and street guides. Part Two begins by focusing on women in Sosrowijayan, with subsequent chapters mapping out manifestations of gendered physical behaviour at musical events that took place in kampung and commercial venues across the city. By analysing and comparing nonverbal forms of communication and interaction in these cultural spaces, I seek to identify connections between intergenerational/communal and cross-cultural/commercial influences on gendered identities, and in turn between the kampung and commercial activities that took place in and around Sosrowijayan's public spaces. These influences can thereby be related to the village/urban, *campursari/musik jalanan* and *becak* driver/street guide divisions already identified and scrutinised, but now analysed across multiple spaces and genres.

The lives of male street guides and/or street children have been the subject of rigorous research on inner-city Yogyakarta.[1] A useful starting point for the present discussion is to schematize the public life of women in Sosrowijayan. I suggest that three broad groups interacted socially around the neighbourhood during my research, each of which tended to gravitate toward some musical worlds and not others. First were those not especially kampung-bound nor commercially exploited. These included public-oriented wives of kampung association leaders, as well as some university students and NGO workers. Second, some women in staff positions, approaching the age of 25 and facing expectations of marriage and children, sought financial and other means to escape 'kampungan' pressures and avoid dependency on men by developing their English language, business and, in some cases, musical skills. And third were a dozen or so women I wish to call '*perek*', from *perempuan eksperimental* and meaning 'experimental girls' (Murray 1991; Richter 2008b). These women regularly sat about in tourist cafés and hotels, often meeting up with western travellers and entering

---

1 Dahles and Bras 1999; Dahles 2001; Solvang 2002; Beazley 2000; Berman 2000.

into sexual encounters with them, in the process entering a murky middle ground between prostitution and relationship. *Perek* were emblematic of commercial zone sexuality, in both their day to day clothing, makeup, and mannerisms, and their frequenting of commercial establishments by night.

Building on Part One's analysis of the roles of music in street-based capital conversion strategies, in Part Two I broaden the focus to gender and physicality across multiple settings, guided by the following questions. Do kampung environments provide safe havens, or are they unduly constraining? Do commercial-venue activities increase personal freedom for women, or are they sites of sexual exploitation? To what extent are westernism, Islamisation, and indigenist Javanism related to these tendencies? What insights might comparisons between these citywide and Sosrowijayan-specific cases lend to these questions?

In the following chapters I examine intergenerational and cross-cultural influences on gendered and sexualised interactions as they emerged during music performances in kampung and commercial venues. In kampung there was great age and generational variation, while class and ethnic markers were especially prominent in commercial venues. As will be discussed, *campursari*, *jalanan*, and related genres such as *dangdut* and rock influenced, and were influenced by, factors such as setting, event theme, and audience characteristics. Attending to particular actors and variants of the central genres will further demonstrate how musical performers, participants and organizers contributed to peaceful exchange and coexistence between social groups during the early post-Soeharto years.

HABITUS, GENDER, AND SOCIALISATION

Bourdieu's concept of *habitus* helps to link musical performance to everyday gendered relations. *Habitus* conveys the idea that people's dispositions and habituated physical movements are products of their structured social worlds. The concept attempts to transcend both excessively 'objectivist' and 'subjectivist' accounts of the roles of structure and agency in social phenomena (Bourdieu and Wacquant 1992:115-40). Bourdieu developed the concept of *habitus* in his studies of the Kabyle peoples in Algeria, where binary oppositions were manifest in housing arrangements and in women's downcast expression and modest behaviour, as against men's outward engagement with other men (Bourdieu 1977, 2001). Excessive emphasis on structure reduces the *habitus* to, at most, a semi-conscious habit. In the current context, the concept of *habitus* could thereby be invoked in claims that generational hierarchies determine kampung interactions, just as money drives the *habitus* in commercial venues. Too much agency, on the other hand, reduces the social world to a 'discontinuous series of instantaneous mechanical equilibria between agents who are treated as interchangeable particles' (Bourdieu 1986:241), thereby providing no way of accounting for the buried structures perpetuating the social reproduction of inequality.

Bourdieu attempts to account for structure and agency when he states that *habitus* is 'a product of history [,] an open system of dispositions that is constantly subjected to experiences, and therefore constantly affected by them in a way that either reinforces or modifies its structures'.[2] *Habitus* is therefore a way to explain how people's senses of reality and perceptions of life chances are conditioned by mental structures they have developed through experience. By shifting the emphasis somewhat, I want to suggest that a person's involvement in a variety of experiences can broaden their scope of imaginable and realizable positions. In this light, the idea of *habitus* 'plasticity' helps to focus attention on the fact that deeply embedded, habitual behaviour, or what Bourdieu (1977:78) calls 'history turned into nature', is at the same time influenced by the physical and mental agility for 'playing the game' that interaction in differing social settings enables.[3]

Without a doubt, a person's *habitus* in Sosrowijayan is tied to shifting social fields and their enactments in the politics of kampung and commercial-zone identity. Where I depart from Bourdieu's foregrounding of social-structural constraints is in my contention that a person's habituated thoughts and behaviours do not merely reflect deeply embedded structures developed through (especially early-)life experiences. Rather, I would argue, experiences throughout life to varying degrees allow actors to actively and consciously shape and reshape such internal structures and the thoughts and behaviours that manifest from these. This will be seen in the following musical events, wherein animated inter-gender interactions sometimes increased participants' agility at playing the game in multiple social and musical worlds, while at others they increased tension and volatility and thereby shut off scope for such social adaptability.

---

2   Bourdieu and Wacquant 1992:133. 'Disposition', Bourdieu (1977:214, note 1) notes, 'designates a way of being [,] in particular, a predisposition, tendency, propensity, or inclination.'
3   In an earlier publication I suggested the idea of an 'enriched *habitus*' (Richter 2008b), although I had reservations about the term. Here I posit that 'plasticity' better captures my intended meaning. This is adapted from studies of 'neuroplasticity' (Doidge 2007), which demonstrate how thoughts are not mere reflections of the brain's hardwiring, but can change the brain's very structure and function.

In relation to gender and power, Norma Sullivan's account (1994:83-7) of gender socialisation in an inner-city Yogyakarta kampung depicts women as dominant in the 'informal, private, domestic zones of everyday kampung life', but lacking the all-important prestige gained through public social affairs. Sullivan argues that from an early age domestic and neighbourhood socialisation prepares females for the more restricted communal life of the kampung, while males are on the other hand groomed for the wider, freer world of public life. By contrast, Shelly Errington (1990) cites the overriding sense, especially among western observers, that Southeast Asian women enjoy higher status than their traditional Indian and Chinese counterparts, with such complementarity between the sexes in Southeast Asia readily evinced through language and work practices as well as systems of kinship and inheritance.

I contend that an analysis of gendered and related dimensions of identity at music performances can place such seemingly irreconcilable interpretations of gender oppression and complementarity into the same framework. Nonverbal communication and interaction at musical events demonstrate both a measure of agency and changing levels of autonomy or oppression during adult life. In the following chapters I shall interpret consequences of the breaking down or maintenance of social barriers, whether negative, in social marginalisation or conflict, or more positive, through increased and diversified experience for those involved. The analysis is informed by Howes' 'bodily modes of knowing' (1990:3-4), and rests in particular on the identification of, and comparison between, three manifestations of physical behaviour at kampung and commercial-venue events.

THREE FORMS OF MUSICAL PHYSICALISATION

Building on the everyday structure/agency tensions inherent in Bourdieu's concept of *habitus*, I use the term 'musical physicalisation' to describe the manifested physical behaviours and gendered interactions that arise around or through music (Richter 2008a, 2008b). Musical physicalisation is any bodily movement that occurs through music. In addition to all forms of dance, this also encompasses other behaviours such as largely unconscious toe-tapping or trance motions, and even altered conversation postures. There are, I would argue, three principal kinds or variants of musical physicalisation manifested in Yogyakarta, which I will describe as 'detachment engagement', 'other worlds', and 'sexualisation'.

The first type of physicalisation, detachment engagement, refers to behaviours around music that proceed from complete physical immobility to active but still relatively understated engagement, and finally back to disengagement.[4] People's detached and neutral appearance in the immobile phase may be deceiving. As will be further discussed, the symbolic importance of kampung wedding receptions can forestall inter-group interaction, and the *habitus* of many guests at high-class hotels may be so at odds with the surrounding environment as to render them stiff. In both cases, greater engagement occurs as social distancing is in various ways bridged, most often through music, though this tends to remain relatively subdued.

The second musical physicalisation, other worlds, refers to highly physicalised dance and/or related bodily movements that indicate a person's or group's attempted or actual entrance into another consciousness or alternative state of being. In kampung, women, men and children alike enjoyed viewing the *jatilan* trance dance, while in commercial venues other world physicalisation was most evident at the Kridosono sports hall. The third and final form of musical physicalisation is sexualisation, which refers to the physical movements at musical performances that individuals more or less explicitly model on sexual intercourse. Even when performers displaying these movements are not themselves sexualised, these may still be referred to as sexualisation to the extent that they charge the atmosphere with sexuality.

I seek to link these physicalisations with interpretations of Indonesia and particularly Java as, alternatively, Muslim, refined, and conservative, or home to a sexually uninhibited indigenism. Detachment engagement in part stems from analyses of Javanese culture that place great emphasis on how notions of prestige and potency mask realities of gender relations in social life (Sullivan 1994; Keeler 1990). As Errington notes, Javanese concepts of power do not readily equate with forcefulness and instrumentality. On the contrary, power may be exercised principally through agents that appear and act with a delicacy generally seen by observers as effeminate (Errington 1990:41-2), actions that can to varying degrees be seen in their artistic representations (Hatley 1999).

The other worlds and sexualisation variants of musical physicalisation question whether highly animated behaviours, rather than being mere outbursts of expression from the underclass, may con-

---

4 The period of physical engagement that occurs during 'detachment engagement' musical physicalisations can be seen as an unspectacular version of Victor Turner's middle, 'liminal' phase (1982) that occurs during rites of passage.

| *Musical worlds in Yogyakarta*

stitute exercises in power. At the least, actors at dance events can become acutely aware of the roles of their bodies in power plays, as Jane Cowan (1990:24) notes in relation to rural Greece, thereby providing a corrective to the overly 'habituated' connotations of *habitus*. Through the analysis of the following performances, I seek to highlight some of the difficulties in disentangling the various forms of musical physicalisation, especially among offstage dancing men and onstage dancing women. I will seek to show how this helps to complexify correlations that are sometimes made between power/oppression and physical immobility/mobility in the context of Javanese social relations.

Entertainment venues and commercial zones discussed in Part Two

4

Detachment engagement

The kampung and commercial-venue sections of this chapter both begin with events featuring extremely immobile participants. This, I will argue, was primarily a result of levels of formality and economic disparity respectively. Other events in these settings involved transitions into greater inter-gender engagement, though still in comparatively subdued forms. While musical detachment in these contexts generally reflected significant power imbalances among the participants, I will seek to show how engagement in various ways challenged and addressed these imbalances.

KAMPUNG TRANSITIONS

Wedding receptions that I witnessed in 2001 were sites of markedly detached bodily postures among guests and hosts, a situation at least partly a result of the symbolically important transitions underway.[1] For guests, the reception phase most often consisted of arriving in formal wear of *kain* and *kebaya* for women, and shiny batik shirt and tidy pants for men, shaking the hands of the wedding party, and then sitting down to a meal in a spatial and social arrangement not conducive to conviviality. Throughout the reception, the bride and groom sat on display in a separate chamber.

The musical detachment pervading wedding receptions was not especially related to class position. I attended the predominantly middle-class wedding reception of a senior police sergeant's son at a national police training school outside the city, where music was provided by an 'electone' keyboard player accompanying various singers. Most of the 200 or more generally wealthy guests conveyed the sense that they were fulfilling their duties as witnesses and were eager to leave. There were parallels to this at the wedding involv-

---

1   Geertz 1960:61-77; Robinson 1986:230-8; Bourdieu and Wacquant 1992:173.

ing the brother of an Astro Band street musician held near their humble home by the river near the city centre. The band dressed in newly acquired cowboy shirts and played with great exuberance, yet the lower class but well-dressed guests were visibly detached and preoccupied from start to finish. In both cases the event took little more than two hours of a late morning.

Of marked contrast was the wedding reception for a Javanese man and a young French woman held at their Niti Prayen house on the south side of town, where many artists lived because rents were more affordable. Preparations involved clearing out the two large main rooms, laying down dozens of straw mats and installing a series of gallon-sized alcoholic drink dispensers. The 60 guests, consisting mostly of adults in their mid-twenties to late thirties, sat on the mats and against the walls, talking, drinking and eating as a few people quietly played electric bass, two acoustic guitars and *dangdut* drum, while a dozen children ran about and played. By eight-thirty pm, most of the young families began making their way home, while those remaining turned to drinking and music making. Six men, all members of a bus-terminal busking combo rumoured to be 'communists' and now wearing bandannas, sang and danced by running on the spot, casting their knees high toward their chests, and stepping in formation. The half-dozen remaining women sang and swayed along to increasingly raucous and animated renditions of 'Tolonglah tolong' (Oh, please help me [to find a girlfriend]), 'Kegagalan cinta' (Failure in love) and 'Rambut sama hitam' (We both have black hair), until ten o'clock when the party broke up due to kampung regulations.

Changes in musical genre and physicalisation often signalled and helped to smooth generational transitions in the course of other kampung events that I witnessed. The following two events included a number of street guides and *jalanan* leaders, but were quite genteel relative to the kampung physicalisations explored in the next chapter. The following events demonstrate subtle transitions between physical detachment and engagement based largely on generationally based groups and their favoured musical genres. The first event began with older pop tunes (often called *pop lama* or *pop nostalgia*) among the elder group, and ended with the younger participants playing *musik jalanan*; the second moved in roughly the opposite direction.

The first case revolved around music making at the opening party for DeBroto Café in Sosrowijayan, just behind Malioboro Street. The party also had features of a *selamatan* (Geertz 1960) in that, not unlike most wedding receptions, guests shook hands with the hosts on arriving and then moved to the serving area. At the

DeBroto reception, each guest received boiled duck and rice before settling in, with most then consuming alcohol. At eight-thirty pm, there were around 80 guests, mostly seated at tables. Except for a few children and elderly participants, the guests were in their late twenties to forties with an even distribution of married men and women. Notably, none of the *perek* was present, despite a number of them living only ten metres away. Conversely, some female staff and leaders did attend, but they were to go home early due to kampung regulations. Younger male street guides and Sosro Boys gathered and shared drinks in a back room.

Changes in musical genre influenced and reflected participants' levels and kinds of physical engagement over the next few hours. During the first half of the party, a solo 'electone' keyboard player accompanied singers from among the seated guests on a clearing by the tables. They began with older pop songs such as 'Perpisahan' (Parting), with those at the tables singing and swaying along. Manthous's 'Kempling' (Sexy), a popular regional tune now often included in *campursari* sets, signalled a shift to greater physical engagement. This further enlivened the participants, in part through the 'owei owei' sing-along choruses, and because a normally 'refined' homemaker was now singing and acting out like a star. Third, *dangdut* songs such as 'Terlena' (Complacence) gave rise to hoots as a youthful mother danced in *joged* style and sang, and many sang along with semi-parodic tones. Finally, they played a slow doo-wop 'Surti Tejo' by the ex-*jalanan* pop group Jamrud, now with greater handclapping and parodic choruses by a number of the newly enlivened Sosro Boys. Physical engagement among the older people peaked at this point, and soon after all rose from their chairs, shook each other's hands, and made their way home.

With the older generation gone, the Sosro Boys and their associates, which included a few young western women, moved from the back room to the café's open area. Half a dozen young men mounted the hitherto unused small stage and, with acoustic guitars, bongos and vocals, played sing-alongs such as 'La Bamba' and improvised 12-bar blues. Most participants enjoyed the music, singing, clapping and/or swaying along. The notable exception to this was half a dozen teenage boys in a corner who jumped about at the start of each song but quickly aired their disappointment when each new song was not Padi or another current 'alternative pop' group: by around ten-thirty pm they gave up and left.

The remaining 25 of us settled at the tables and chairs and sang an Iwan Fals medley beginning with 'Kumenanti seorang kekasih' (Waiting for a lover) and then through to 'Wakil rakyat' (People's representatives), 'Bento' and 'Pesawat tempurku' (My fighter pilot). The lyrics of these and other *jalanan* evergreens variously express themes of love and of political opposition and urban alienation, including the mellow and pleasant 'Serenada' by KPJ founder Anton Baret. The two guitars were regularly rotated and many employed makeshift percussion such as forks with empty bottles and tapping tabletops. As was the case during the first half of the party, participants increased their musical engagement over time, but now the amount of alcohol consumed increased levels of physical engagement but at the same time dulled senses of timing. Rather than moving into sensual dance music, the partakers increasingly immersed themselves in the lyrical themes of familiar songs. Soon after the midnight curfew, the party quietly broke off into small groups and dispersed.

In contrast to the DeBroto party's transition from semi-parodied nostalgia and *dangdut* inflections to balladeering youthful rebellion or camaraderie, detachment engagement processes at a Joglo Jago party shifted in the opposite direction: from youthful protest and alienation to animated and humorous Melayu songs and, finally, patriotic and nostalgic *kroncong* and *langgam*. Also unlike the DeBroto party, the performance at Joglo Jago, a studio and house toward the southeast outskirts of town, was more formal and pre-planned, and Sawung Jabo, *jalanan* folk/rock legend and co-owner of Joglo Jago, had designed the venue to allow for music performance. The party was held to celebrate the eighty-seventh birthday of Pak Suharso Sugiyanto, a renowned artist and an unashamed 'lady's man', though this latter characteristic did not lead to any musical sexualisation at the party. Among the hundred guests were numerous *jalanan*-connected figures, including the then Jakarta-based reggae artist Aniesenchu and around half a dozen Sosro Boys.

The enclosed, outdoor party featured the low lighting of traditional oil lamps, a hired *angkringan* complete with Javanese snacks, and two rows of bench seats facing a small stage in the studio's open pavilion. The first act was a female duo singing Jabo's 'Mengejar bayangan, menangkap angin' (Chase a shadow, clutch the wind), followed by a male soloist – all performers were young adults playing folk guitar. The *jalanan* songwriter Untung Basuki followed with a short speech about Pak Sugiyanto's relationship to Indonesia's first president, Soekarno. Then, continuing the theme of nurturing young performers, he sang his 'Parang Tritis' accompanied by two young men from Sulawesi about to begin musical studies at the Arts Institute. Then Tyas, other KPJM members and I played Javanese *jalanan* and extended versions of a few of their minor key songs.

Audience/guest involvement in the music up to this point was not so much detached as drifting between conversing over it, listening, and swaying a little. Physical engagement increased with Jimi Do Re Mi, a *jalanan* musician famous locally for his homemade multifunction red guitar and original compositions. A number of guests persuaded Jimi and his two percussionists to play 'Cinta hampa' (Unrequited love), this being of the *pop melayu* genre and predecessor of *dangdut*. A couple from among the guests rose to sing in duet, and the band began the song with a pronounced Arabic/*melayu* rhythm. This caused a few sectors of the party to engage physically, beyond their hitherto chatting and polite applauding, by swaying on their seats and singing. This in turn set the stage for Mas Tono to sing over Jimi's group and dance about clownishly, which led many seated women to guffaw, stamp their feet, and cheer. Mas Tono then sang 'Semalam di Malaysia' (One night in Malaysia), a heartfelt ballad that with his out of tune but comical treatment also provoked laughs and cheers.

In contrast to the turning point at the DeBroto party, for Pak Sugiyanto's eighty-seventh at Joglo Jago a *kroncong* orchestra followed the height in musical physicalisation. This group sang 'Bengawan Solo', 'Sewu kuto', 'Yen ing tawang ono lintang' (When there are stars in the sky), 'Prahu layar' and 'Ojo diperoki', the latter with such sonorous beauty that it reduced Pak Sugiyanto to tears. Many of these songs were also popular in the *campursari* genre, but here did not include synthesiser keyboards or retuned gamelan gongs. Some sang along, and Mas Tono and a friend sat on the side of the stage clapping, shuffling and singing 'ei oh ei' in a style similar to the West Javanese *senggok* described by Jeremy Wallach (2004). Most others at the party sat back and enjoyed the music, after which most people made their way home.

The above kampung events displayed little evidence of detachment based on status-marking clothing, elevated seating, and/or deferential pronouncements. Nonetheless, participants of various class positions were notably detached around music at daytime wedding receptions. By contrast, the DeBroto and Joglo Jago cases demonstrate inter-generational transitions to physical engagement, but with differing musical tastes and genres. In both of these latter cases, music was central to the overlap between, and transitions through, the roles played by different generations. Public-oriented women sometimes led these transitions; the two other groups outlined earlier, younger staff workers and *perek*, were in some cases not present let alone involved in musical performance. As I discuss next, notable parallels and differences of musical detachment engagement were evident in Yogyakarta's commercial hotels and *kafe* nightclubs.

| *Musical worlds in Yogyakarta*

Harsh contrast between riverside kampung and a high-class hotel

FROM HOTEL GAMELAN TO *KAFE* POP

International, high-class hotels located in economically struggling zones constitute some of the starkest cross-national and class-based disparities imaginable. Shiny limousines pull up to regally clothed bellhops under marblesque entranceways, while only metres away members of the dusty underclass perch on old wooden stools under torn plastic awnings. These contrasts exert an influence on the nature of physical engagement with music inside these hotels, with detachment reflecting not kampung formality but rather a discomforting awareness of surrounding class disparities. Many of Yogyakarta's high-class hotels flank a section of the eastbound Solo Road that runs to the airport and out of town (see Map to Part Two). Here in 2001 were the Santika and Novotel hotels and, slightly to the north, the Radisson. Each of these hotels officially charged from Rp 1 Million (US$100) per night, and a cup of tea cost around Rp 17,500 (US$1.75) while that at a bordering street stall cost Rp 500 (US5c).

Most reception areas in these hotels featured music that complemented the air-conditioned and sofa-seated replication of an authentic Javanese culture. In the mansion-style, single-story Radisson Hotel, the courtly music of a gamelan trio echoed softly against the chatter of hotel guests and clinking of cups and glasses, with the group's presence designed to appear incidental. By evening, music in the hotels' restaurants and bar sections could move guests from physical detachment into more engaged modes. For example, one evening at the Novotel a local trio performed European and Latin folk songs to a tour group of 20 elderly continental Europeans as they ate their buffet dinner at the candlelit poolside tables. The all-singing trio moved from table to table, and later accompanied the guests as they waltzed in small, upright circles. Such physicalisation served to engage the guests and the musicians, with the surrounding tidy and under-occupied staff only able to feign enjoyment through polite hand clapping.

4 Detachment engagement

Calypso Band at Santika Hotel

Many people I spoke with in Yogyakarta sought involvement in the high-class hotel scene. However, despite the increasing demand for jazz among the middle classes, musicians often found themselves exploited and under-appreciated in these environments. One case of this was my guitar teacher, who played with his Latin band 'Calypso' at Santika Hotel. On their first night, less than a dozen people attended the hotel's large restaurant. Most did not acknowledge the group and their creatively crafted arrangements, the only exception being three Japanese women who posed for photographs with the performers' guitars while they were on a break. In the cut-throat hotel environment, intensified by the economic crisis and downturns in the tourism industry, the hotel management cancelled the group's contract soon after the show.

Hotel staff and most musical performers complied with the hotel management's demands for deferential behaviour. By contrast, freelance *perek* would fraternise directly with the mostly foreign clientele. At the Hotel Ibis' foyer adjoining Malioboro Mall, a few *perek* regularly played pool, drank alcohol and were forward with patrons. It seemed clear to me that their sexy dress, make-up and mannerisms generally made both managers and guests very uncomfortable. In contrast, Yayi was also involved in the hotel business, but as a performer and with relative financial success and autonomy. As a lead singer she performed in these hotels around five times a week, and was able to traverse a wide range of genres. As I will further discuss, Yayi's performing skills and experience enabled what I am venturing to call *habitus* plasticity, an important indicator of which was her ability to balance polite deference and controlled crowd-rousing across several settings.

| *Musical worlds in Yogyakarta*

High-class international hotels in Yogyakarta were the sites of acute social divisions based primarily on class, nationality, and age. Rallies and threats centred on high-class hotels in neighbouring Surakarta ('Solo') were among the most overt expressions of anti-foreigner sentiment in pre-'September 11' Indonesia. In Yogyakarta in the same period, social divisions at high-class hotels were maintained with minimal security presence. Music performances in the hotel receptions were, in line with the service and décor, designed to ensure the comfort of high-paying guests. Physical engagement among guests sometimes arose, but more often the best efforts of music groups and their spokesperson/singer could not overcome the under-patronised and economically imbalanced atmosphere of social and musical detachment. This made the gaudy gestures of the *perek* even starker, and the less experienced hotel staff walked about nervously attempting to convert their college training into gestures of respect for the wealthy guests. Most guests in turn were polite but kept their gaze downcast. Musical performance in the high-class hotel scene was therefore a difficult arena in which to foster engagement within and across social groups.

The Hotel Natour Garuda musical scene was more representative of the experience of specifically Indonesian middle- to upper-class hotel guests. A building of some historical significance (Artha 2001:26-32), Hotel Garuda was refreshingly cool and dutifully maintained, standing in contrast with the ramshackle venues of nearby, bustling Malioboro Street. During my research, four regular arenas for live music were located within the hotel and its grounds. Firstly, during most lunch periods a seven-member gamelan ensemble played on a floor-level stage adjacent to the open-plan restaurant in the reception area. This was a larger and more elaborate version of the Radisson group; however, given the high ceilings of Hotel Garuda's lobby, their music sounded somewhat like it was taking place in a shopping mall. The gamelan served primarily as background for the Indonesian businessmen dining in various sized groups, and wealthy Indonesian families gathering in the spacious reception area either newly arrived, preparing to check out, or setting out on excursions.

Second, a *kroncong* orchestra sometimes played through the mid-evening hours, with the two middle-aged female singers and all-male musicians crowded into a small but prominent part of the restaurant. The *kroncong* group's location, timing, song choices and volume allowed them to shift between atmospheric background and being the central attraction. Their presence was often largely unnoticed, although audience engagement tended to increase when the female MC/singers addressed guests directly, or when someone requested a song or got up to sing. A sonorous and more mobile West Sumatran Batak vocal trio also occasionally played in the restaurant.

A third performance arena was the halls, restaurants, and mezzanine rooms within the complex where various groups held functions, some of which physically engaged participants. On one occasion, the street-based Astro Band entertained a group of tax officers from Surabaya in a small function room. The tax officers also hired a woman MC, who soon got the officers involved in clapping along. Then a number of them sang songs ranging from 'Cotton fields' to the Javanese 'Poco loro' (Two wives). Later the officers formed two lines and danced opposite each other to the eastern Indonesian song 'Poco poco'. In these ways, the MC and band helped to facilitate physical musical engagement, at least among the officers. Another function was a fashion show held in the hotel's grand hall. Again a woman MC induced guests to get up and sing. The formal part of the evening featured parades of everything from sleek Islamic wear to stylishly torn jeans, all to sophisticated recorded music.

Finally, performances took place at the outdoor Garuda Kafe, which could seat up to 50 guests under an awning covering much of the area, including the small stage and a bar/serving area. Unlike the hotel's other settings, the *kafe* was a site of loud, up-tempo music which, merging into the traffic noise on the nearby Malioboro Street, effectively precluded conversation. The *kafe* hired bands to play weekly, generally over one-month periods, with different groups featuring most nights of the week. Significantly, a loose-knit group of musicians that became central to my research into *jalanan* and *campursari* also performed at Kafe Garuda, and with the aforementioned Yayi on vocals. Given the general lack of business and meagre pay, the band treated the venue very casually, not unlike the gamelan group indoors. Their set times were flexible and their repertoire moved freely between heavy metal epics (the guitar sound-effects programmed to various distortions; compare with Sutton 1996) to 'My way', 'Sad movies', and open blues jamming. By contrast, while some among them knew many *campursari* songs, the group considered them completely out of place here. Nonetheless, like other hotel and *kafe* bands, they were always receptive to audience requests, and Yayi maintained a professional air.

Hotel Garuda could therefore become a hive of musical activity. Most of the events at the hotel did not exclude women, some indeed regularly playing leading roles as MC or singer. The hotel nonetheless remained exclusive in terms of class and acceptable behaviour, with outsiders such as street workers and *perek* rarely entering the grounds, let alone the hotel proper, and physical engagement with music was for the most part understated.

The final type of commercial venue explored here, *kafe* nightclubs, was distinct from high-class hotel bars and restaurants, even when adjoining them. Detachment engagement transitions at *kafe* nightclubs often centred on very loud rock or pop music, dim lighting, and varying levels of alcohol consumption. As venues whose central purpose was the melding of loud music, physical interaction (especially dancing), and economic transactions, *kafe* fit within a broader category of music-oriented commercial establishments. In 2001 these included: Bambu Resto, a late-night musicians' venue often featuring music of the Beatles and Elvis; the relatively seedy Bar Borobudur; Papillon, a discotheque with a pitch-black interior and musics combining 80s disco for the 'young executives' and for the 'youth' various subgenres of 'hip' such as techno and hip-metal; Jogja Jogja, another disco, characterised by a young clientele, thudding techno music, and high levels of *shabu-shabu* methamphetamine consumption; and Takasimura, a sordid nightclub on Solo Road patronised by army generals and domestic and foreign businessmen. Most of the upwardly aspiring *kafe* in Yogyakarta were located on Magelang Road to the north of the city centre (Map to Part Two), each of which was large, featured live music and catered mostly to a moneyed, domestic clientele.

Entrepreneurs and business groups established a number of Yogyakarta's *kafe* in the early days of Reformasi, in an atmosphere of new political freedoms. However, economic and other problems meant there was a dearth of middle-class Indonesians and foreigners with disposable cash, leaving bands and *kafe* underpatronised. For example, Java Kafe opened during the economic crisis in early 1999, yet the owners were evidently optimistic about the business they would generate. The *kafe* was set up to seat over 200 people, with stylish bamboo-laced chairs and green-lit palm trees creating a pleasant ambience, and an overall layout designed to cater to anything from family functions to sizeable rock gigs. However, this arrangement did not readily encourage dancing among audience members. Seats faced the band all the way to the stage, thus foregrounding the band yet allowing no room to dance, and the blasting volume of the band again made the option of conversation very difficult. Over a few hours on one occasion when I visited, the 20 customers all sat silently next to their friends for long periods. While economic divisions were not as great as those at luxury hotels, disengagement here seemed to extend beyond musical physicalisation and into social interaction.

At the same time, *kafe* bands evidently drew in and held audiences for reasons other than dancing to and/or talking over the music. For example, at Java Kafe one evening the Bintang Band played bass, drums, percussion and keyboards with great exuberance, while the central female singer and two males flanking her danced in formation by stepping forward-left-back, forward-right-back in time with the music. The singers also employed humorous but polite and inclusive MC techniques, as with the transnational Filipino bands described by Stephanie Ng (2005). Like talk-show hosts of popular MTV Asia shows, the singers bantered into their microphones to include the *kafe* guests. They welcomed newcomers, mentioning their table number and inviting them to make a request at any time, then went back to lightly flirting among themselves before announcing the next song. Songs on this evening included Sting's 'An Englishman in New York', the then globally popular 'Vengaboys are coming', and 'Kemesraan' (Intimacy), a song made famous by Iwan Fals.

In terms of both the degree of detachment engagement and the socioeconomic positions of participants, Yogyakarta's *kafe* nightclubs generally fell between high-class hotels and the seedier Bar Borobudur (discussed later). Dancing at *kafe*, as with discothèques, usually involved two lines on the dance floor, with partners facing each other. Most *kafe* bands played Top 40 and other popular cover versions and thus were not known for originality or social statements. It was nonetheless evident in their presentation that members took themselves very seriously, and one member explained to me that her group followed an individually devised five-point philosophy. Instrumental and vocal arrangements of groups such as the Bintang Band were part of an active but underemployed middle class popular music scene in Yogyakarta; as was their name, with others including New Colors Band, S@toe Band, and Galaxi Band.

Finally, Yogya Kafe departed significantly from these commercial-venue conventions of loud Top 40 bands and generally few and immobile customers. This venue comprised several tables and chairs (some being in a quiet section), a pool table and bar and, accompanying the musical activities, a sunken marble dance floor, sophisticated lighting, and a big screen projecting the band in action, often with hi-tech freeze framing. Many people in the rock and *jalanan* scene valued the uniqueness of Yogya Kafe, especially because the owner promoted local bands and housed many touring acts. An evening's entertainment often consisted of a number of bands, and there was greater emphasis on original music. Yogya Kafe's wooden décor had the worn-in hues of Bar Borobudur, yet it also had the spaciousness and elegance of other *kafe*. The behaviour of the clientele generally reflected this, in that attendance and alcohol consumption tended to be relatively high yet contained, and inter-gender interaction was unusually high without necessarily being premised on sexual transactions.

In sum, international hotels housed live music that varied from exotic background to functional entertainment. The path for outsiders, especially female ones, to become involved included staff, musical, or *perek* work. At all *kafe* nightclubs, the music was generally of very high volume, making conversation virtually impossible. Many educated middle-class Indonesian women nonetheless evidently saw these venues as outlets conducive for mixing with people outside their daily *habitus*. As at nightclubs more generally, high volumes and dark atmospheres encouraged physical rather than verbally oriented interaction among clientele, which here generally remained relatively polite and sexually understated. Variations in degrees of musical detachment engagement, therefore, seemed closely related to the degree and type of social divisions prevailing with commercial establishments.

At the kampung and commercial-venue events discussed in this chapter, power-laden immobility was in greater evidence at more formal kampung events and with greater class disparity in the commercial establishments. The correlations I have posited between, on the one hand, a decline in levels of formality (in kampung) and class differentiation (in commercial establishments), and on the other greater cross-group interaction, suggest patterns, or at least tendencies, regarding women's involvement in the generally male-dominated world of night-time musical performances. In the kampung events, physical engagement among guests rose and ebbed broadly according to age, but these processes were not mono-directional. In other words, the smooth and trouble-free transitions that occurred through the DeBroto and Joglo Jago kampung events can be seen respectively in the retirement of older party-goers to make way for the more youthful participants, and in the younger generations' bowing to the elders' music and its conventions. In both cases, women seemed quite relaxed clapping along and acting out towards the performers. However, while adult women led the intermediate phase at DeBroto, at Joglo Jago women performed both early and late in the proceedings, but did not take on comical, sensual or otherwise spectacular centre-stage roles.

Detachment engagement transitions in kampung and commercial zones both influenced and reflected the gendered *habitus* of participants. Some women at the DeBroto event in Sosrowijayan demonstrated their performance skills, and thereby their ability not only to keep house but also to entertain. For the few women who did this, their management of multiple roles was reflected in the confident bearing they carried around the kampung. Similarly, in commercial-venue situations with large class disparities, most notably at high-class hotels, women holding a formal position could exercise some authority without having to trade on their sexuality. However, musical performances in these establishments to some extent rendered problematic the equation of power and immobility. A number of women in MC and singing/dancing lead roles successfully occupied a middle ground between immobile, subservient staff employees and excessively sexualised *perek*.

Middle-class *kafe* nightclub music generally encouraged a less structured, more relaxed, and widespread form of inter-gender interaction. However, relatively small numbers attended *kafe*, which hampered the influence of this commercial-venue variant of music and inter-gender relations on wider society. Such connections between musical detachment engagement and the everyday *habitus* is evidence that the 'Javanese tradition' of exercising power through immobility is not absolute. Building from these observations, the following chapter explores musical physicalisations that were distinctly more animated.

5

Other worlds and sexualisation

In contrast to detachment engagement transitions, the musical events in this chapter reveal ways in which gender and other social boundaries were negotiated in situations of intensified musical physicality (Cowan 1990; McIntosh 2010). More specifically, the other worlds and sexualisation forms of musical physicalisation that variously arose and merged in Yogyakarta's kampung and commercial-venue events challenge conventional understandings of Javanese power. These physicalisations, I argue, shine light on the relationships between musical performance, gendered bodies and the social dynamics characteristic of downtown Yogyakarta in the early post-Soeharto years.

KAMPUNG *JATILAN* AND KRIDOSONO METAL/ELECTRONIC

'Other worlds' refers to the highly physicalised dance and/or related bodily movements that reflect an actor's entrance into an alternative reality or state of being. While political campaigns in early post-Soeharto Yogyakarta sometimes included menacing other worlds-style hysteria, the more popular and widespread cases derived primarily from Javanese mysticism and western-influenced metal and electronic musics. This section seeks to demonstrate how these latter cases produced outlets of expression that helped to transcend performer/audience and gender-based social divisions, which in turn influenced and were influenced by the gendered *habitus* in daily life.

Of the numerous indigenist and regionalist performance types that have long challenged stereotypes of conservatism in Java (Richter 2008a:180, note 6), in 2001 the *jatilan* trance dance was immensely popular.[1] *Jatilan* is generally performed in a cordoned-off arena, within which the dancers enter into a trance, as reflected in performers' trance-like or possessed movements and facial expressions. M. Wienarti (1968) has discussed *jatilan* and its animist

---

1 On the related *jaranan* trance dance popular in East Java, see Clara van Groenendael 2008.

associations, as well as its historical function in rites of passage such as marriage. Margaret Kartomi (1973) has explored 'folk trance art forms' more broadly in terms of their pre-Hindu origins and contemporary entertainment functions. I found the performances noteworthy for the way in which the trance phases signalled the submergence of performers into an 'other world', and also because audiences consisted of women, men and children.

The first *jatilan* I witnessed took place late at night in a village north of Yogyakarta, where two rows of four men in matching red costumes and make-up and holding a hobbyhorse lined up, and then began stepping delicately in formation as the music built up in tempo and volume. Within minutes some of the dancers' eyes began to roll, and soon after that mayhem broke out with whip cracking, flame swallowing, and much frenzied running and hopping about, all to great shrieks and laughter among the 200-strong audience. I also watched a number of *jatilan* events in urban kampung. These took place in the middle of the day, generally around Independence Day, with audiences comprised largely of mothers with young children and young men with dyed hair and other signs of western punk and grunge affiliation. Also in contrast to the village *jatilan*, where the build-up to the trance was more gradual, in the urban cases all of the dancers simultaneously fell into a violent heap and, upon rising to their feet, began trance dancing together.

Jatilan dancers in an urban kampung

5 *Other worlds and sexualisation*

Jatilan dancers in an urban kampung

Kampung *jatilan* performances allowed onlookers to view familiar neighbours entering into an unfamiliar, other world of trance. Audiences remained physically immobile and separate from (though in thrilling proximity to) the performers, except for the occasional audience member who, entranced, entered the arena. In turn, performer actions on centre stage can be related to gender roles and relations. The shaman (*dukun*), always a male, along with the deep gong players wielded the transformative power needed to transport the dancers to the other world. The shaman's movements were poised and deliberate, while those of the trance dancers were its unpredictable and unwieldy opposite. These roles in turn can be related to factors of gender, physicality, and power. The 'feminised' appearance and movements of the dancers can be seen to draw on ideas about the subordinate 'irrational' female, something Norma Sullivan (1994:170) points out in her discussion of communal rituals. By contrast, the poised and deliberate moves of the shaman may be seen as masculine and potent (Errington 1990:41-2).

In contrast to the *jatilan* trance dances, many western scholars associate 'underground', 'punk', 'black metal' and related genres at the more abrasive end of Indonesia's pop-rock spectrum with symbolic protest, self-expression, and democratic progressiveness (Baulch 2007; Bodden 2005; Hill and Sen 2000). The following performances fit broadly within this cluster of genres, but I view these within the specific context of other world physicalisations that occurred at Kridosono sports hall. This was a popular venue for events involving the chiefly youth-oriented hard rock and 'electronic' musical worlds or subcultures, and which in many cases relied on the organizational skills and networks of the ethnic-Chinese rock legend Log Zhelebour. Kridosono events were commercial in the sense that they included admission charges and involved prominent sponsor signage, although in practice they foremost created situations in which performers, and to varying degrees audiences enacted other world physicalisations to express themselves and release tensions.

For example, contestants in a 'Twelve best student bands in Central Java' competition at Kridosono included a teenage-girl dance troupe, who alternated between precise but mechanical cheer-squad movements, and looser, highly sexualised hip swivelling; and No Rain, a smartly dressed group featuring wall of sound effects reminiscent of British post-new wave groups. The attentive but largely placid and immobile crowd receiving these acts soon erupted when 'grindcore' group Radikal Corps appeared and a sizeable black-clothed sector of the audience ran to the stage. As band members pounced and growled around the stage, their fans before them broke into tortured dance moves, some casting their knees into the air while marching in circles, some pounding their upper bodies back and forth in a haze of hair, and others clasped onto the stage fence and imitated thumping their heads against a wall. Later, guest stars BIP, containing three former members of Slank, transformed the hall into an arena full of dancing women and men. Most people in the audience variously swung their heads, arms and/or whole bodies to the music and the rock stars performing on stage.

The third annual ParkinSound Performance also included widely participatory other worlds dancing at Kridosono. The audience steadily increased through the afternoon, by ten o'clock in the evening numbering well over a thousand. Many were university students and their friends, including many visitors from Jakarta. The average age was around 20 years, with many dressed self-consciously in secondhand or homemade clothing; and almost half was female, an unusually high proportion for evening public entertainment in Yogyakarta City. The most outstanding feature in common among the 18 bands was that, unlike most techno music and performance in the West, here the practices of sampling, drum machines and DJ scratching were in almost all cases combined with musicians playing standard pop/rock instruments.

While the generally subtle and expressionistic musings of several of the groups received appreciative applause and gentle swaying from among the audience, the appearance of 'Teknoshit' heralded a phase of overtly political messages and anguished onstage other world physicalisations. Following them, Marzuki the organizer urged the audience to get up from their seats, prompting hundreds to descend from the stadium seating to the floor and dance to the pumping beat. Soon practically everyone in the hall, including young women in red and other brightly coloured *jilbab* (Muslim headscarves), was now dancing. Covering the floor from one end of the hall to the other, the dancers threw their arms high into the air and stepped in time to the pounding beat while facing the stage, swinging their heads from side to side for half an hour.

At Kridosono sports hall, the vast majority of those involved were lower middle- to middle-class youth and young adults. Although the performance stages were largely separate from audiences, audience physicalisation at times blended with that of the performers. For most, the thundering volume and bass rhythm induced some form of physical movement, even if at times being involuntary or only semiconscious. At a minimum, this might involve perching forward or head nodding. When physicalisation became more extreme, performer and audience actions did not manifest themselves in sexual display, but instead demonstrated socio-political expression through exhibiting a kind of bodily anguish. Kampung *jatilan* performances on the other hand induced thrilled giggles and gasps from the audience, especially from women and children. Despite differences of age, spatial arrangement and musical genre, both forms of other world physicalisation were highly animated, and at the same time often played down rather than accentuated gender differences and sexuality.

According to the 'traditional' idea of power in Javanese society, immobility reflects and conveys power while high levels of physical movement do not. I am arguing that the musical performances under analysis here help to problematise overly simplistic readings of the relations between gender, physicality, and power in Java. This has been demonstrated through the animation and empowerment of women in detachment engagement musical situations, in the relatively gender-neutral *jatilan* performances, and among youth at other world commercial-venue events. In the following sections I discuss cases involving musical sexualisation, and explore further the relationships between music, physical mobility, gender relations, and social stature. The first of these focuses on a small number of musical events that took place in kampung, and which highlight interrelationships between the three physicalisations and the main groups and genres under study in this book.

CAMPURSARI/DANGDUT AND *JALANAN*/ROCK IN THE KAMPUNG

Among the several kampung events I witnessed in Yogyakarta in 2001, the performance of *campursari/dangdut* crossovers was an especially prominent feature (see also Mrázek 1999:53-4). This in turn reflected and reinforced other world/sexualisation tensions and accommodations. By contrast, rock bands and their *jalanan* counterparts at kampung events tended to be loud, inducing physical detachment, and perhaps internal appreciation, among audiences. As I will show, a performance in the Kusuman kampung traversed all of these genres, and highlighted roles played by lead female performers and (generally all-male) musical groups in steering the proceedings and overall musical experience for all participants.

Campursari-dangdut/other worlds-sexualisation transitions occurred at a village reception for a boy's circumcision that I attended with Pak Harno, a *becak* driver and leader of the Sosro Bahu association addressed earlier. On this occasion, the musical performance gave rise to intergenerational sexual and other tensions and accommodations between men. Before the orchestra began, five *pesinden* (female singers) gathered from different directions to settle at a table to the side of the performance clearing. The 200 village men there all sat chatting before the performance area in their shimmering batik shirts with stovepipe pants. The *campursari* music began a little after eight pm, and moved through its characteristic tempo changes and gradual increases in volume, with the sounds blending Javanese gongs and deep percussion with synthesiser

Genre-bending kampung performance

sounds ranging from violins to 'space age'. Over the next couple of hours, a series of humorous and musical interchanges between lead performers and guests took place to the accompaniment of the orchestra.

In the meantime, 15 teenage boys, distinguishable not only by their age but also their pink body shirts and white ties, served a three-course meal at the tables set in rows before the men. The boys periodically returned to the tables to provide refills of tea and to clear up, carrying out these duties with quintessentially polite Javanese gestures of deference, dragging their right hands low to the ground upon passing their elders, and speaking only to be of assistance. By ten-thirty pm however, their duties completed, half a dozen of the young staff suddenly tore off their shirts and ties, kicked off their shoes and, in white undershirts, black formal pants and bare feet, began other world dancing (*joged*) around each other. Continuing to hop about and sweep their arms, the boys slowly swarmed toward and then onto the performance clearing. A few of them shouted repeatedly for *dangdut* songs, launching into ever more ecstatic dancing upon the fulfilment of their requests. The more the musicians complied, the further the catering group overtook the performance clearing. When a few of the teenage boys began circling the young female singer however, the village head and his colleague, who up to this point had been watching from a distance, ran into their path and herded them to an enclosure behind the guests. From there the young caterers continued to shout for more *dangdut* songs while dancing merrily among themselves.

Entertainment at this village circumcision reception, attended exclusively by men, became an occasion to mark transitions between youth and adulthood, *campursari* and *dangdut* musical genres, and other world and sexualised physicalities. The young staff members were able to challenge their marginal status through dance, a phenomenon Cowan (1990:185-6) also notes in relation to dance in rural Greece. However, here the youth overstepped their limits by invading the female performers' space, and with sexualisation overtaking other worlds, the authorities were compelled to step in and steer them away.

Performances around city kampung also became arenas for the playing out of tensions and accommodations between *campursari* and highly sexualised *dangdut*. At one Independence Day performance, the *campursari* singers' refined dress and subdued mannerisms contrasted sharply with the denim street wear and erotic dance moves of the guest *dangdut* singers who followed. The first *dangdut* singer, a denim-clad woman in her early twenties, broke into a song. Aided by the swooping trumpet sounds on keyboard and insistent drums from the orchestra, she interspersed hoots and wails with her singing. Along with her increasingly erotic movements, these roused large and surprisingly diverse segments of the audience. Another young woman sang 'Terlena', with her air of cute vulnerability in the introduction leading into brash and explicitly sexual dance routines. Some among the seated families appeared uninterested or mildly offended by this, but many more became animated with laughter, hand clapping, and rib poking.

To the extent that musical genres can be linked to their broader cultural associations, these kampung examples indicate that westernism was not prominent; the polite, Javanist engagements between performers and audience took place earlier in the evening; and heightened sexuality later in the events was the product of a conglomeration of nationalist, *melayu*, Indian and Arabic influences. While *campursari* and *dangdut* were central to contests around permissible sexuality at evening kampung performances, rock music in these settings was only likely to invoke other world and/or sexualised dancing if injected into, for example, the repertoire of a *dangdut* group. More often, rock music here was a vehicle for the expression of urban alienation and/or teen angst. Kampung rock physicalisations were akin to the immersed yet physically immobile audience receptions characteristic of Kridosono events dominated by teenage males.

Live rock music at kampung events was most often an early segment in a several act show, and the performers were typically male teenagers. For Independence Day in one city kampung, the first two acts were groups of teenage boys playing two songs each, all of which were versions of Indonesian alternative pop groups such as Padi and Dewa. Their raw and distorted renditions added an air of urban alienation to the original versions. A variation on this occurred with the Malioboro Arts Community at the Pajeksan kampung south of Sosrowijayan. Independence Day here featured 12 western-style rock bands playing music ranging from teenage 'hip-metal' to older generation pop (1950s and 1960s Beatlesque). The headline act was KPJM, who performed extended versions of their locally renowned *jalanan* songs. Here the audience applauded often and enthusiastically, but head nodding was the closest they came to dancing, and the large space before the stage remained empty.

The final event to be discussed in this section took place in Kusuman kampung, and warrants more extensive description. Musically, this performance combined *campursari* and *dangdut* with rock and soul music, and the different forms of physicalisation – detachment engagement, other worlds and sexualisation – were

5 Other worlds and sexualisation

clearly demarcated in space. Kusuman was more socially and ethnically uniform than Sosrowijayan, but it also housed a number of Sosrowijayan-based street workers and is only ten minutes by bicycle from Malioboro Street. The performance also involved members of the Tombo Sutris *campursari* orchestra (discussed later), as well as Yayi, who specialised in highly sexualised performances in a number of different settings.

The performance took place as part of the *selapanan* celebration that occurs 35 days after the birth of a child, one of many lifecycle rituals practiced in Java (Geertz 1960:38-50). When I arrived at nine pm, the event was already underway. In addition to those formally invited, anybody living in the kampung could attend, with the result that by mid-evening attendance had reached over 200 people. These included both males and females of all age groups, and dressed with varying degrees of formality. While there were no formal demarcations, the guests nonetheless settled into distinct areas: the relatives and closest associates of Visnu and his wife enjoyed an elevated view midway back from the stage; a number of women, including those with older children, stood behind this row; most of Visnu's male friends crowded to the left of the stage; and a group of young mothers and their children sat directly in front of it. Most others stood or sat outwards from these circles, broadly reflecting their social distance from the hosts. Most physically distant but audibly dominant was a group of mostly young men dancing in a clearing over a waist-high wire fence five metres to the right of the band.

The 12 member group took up much of the large stage, with a narrow section at the front reserved for the lead performers. The players' wide range of musical skills enabled them to respond to audience requests and to the performances of the numerous local girls who got up to sing. These factors also became the basis for the group's improvisatory and/or comical passages. Musical styles shifted from *campursari* to combinations of *campursari, dangdut,* western rock, and soul.

Yayi, the 17 year-old professional singer discussed earlier, was the lead performer. Well experienced in the art of rousing yet containing an audience, each time she re-emerged to sing a few songs the atmosphere became more sexually charged, and yet she was also able to utilise her sexuality to steer audience behaviours. At ten o'clock she appeared wearing a skimpy lace top and jeans. However, seeing that the raucousness among the men dancing in the side enclosure was getting out of hand, she instructed the band to keep the tempo up but, with the air of having won the dancing men's consent, changed the theme to 'rock and roll'. She sang

James Brown's 'I feel good', with orchestral accompaniment combining rhythmic precision with comical syncopations. The men to the side continued to dance but now with less gusto and bravado.[2]

Near the end of the show, people increasingly called on a number of teenage kampung girls to perform on stage. I found it difficult to determine whether the girls were enthusiastic about performing, or whether they were coerced into it. Their initial responses were gestures of unwillingness – arms folded and turning slightly away from the stage – although some men insisted that they were '*malu-malu kucing*' (feigning shyness). In any event, when the girls performed, always in groups of two, the most vocally insistent in the audience urged them to display their sexuality as erotically as possible, especially in the instrumental passages. As I had seen at other kampung performances, most of the girls corkscrewed slowly to the ground and back up in an especially sexual manner. Physical responses from the audience varied. The men dancing in the side area hooted toward the stage, then returned to face each other and swing their arms ever higher into the air. Much like at the Purawisata events to be discussed next, the men's dancing combined other world mythical styles with a sexual charge. Most audience members at the Kusuman performance, including the hosts, did not seem offended or uncomfortable, appearing rather to treat the display of young female sexuality as a normal part of such festivities.

Musical physicalisations at this Kusuman event highlight patterns of spatial segregation and musical/genre divisions. Attendants were more or less segregated according to gender, age, and social proximity to the hosts. As the evening progressed, other worlds and sexual movements increased, the former prominently among the men dancing in a separate enclosure, the latter among female lead performers. Given the high volume and cramped conditions, simply being at the event meant engaging physically with it. Only the mothers of young children seated before the stage were able to stay relatively detached from the rest of the crowd. The other world moves of the men to the side were on the verge of becoming sexualised and dominating proceedings, as they did at the village ceremony discussed earlier, but here they were successfully contained. In part this was because the organizers had assigned them a separate area, but it was also due to Yayi and the orchestra's deft crowd management.

Are these overt displays of sexuality evidence of female autonomy, or of gender oppression? They can be seen as oppressed to the

---

2 The unwieldy behaviours of the adult males at this kampung event are of course but one of the great myriad of shifting 'masculine' cultural expressions found in Indonesia (Clark 2010).

extent that they were objectified and given attention largely for their ability to display sexual allure. This position is further supported by the fact that the audience called for sexual displays only from teenage girls and not, for example, women in their twenties or thirties. On the other hand, Yayi in particular was able to direct guest behaviours even more effectively than the adult male MCs, providing a positive role model for the younger girls.[3] Moreover, older women, including Visnu's mother, encouraged the girls' sexualised roles.

The music on this occasion did not fit into distinct genre categories. This was in part a result of the equipment available, but also of deliberate choice. Rather than presenting music with specific and distinct cultural associations – *campursari*: village-Javanism; *dangdut*: nationalism, and South and Central Asia-bound quasi-Islamic internationalism; rock: US and UK westernism; and soul: African-Americanism – the music ranged across and between these. The refined/rough divide of 'high' and 'popular' art as described by Geertz (1960) is also difficult to maintain in this case. The relatively refined aspects of *campursari* were interwoven with the more salacious *dangdut*, with gamelan gongs featured in otherwise standard *dangdut* songs; *campursari* songs were given *dangdut* and rock flavours, for example with funk-style bass.

Nor was sexualisation confined to the performance of *dangdut*. 'Kuda lumping', a Javanese folk song with an 'other world' title referring to the toy horse used in *jatilan*, encouraged sexualisation on stage, while Yayi used the music of James Brown to curb sexualisation among the off-stage dancing men. In these ways, performers were able to deploy a variety of musical and cultural associations to steer the general behaviour and mood of the event in particular directions. The final section of this chapter returns again to Yogyakarta's entertainment venues. These cases will demonstrate a narrower scope for experimentation between genres and physical engagements and, consequently, different prospects for *habitus* plasticity.

DANGDUT SHOWS AND PUB ROCK

Two venues in Yogyakarta were unusual public spaces in that both centred on women dancing in highly sexualised ways. The first, Taman Ria, had clearly defined spatial separations between the female performers and the predominantly lower-class male Muslim audience. The second, Bar Borobudur, had porous spatial bound-

---

3 On creative dimensions of on-stage female *dangdut* performance, see Bader 2011.

aries, attracted a mixed clientele including foreigners, and as a result generated and maintained contrasting gender relations.

Taman Ria at the Purawisata venue revolved around highly sexualised female *dangdut* singers performing on stage. Located on busy Bridjen Katamso Road outside the eastern walls of the Greater Kraton, Purawisata was a multi-function amusement park and cultural arts centre. *Dangdut* performances had been taking place there from nine pm through to one am virtually every night of the year over the past 12 years, meaning that tens of thousands of spectators and hundreds of lead performers had participated. We can therefore expect *dangdut* performances at Taman Ria to reveal significant patterns of behaviour in relation to musical sexualisation in Yogyakarta's commercial venues. During my research, *dangdut* singer/performers at the venue defied government and Muslim group bans on dressing and dancing in an overtly sexual manner. Their dresses had either long splits up to the hip, or were mini/see-through combinations, and their slow simulations of sexual intercourse always induced mild frenzy among the men below them.

At the album launch event for a young star named Vivin, the audience was dressed especially tidily. While as usual the majority of the audience were young men of around 18 years of age, there was a slightly greater proportion of women in the audience than on average nights. Dancing was widespread through the audience, mostly comprising men dancing in couples. Despite being the occasion for an official album launch, the audience persistently shouted for evergreens like 'Terlena', 'Rindu' and 'Malam terakhir'. The singers and the band for Vivin's show were markedly more professional than on standard evenings. A new singer – there were over 15 in total – would emerge for each song in glamorous dress and makeup and evidently adept at sexualising her performance. Vivin engaged in a running commentary throughout and, as with Yayi in other settings, both roused and controlled the audience at the same time. Although from Jakarta, the singers spoke using polite forms of Javanese to keep the audience onside. They sang from a pre-planned repertoire, but also accepted requests from the audience, responding to bouts of excited shouting with calming phrases like 'What is it, darling?' (Apa, sayang?). During instrumental passages, they reminded the men to smile as they danced. The show began at ten pm and finished promptly at midnight, at which time the audience dispersed in an orderly fashion.

Bar Borobudur near Sosrowijayan differed from Taman Ria in many ways: it was a ranch-style bar featuring loud live rock music, high levels of alcohol consumption, and a distinct variation of musical sexualisation. Through much of the 1990s, the bar was a popular meeting and drinking spot for expatriates, travellers, and educators, along with a large number of Indonesians. By 2001, an increase in the number of sex workers and an overall decline in diversity of clientele had given the venue a seedy edge. The clientele generally numbered between ten and 80, depending mostly on the popularity of the band. Some customers stayed only a short while, but many would stay on at the bar until the closing time at one-thirty am, some then moving on to Prada eatery.

Physical movements at the bar were linked with alcohol, a relatively diverse clientele, and loud rock-oriented music, all of which influenced each other. Live bands sometimes transformed the venue into a crowded dance floor with sweaty singles and couples dancing, some becoming highly sexualised, that spilled over into the seating area. *Perek* clearly pursued money and/or a partner at Bar Borobudur, although it was also evident that they sometimes danced for their own pleasure. *Perek* and others especially enjoyed the Alaska Band, whose cover versions of Robbie Williams' 'Better man', a song by the world beat, Benin-born female singer Angelique Kidjo, and an extended, funk version of 'I will survive', stressed agency and personal responsibility. On the other hand, no one at Bar Borobudur played *dangdut*-style music.

Despite the many rough, even exploitative, aspects of Bar Borobudur, it remained one of very few inner-city venues conducive to after hours, mixed-gender, intercultural socialising. Bar Borobudur was to most *kafe* nightclubs and hotel bars what Opposite Resto was to the TransWeb hangout discussed earlier. In other words, both Bar Borobudur and Opposite Resto could become somewhat volatile; and yet, unlike during the Soeharto era, people here openly aired their opinions on social and political matters in ways that seemed at least as often socially bonding as tension inducing. Additionally, the regulars at the bar were more diverse than they may have at first appeared. For example, sex worker Lia had a penchant for Swedish and Greek folk musics, as well as the music and philosophy of Islamic culturalist Emma Ainun Nadjib (discussed later). And many of the apparent 'outsiders' at the bar were actually on familiar terms with influential Malioboro Street figures.

The *perek* at times seemed to revel in sexual exhibition, and many of them enjoyed the material spoils offered by foreigners such as all-expenses-paid journeys, jewellery, and fine clothing. However, in the longer term their situation is more complicated, with the success rate of such relationships being quite low (Dahles and Bras 1999:285). The sexualised behaviours of *perek* at Bar Borobudur were by no means separate from their daily interactions around Sosrowijayan. Unlike the male newcomer street guides, who could fraternise with foreigners and both bring in money and earn credibility with the Sosro Boys, any financially-based kudos that the *perek* could potentially gain through their attention grabbing clothing and mannerisms was offset both by this ruthless and often harsh form of commerce, as well as by kampung disapproval.

By contrast, at Purawisata's Taman Ria the highly sexualised dancing of the female *dangdut* singers was professional and separate from the audience, who were generally happy to dance among themselves. There were virtually no women in the audience. The lead performers combined their bodily displays with leadership and a command over the audience below. *Perek* at Bar Borobudur instead mixed with the clientele in their pursuit of money, and often danced around the customer tables in overtly sexual ways.

Conclusion

In Part Two, I have classified music performances that took place in Yogyakarta's kampung and commercial entertainment venues according to detachment engagement, other worlds and sexualisation forms of musical physicalisation. Musical performance created arenas in which gender and other aspects of identity were negotiated, maintained, celebrated and/or contested in these venues, and by extension in Sosrowijayan. Among the kampung events discussed, wedding receptions were characterised by musically detached guests and hosts, regardless of class position. Physical engagement with music was greater at kampung events premised on other themes. On these occasions, inter-group animation generally reached its peak in the middle segment of the evening, as did transitions between generational groups and their favoured musical genres. Often an intermediary period of *dangdut*-related music and performance briefly enlivened the proceedings. Few young women and *perek* attended the kampung parties I witnessed, but some of the older, established women played leading roles at them.

Gendered behaviours in high-class hotels were broadly consistent with arguments that equate physical immobility with the expression of power in Java. Nonetheless, female staff, performers, and *perek* in these settings sometimes mobilised their physicality to enhance their positions in such high-stakes environments, characterised as they were by great economic disparities and a musically detached clientele. Performing work was generally insecure and unreliable. Nonetheless, performers' engaged and animated roles sometimes generated interactions, and arguably a kind of *habitus* plasticity, that were denied both general staff and *perek*. In the more middle-class *kafe* nightclub scene, spaces opened up for performers and clientele to mix across genders and outside kampung and other more traditional contexts. With the exception of Yogya Kafe however, music at *kafe* was not a central focus to the same extent as at Kridosono sports hall.

Other world *jatilan* events seemed to soothe gender tensions rather than intensify them. However, these kampung events differed from those at Kridosono in two main ways. Firstly, a broader audience attended *jatilan*, in generational and to an extent class terms; and second, audience/performer lines generally remained separate, both spatially and in terms of other world bodily movements. Another variant of other worlds physicalisation, distinct to both *jatilan* and the metal and electronic scenes, involved male audience members in kampung dancing in a *joged* style that to varying degrees merged with sexualisation. Other world commercial-venue events involving metal or electronic music displayed some class and inter-generational restrictions on involvement, but at the same time dance and performance here were markedly unconstrained by gender division and sexual tension. Other world commercial events therefore to various degrees challenged and transcended both conservative and sexualised gender roles.

Finally, variety and degrees of musical sexualisation are noteworthy in relation to questions of gender, *habitus* and autonomy in Yogyakarta. In some of the kampung musical events discussed above, participants contested and merged sexualisation with the other physicalisations. These interplays influenced and were influenced by shifts in musical genre. Loud live rock music at kampung events rarely resulted in high levels of physical movement while, by contrast, *campursari/dangdut* hybrid music often brought out intergenerational tension over acceptable or appropriate displays of public sexuality. These were occasions for other world dancing on the part of the men offstage, and onstage sexualisation on the part of lead female performers. Young men often fuelled this drive toward *dangdut* sexualisation, but so too did others. At the Kusuman event, much of the audience called for teenage girls to sing and dance on stage with overt sexuality. While this may have served to reinforce the sexually objectified role of women, Yayi's performance techniques suggest that processes of individual empowerment, as well as the generation of in-group solidarity among teenage girls, were also at work.

Purawisata centred on quasi-Islamic, lower-class versions of *dangdut*, whereas Bar Borobudur was heavily westernised, in both music and clientele. At both establishments, men variously introduced other worldly behaviours into a sexualised environment, through mythic-style dancing and alcohol consumption respectively. The forms of female musical sexualisation differed across the venues. At Purawisata, women performed in a sexual manner from the safety of a separate stage. At Bar Borobudur by contrast, *perek* mixed with clientele; they often spent time there, and in Sosrowijayan generally. *Perek* were emblematic of women in the nocturnal world of music, alcohol consumption, western influence, and sexual objectification.

Conclusion

The manifestations of detachment engagement, other worlds and sexualisation explored above suggest that music played a role in shaping neighbourhood gender relations far beyond that of merely producing temporary ruptures to everyday life. Kampung events involving music take much planning and preparation, making such events the enactment of 'social drama' (Turner 1982). The young women and men involved were at important developmental and social stages in their lives. Many teenage girls were compelled to perform in a sexual manner at kampung events and to be married and have children by the age of 25. Through such ventures, women in particular risked social isolation by overstepping the bounds of acceptable kampung behaviour (Sullivan 1994), as had occurred to some of the older *perek* and street guides. However, some young women would branch out into different social situations, interacting with people whose class, ethnic and national backgrounds were different from their own, thereby providing material with which to reflect on and rethink any kampung-based dimensions of their habituated behaviours and roles.

Throughout Part Two I have discussed variants of musical genre and physicalisation in kampung and commercial-venue events. I reflected on intergenerational, class and other factors that intermingled with gendered aspects of the events, and of social life in Sosrowijayan and Yogyakarta more broadly. Having now addressed capital conversions around street music and gendered physicalities at kampung and commercial-venue events, Part Three completes the study by applying the notions of bureaucratic field and grounded cosmopolitanism to musical performances in Yogyakarta's state institutions, noting in particular *campursari*/village, *jalanan*/city and related musical associations and their relationship to issues of state power and intergroup relations in the early post-Soeharto era.

PART 3

State power and musical cosmopolitanism

Background

It is for good reason that many academic studies of Indonesia centre on the nation-state. Historically, as Benedict Anderson (1990:41-5) explains, in the Indonesia/Malay world the term *negari* designates both a capital city and a kingdom, reflecting centuries of empires and statehood in the region. Since World War II and the period of decolonisation, arguably the first major phase of the Indonesian state ran from Independence through Guided Democracy, the downfall of Soekarno and the horrendous killings of suspected communists. The second phase was the 32 year reign (1966-1998) of President Soeharto and his New Order government, in which the state party Golkar exercised control over the state, and in its development drive implemented repressive measures over the wider society. Appeals to national culture were both widespread and diverse in their sources and aims during this period.[1]

By 1997 the Reformasi movement had begun to gain momentum, signalling the beginnings of a third phase in the history of modern Indonesia. Following the toppling of Soeharto as President in 1998, the legitimacy of the Indonesian nation-state was challenged on many fronts. Economic collapses that preceded and were not resolved by Soeharto's downfall further exacerbated intergroup and interpersonal sensitivities, not least in Javanese cities hit heavily by unemployment. Concerns over the integrity of the nation-state were also acute, with East Timor gaining independence from Indonesia, and powerful groups in numerous provinces seeking autonomy or independence. Added to these were long-term issues concerning roles of Islam and the Military in state affairs. When I was conducting fieldwork, the brilliant and worldly yet administratively challenged President Abdurrahman Wahid (Gus Dur) underwent a protracted impeachment process. Major shifts were underway in local government, and protests over labour issues and fuel oil prices were commonplace.

---

1 As Keith Foulcher (1990:301-16) explains with reference to New Order Indonesia, states attempt to exercise hegemonic control over their citizens through appeals to notions of national culture, just as both disenfranchised and middle-class citizens may deploy cultural expression to resist such state impositions.

Despite these major political and economic crises and heightened inter-group sensitivities, as well as growing links with international terrorism, Indonesia had a great deal of success in adjusting to a new era, notably in areas of regional autonomy, press freedoms, legal reforms, and the democratic election process more broadly. The extent to which 'the state' facilitated or impeded these developments is open to debate. However, areas of cultural expression like music present possibilities for new ways of analysing coercion, resistance and pleasure in the Indonesian context. Focussing ethnographically on music performances at Yogyakarta's state institutions highlights spaces where government authorities and popular oppositionists engage both each other and the wider public.

In downtown Yogyakarta in 2001, the streets became contested spaces for exhibiting and promoting popular support for the various parties, leaders, and their ideological positions. Neighbourhood groups displayed red or green flags to mark their political allegiance; banners over main roads warned of the new 'communist' threat or pleaded for peace; and marauding motorcycle campaigners roared through the streets brandishing flags and sometimes weapons.[2] In the midst of these political actions, public musical events merged routinely annual themes with specifically political agendas. By describing several such events that took place at Yogyakarta's state institutions, in Part Three I identify and discuss tensions and accommodations between bureaucratic and cosmopolitan practices.

Bourdieu (1994:4) uses the concept of the bureaucratic field to describe the social arena where people and their interests converge and compete over various 'species of capital' in their quests to secure 'properly statist capital'. The concept of grounded cosmopolitanism refers to openness to, engagement with and even celebration of cultural otherness that is based primarily on experiencing the world's diversity at home. Music performances at Yogyakarta's state institutions merged deliberate organizational agendas with incidental recreational pleasures. As such, these events were never fully immersed in, nor completely removed from contests over national identity and power. Collectively they demonstrate the generally positive roles that music played in promoting and maintaining peaceful social relations during the early post-Soeharto years.

All of the following musical performances took place at the sites of one of four arms of state power – the Regional Parliament, universities, the armed forces, and the Sultan's Palace. The first three, it can be argued, constitute a significant part of the machin-

2   On political campaigning in Yogyakarta during 1997, see Brata 1997.

ery of the state. The final site, the Sultan's Palace in Yogyakarta, is the site par excellence of symbolic power. Music performances at these institutions in various ways involved the *campursari* and *jalanan* musical worlds. The events were invariably occasions for the expression of nationalist agendas, sensibilities and contestations. Contests ranged from global concerns over contemporary Islamic, western and other influences, to national, regional, and ethnic issues. At the same time, a focus on grounded cosmopolitanism also highlights intellectual, social, romantic, and other motivations, sensibilities, and behavioural manifestations associated with music making in Yogyakarta.

THE BUREAUCRATIC FIELD

Bourdieu developed the concept of 'field' to designate the social arenas where battles over certain forms of capital take place. He first developed the concept in the 1960s, in relation to artists and intellectuals in France. This helped Bourdieu to articulate an alternative to the notion of an autonomous art world (Swartz 1997:118), and to refine his analysis of forms of intellectual prestige (Lane 2000:73-80). It is noteworthy that, while ethnographic sensibilities continued to inform his studies of French society, Algeria as an area of study in general receded, surfacing primarily to illustrate 'paradigmatic forms [of] preserved structures' (Bourdieu 2001:6). Such considerations are important when applying Bourdieu's concepts and methods to a study of Indonesia, and highlight the need to clarify its characteristics and parameters.

While Bourdieu is widely renowned for identifying power struggles in cultural fields, his less known concept of bureaucratic field can aid analyses of the evolution of state structures. In contrast to my earlier use of 'capital' in the minutiae of street life, in the present context the various capitals are major institutional forms of social-structural power. Ultimately, it is by identifying connections between these 'simple' and institutional capitals that we can expect to locate the power dimensions of social fields as they are enacted through the *habitus* in everyday life.

According to Bourdieu (1994), there are four 'species of capital' in the bureaucratic field: economic capital, the capital of physical force, and informational (or cultural) and symbolic capitals. Primary centres for contests over these species of capital overlap with the state institutions at which I observed musical performances in Yogyakarta: government institutions such as regional parliaments are central to the development of an efficient tax system and national markets; military and police forces exercise physical coercion to mandate the state's legitimacy; universities contribute (among other things) to the concentration and standardisation of information (including language); and, finally, seats of hereditary leadership yield enormous symbolic capital. This was certainly the case at the Sultan's Palace (Kraton) in Yogyakarta, given its authority over ethnic (Javanese) and religious (Islamic) matters. Gaining control over these capitals, Bourdieu (1994:4) contends, allows dominant actors in society to procure what he terms 'properly statist capital'. In the current context, the bureaucratic field provides a useful means of identifying connections between musical performance and competition within and between institutions.

While the bureaucratic field is a constant consideration in the following chapters, I also work from the premise that restricting analysis to this or any other field risks reducing all social change to matters of contestation. Bourdieu (1992:100) himself seems to concede this when he states that '[t]he limits of the field are situated at the point where the effects of the field cease'. Restricting the study of social phenomena solely to fields of contestation and conflict in post-Soeharto Indonesia would threaten to close off scope for appreciating ways in which local-level actors dealt successfully with cultural difference and social change, whether at global, state, or local levels.

GROUNDED COSMOPOLITANISM

Contemporary cosmopolitanism debates in the human sciences have in large part grown out of those over cultural globalisation. Schematizations in globalisation theory, such as Roland Robertson's differentiation (1995) between 'homogenizers' and 'heterogenizers', along with the increasing realization that the world is becoming more diverse and heterogeneous, led to theorizations over how concepts such as cosmopolitanism can contribute toward peaceful coexistence in the globalised world. Cosmopolitanism in its general sense points to respect for, and interest in, other cultures (Jurriëns and De Kloet 2007), 'a willingness to engage with the Other' (Hannerz 1996:103), and being a 'citizen of the world' (Appiah 1997:618). As Pnina Werbner (2004:11-2) notes, cosmopolitanism in the popular imagination has grown out of associations with particular places and classes, most notably the high culture of early twentieth-century Paris, while in a more sociological reading a cosmopolitan 'contributes to the creation of ... trans-ethnic cultural and ideological worlds'. The concept of cosmopolitanism provides a way to account for social practices and sensibilities that cannot readily be explained within the framework of hegemony and resistance in the bureaucratic field. Cosmopolitanism cannot be reduced to political ideology; nor is it somehow outside it (Appiah 1997:619).

A body of studies over recent years underline the need to engage cosmopolitanism with other, coexisting sentiments and/or ideologies. For example, Pnina Werbner (1999) offers the concept of a 'working class' cosmopolitanism, while Richard Werbner (2002) explores the notion of 'cosmopolitan ethnicity'. Kahn (2003:408-9) emphasises the culturally embedded aspects of pluralised cosmopolitanisms which, conceived as practice, may help to explain 'culturally embedded [,] relatively peaceful' inter-group relations. As well as illustrating how cosmopolitan practices coexist with other practices around, for example, local clubs or national bodies, Kahn (2003) also draws attention to the fact that even 'remote' peoples are and have long been very much part of the contemporary, intercultural world.

Kwame Anthony Appiah (1997:622) employs the term 'cosmopolitan patriots' to show people can both 'lov[e their] homeland [and possess a] loyalty to humankind'. This term is relevant to the current context. However, given that it applies primarily to geographically mobile citizens, I suggest instead the concept of 'grounded cosmopolitanism'. Firstly, to be grounded is to be forced to stay in one place. This suggests prevention or prohibition, as when a pilot is grounded due to inclement weather. In this sense, grounded cosmopolitans in Yogyakarta are prohibited from experiencing faraway places due largely to economic constraints. Categorising people as grounded in this sense highlights their preclusion from engaging in world travel, but it also risks setting up false dichotomies between the 'mobile west' and 'sedentary rest' (Bauman 1998). It was clearly the case that relatively few citizens of Yogyakarta had travelled extensively (many had very little money and had never left the province, let alone the island or nation); but it also needs to be noted that considerable numbers, ranging from state actors and academics to individual artists and *perek*, often experienced other parts of the globe.

But there is a further reason why being a 'grounded' cosmopolitan is not necessarily to be left behind in the global age of mobility. This is due to its second meaning, the sense of being in touch with one's immediate surrounds, of being ecologically aware, and having a stable sense of place. This sense of being grounded may go some way toward explaining the ongoing reverence for the Kraton. The cosmopolitan aspect of grounded cosmopolitan sensibilities in Yogyakarta is to a significant extent enabled because 'the world' comes to to the city, through cultural tourism, education and, to a degree, information technology, even if global politics and markets assert considerable influence on directions and levels of such interaction. In short, grounded cosmopolitans are characterised by being attuned to the local surrounds and well equipped to interact with cultural diversity. In the realm of musical practice, this openness to difference helps musical forms and styles from around the globe to be selectively incorporated and localised, as reciprocally there is openness toward sharing the region's more indigenous musics with the outside world.

While much political theorizing on Indonesia has been concerned with intrigues in Jakarta, anthropologists have approached the state in Yogyakarta through an examination of the generally powerful roles of state actors in kampung (Guinness 1986; Norma Sullivan 1994). Foreign researchers in Indonesia gain a familiarity with the state when procuring their research visas, an experience that sometimes influences research directions (for example, Pemberton 1994). In a day to day sense too, human faces of the state are evident in the groups of khaki-uniformed workers at any number of institutions, such as those who at day's end can be seen leaving government offices and departments en masse, generally on motorcycles. While *becak* drivers and street guides featured prominently on Malioboro Street, around the city uniformed state employees were an especially recognisable group of people. The further one ventured into village and market districts, 'traditional' wear such as sarongs become more visible, along with the arrivals and departures of schoolchildren and mosque attendants.

The following chapters note how large public gatherings to witness performances at state institutions interweaved with power dimensions of the event organizers and sponsors, the performances themselves, and the institution where the performance took place. Amidst these heated contests for statist power we can also detect degrees of grounded cosmopolitanism. On Malioboro Street outside the Regional Parliament, street workers found some unity against outsider domination not only in the sheer numbers of Javanese and local Yogyanese, but also through their openness to quintessentially Javanist and nationalist art forms, globalist cultural affiliations, and hybridizations of these. The Armed Forces are trained to kill, but individuals also receive the best in state-funded training, including cultural and humanities studies. In theory at least, they functioned to maintain democratic principles. At universities, students and scholars from within the region and across the country both developed their critical faculties and expanded their worldly knowledge; foreign visitors, generally there to learn the national language and local cultures, also contributed to this process.

Hamengkubuwono Asia-Pacific marching band contestants exit the Regional Parliament and turn back onto Malioboro Street

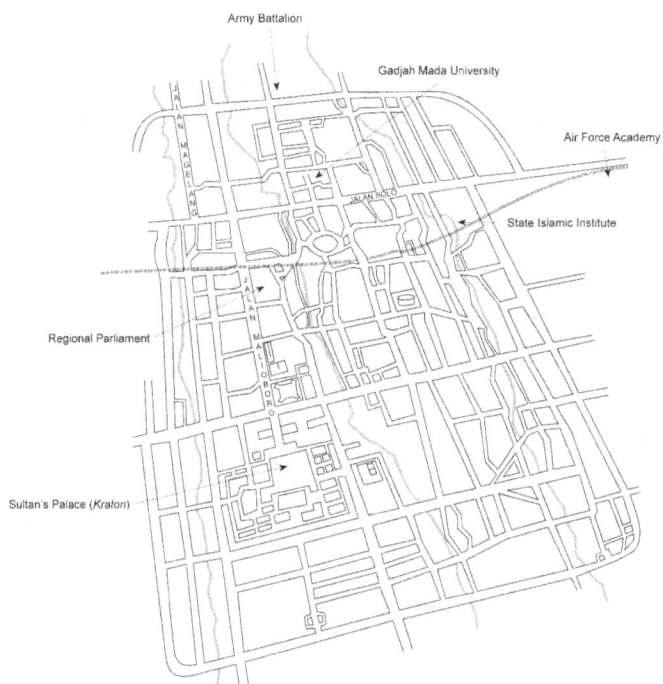

State institutions discussed in Part Three

6

Regional Parliament

During the New Order period, Indonesia's political structure extended from central government to province, regency/municipality, sub-district, and finally the kampung levels of sub-ward and neighbourhood association. Changes following Soeharto's fall in 1998 had profound consequences for this complex structure. The Regional Autonomy Law, implemented in 2001, was especially influential (Ryaas Rasyid 2003; Bubandt 2004; Erb, Sulistiyanto, and Faucher 2005). Under the new law, the functions of the sectoral ministry offices were shifted to the more autonomous 'local service units', initiating Indonesia's largest bureaucratic restructuring since 1974 (Ryaas Rasyid 2003:64-5) and precipitating heated contests between Jakarta and the regions and within the regions themselves. At the same time, regional parliaments, known locally as DPRD, gained greater powers in matters of regional policy and leadership. The regional parliaments thereby gained significance in what Bourdieu (1994:5-7) calls the bureaucratic field. Added to all of this, Yogyakarta remained in the highly unusual position of having a Sultan as governor.

The central location of Yogyakarta's Regional Parliament building reinforces its socio-political importance. Located in the middle of bustling Malioboro Street, it is only metres away from heavily populated street stalls and shops, next door to the Garuda Hotel, and close to Malioboro Mall. Public actions such as student and worker demonstrations often took place here, which in turn served to bring political activists and those involved in everyday commercial activities into close physical proximity. Organized musical events here were staged in various parts of the complex, reflecting power relations between organizers, participants, and political leaders. The Parliament and its grounds was in this way an important interface between struggles over statist capital and wider public protest amidst the multi-ethnic, international and cosmopolitan Malioboro Street.

Performance organizers often conceived of, organized, and finally carried out events according to an established formula. As some street musicians explained it to me, the initial impetus was usually a simple desire to perform; subsequently, an organizer or coalition of organizers sought out a theme that would be acceptable to government officials. The final step was the relatively straightforward task of securing licenses and sponsors for the performance. Put another way, the desire of musicians to perform, rather than any state directive, often initiated and drove state events. At the same time, Sumit Mandal (2003:185) demonstrates how Indonesian artists have often taken on 'public, oppositional and dramatic stances' in settings such as Malioboro Street. These factors further illustrate the complex interplays of political manoeuvring and pleasure seeking that characterise public performances in Yogyakarta.

As will be further discussed, central actors in the following cases were Tyas, a street-arts leader; Roem, private assistant to Yogyakarta's future mayor; and Yanto, gangster, religious leader, and the owner of a *campursari* orchestra. Performances at the Regional Parliament gave rise to distinct contests for state capital coloured by themes of local unity as well as more leisurely pursuits and/or inter-culturally tolerant agendas.

AWARDS NIGHT *CAMPURSARI*

An 'Awards Night' held at the Regional Parliament was of direct benefit to wielders of capital within the bureaucratic field. The Tombo Sutris *campursari* orchestra was the sole musical act for the event and, although it did not explicitly address a nationalist theme, paradoxically there was an overtly political agenda. The event was advertised as an opportunity to honour community service, and yet political, religious, and business leaders used the event to combine public rallying with what can be termed statist capital. Tombo Sutris members included those in the highly skilled and adaptable Kusuman kampung orchestra discussed earlier. The dozen musicians played gamelan instruments in combination with keyboards, bass guitar, and *dangdut* and *kroncong* instruments, and there were six female singers, two Masters of Ceremonies (MCs), and an Imam (Islamic communal prayer leader).

Yanto, the orchestra's owner and manager, was a high-level gangster (*preman*) that some people likened to Robin Hood.[1] He headed

---

1 For other examples of *preman*, see Antariksa 2001; Wilson 2010.

youth gangs attached to particular political parties, as well as pickpocket and gambling rings; he also funded schooling for children in his neighbourhood and bailed out subordinates detained for petty crimes. Additionally, the orchestra regularly performed for and entertained underprivileged groups ranging from sex workers to prisoners. Some casual observers believed that Yanto was a reformed criminal with wholeheartedly benevolent motives. By contrast, a number of Malioboro-based street workers told me that in reality he organized mass prayers and light-hearted entertainment in order to mobilise people for specific purposes. The Awards Night, as one of a series of events leading up to the mayoral selections, was a good example of how *campursari* sometimes became a vehicle for such political ends.

While most DPRD performances took place on Malioboro Street or the roadway inside the grounds, on this occasion the stage was set up in a privileged position at the foot of the main chambers. At seven-thirty pm, as orchestra members readied themselves out of view, most of the audience were immaculately dressed men in white fez-caps seated before the stage. By nine pm over a thousand people had gathered, the vast majority being labourers and *becak* drivers, many of whom sat in groups identifiable by their red, green or blue sponsors' uniforms bearing functional acronymic logos. With the crowd continuing to build in the darkness of the grounds, the orchestra leapt into their signature show tune to accompanying bright lights, following with a series of musically dynamic Javanist pieces. The orchestra then played some popular *campursari* songs, after which they took a break as the MCs took centre stage and mixed Indonesian and Javanese colloquialisms into humorous word plays (*plesetan*) with English, Mandarin, and French. Then the orchestra broke into another fanfare tune as one after another the stunningly made-up young female singers sang *campursari* favourites. The orchestra's slick presentation of familiar *campursari* songs, interspersed with humorous and topical commentary, was very effective in pleasing the audience.

The next break in songs signalled the award announcements and accompanying ceremony. The Tombo Sutris Award was to be granted as a token of appreciation to a leader in Yogyakarta who had displayed outstanding social commitment to, and support for, the community's 'little people'. After another round of humorous banter from the MCs, the orchestra's owner Yanto took centre stage and, in slow, measured phrases mixing Javanese, Arabic and Indonesian, granted the award to Sukri Fadholi, who at the time was head of the Regional Parliament's United Islamic Faction. I later heard many Tombo Sutris members express their appreciation for Sukri, most of all because he championed a more equitable distribution of resources to the poor.

Audience numbers remained large throughout the awards ceremony and speeches. This public conferring of a community service award to a member of parliament in an official setting, covered also by various media, thereby lent legitimacy to the event and its organizers. The speeches drew to a close, after which the orchestra again resumed to accompany each young woman at centre stage that sang and danced with increasingly overt sexuality. The event wound down around midnight and the audience dispersed peacefully soon after.

In contrast to the fanfare of the awards event, later news reports relayed how street violence had occurred earlier the same day. Participants in a mass prayer north of the city had subsequently set out on a large political convoy. Members of this convoy damaged an entertainment venue and a number of houses in the city, including that of a Institut Agama Islam Negeri (IAIN, State Institute of Islamic Studies) lecturer. What was not reported was the connection between Yanto and the convoy, common knowledge among many on Malioboro Street. The political significance of this event became evident in that two months later, as Megawati replaced Gus Dur as Indonesia's president, the mayoral selection process in Yogyakarta intensified, finally resulting in a victory for the Partai Amanat Nasional (PAN, National Mandate Party) and the United Islamic Faction. In light of this, *campursari* entertainment at the Regional Parliament Awards Night was a 'bread and circuses' vehicle in a wider political project. Yanto did not hold an official government position, but his role in combining public activities and entertainment with a community award assisted Sukri to become Yogyakarta's vice-mayor in the following months.[2]

Viewed within the more generalised conception of bureaucratic fields, Yanto's quasi-state control over physical force and economic capital supported Sukri's pursuit of the mayoral position and therefore properly statist capital. Tombo Sutris played *campursari* by mixing gamelan with Arab-Islamic, James Bond, and various other nuances. Replete with humour, glitz, and glamour, the *campursari* orchestra enabled political and religious leaders to draw in a large audience and, through speeches and other means, influence public opinion. Relations of force, Bourdieu (1994:14) asserts, involve cognitive acts that 'are not forms of consciousness but *dispositions of*

---

2   This is not to question the legitimacy of the mayoral team, who indeed were to institute many culturally inclusive changes in Yogyakarta over subsequent years.

the body'. This is especially evident when music engages audiences at the level of bodily sensuality (Howes 1990).

At the same time, the Awards Night *campursari* entertainment cannot be seen as merely a device to dupe the masses. Rather than being a part of the depoliticised Soeharto-era public (Pemberton 1994), many street workers seemed acutely aware of the political context. Some *becak* drivers in Sosrowijayan refused to attend the event because of Yanto's 'gangster politics', and many who did attend were aware of the underlying political meanings, but nonetheless accepted their free sponsor uniforms and chose to stay on and enjoy the show. Furthermore, a number of Tombo Sutris members in other contexts played Latin American music and western rock, Islamic *qasidah*, reggae, jazz, Japanese folk, and Indonesian *dangdut* and *kroncong*. Against these somewhat celebratory readings however, the combination of a gangster-owned *campursari* orchestra, the Regional Parliament, and mayoral selections highlights one role of music in negotiating local bureaucratic power, in particular through entertaining street workers with dazzling renditions of familiar songs.

AWAKENING DAY ROCK AND REGGAE

A set of musical acts for Awakening Day at the Regional Parliament offer a rather different example of the intersection of nationalist and cosmopolitanism themes at a state institution. Awakening Day (Hari Kebangkitan), also known as Resurgence Day, commemorates the early nationalist movement of Budi Utomo (Glorious Endeavour). Founded in Yogyakarta in 1908, Budi Utomo's support subsequently expanded beyond its *priyayi* aristocratic class base (Geertz 1960). In 1935, it merged with the Partai Indonesia Raya (Parindra, Greater Indonesia Party). Budi Utomo adopted the catchphrase 'the will to unite' (Zainu'ddin 1968:174-6). Unity was indeed the main theme for an Awakening Day musical performance at the Regional Parliament in 2001. However, musicians, organizers and audience members used the event to negotiate and promote a sense of unity not confined to the nation.

The Awakening Day events opened with a 'Painting Demo' next to a *jalanan* gathering place midway down Malioboro Street. The next five days featured street exhibits among the trinket stalls up and down Malioboro Street. Under the title Satu Rasa Satu Jiwa (One Feeling One Spirit), the Painting Demo included live painting and music performances by Jagongan and Musik Prapatan

(Crossroads Music), the latter including members of the locally renowned Malioboro Streetside Singers (KPJM). A newspaper article (*Kedaulatan Rakyat*, 21-5-2001) pointed out that the main organizers of the Demo were Malioboro artists and members of the Malioboro Arts Community. Bambang, the committee head, told reporters that shoe shiners, newspaper sellers, and others were all coming together to 'practice togetherness and unity' and, by promoting the artists as a national asset, hoped that the event would help to resurrect the 'people' (*bangsa*). *Bangsa*, an emotive term meaning nation, people, or race, served here to connect the nation and the street, although I heard first-hand that the more specific agenda of the Painting Demo was to support the special status of Yogyakarta and the Sultan.

A week after the official date, Awakening Day was celebrated at the Regional Parliament not before the chambers but on the roadway inside the grounds. From four pm until one-thirty am 11 bands played three songs each. On this occasion, the music was overwhelmingly western, varying from death and heavy metal, good-time rock and roll and pop, to reggae. Each group on stage added to the sense of celebration in the audience, most of whom knew band members, thereby promoting local, Malioboro solidarity rather than national unity. There was very little reference to the specifically Javanese or national themes found in official state-sponsored representations of Indonesian culture. However, some groups used Benyamin S-style parodies and exaggerations in order to both perform western popular culture and at the same time critique its excesses (Hanan and Koesasi 2011:55-7). For example, a band comprising Sosrowijayan street guide 'gigolos' featured Ari on vocals parading and semi-collapsing around the stage, while friends of the band members jumped up to play deliberately out-of-tune harmonica and generally contribute to the carnivalesque air of havoc on stage. The group eventually settled into playing songs by U2 and The Police.

A large banner above the stage read Yogyakarta Tetap Satu (Yogyakarta Forever United), reinforcing the message of unity. Malioboro-based musical groups forwarded their versions of unity not only through their music and general antics, but also in their inter-song commentary. Ari and Agus, both street guides, engaged in comical banter that reinforced the celebratory atmosphere while also articulating the broader agenda of the evening. It was unusual to hear the Muslim greeting, jokes about gangsters, references to the Sosrowijayan community, and calls to support street children NGOs and the wider nation, all within a few sentences. Significantly, Ari also thanked Malioboro Klasikal, one of the three *pengamen* organizations on Malioboro. On doing so, a Malioboro Arts Community member told me with some disappointment that the Malioboro community was actually a single unit and not three factions, and should be presented as such. These representations and comments indicate that local, street-level unity was widely promoted, albeit with contested boundaries.

Around 800 people attended in the 1,200 capacity area before and around the stage. While the event took place in the Parliament grounds, no one wore official clothing or gave formal speeches, and there were no opulent displays of state power that often characterise such a setting. Tyas and other Malioboro Arts Community members had organized the event through their connections with government officials. Most people there wore the street-worn black and denim garb of the Malioboro community, and there were a small but prominent number of westerners. While most audience members sat or squatted some distance from the stage, dozens also 'pogo' danced and strutted merrily in front of the performing bands. Group after group rose to the stage, performed, and then quickly made way for the next act, with dancing in the audience rising and ebbing. Soon after midnight, the event slowly wound down with a reggae band playing Bob Marley and other classics until one-thirty am.

Themes of peace and unity shaped this event. While the performers' methods stood in stark contrast to the roving political campaigns that regularly swept through Malioboro Street, in decibel terms both made aggressive use of the soundscape. We could say, following Bourdieu, that the musicians and political campaigners were both seeking to control and convert different kinds of statist capital. A national theme underpinned the performances, even though the event was held eight days after the official date. During this period in fact, Malioboro Street was an arena for a variety of political actions. For example, a student demonstration to celebrate three years since the downfall of Soeharto was blocked by a large 'anti-communist' group. Also along Malioboro Street there was a United Development Party procession made up of a police-style jeep, a tray truck with a dozen people giving out bags of rice, and around 30 young men on motorcycles in long-sleeved black t-shirts behind them carrying the green Islamic party flags.

Yet these Awakening Day performances present a somewhat ambivalent connection with historical and contemporary national issues and struggles for statist power. Notwithstanding the comical exaggerations of western pop that some groups injected into their performances, it seems difficult to reconcile the fact that Awakening Day, which commemorates an early nationalist movement, was celebrated with 11 bands all of which chose to play western rock music. Both the musical and clothing styles of most performers and audience members at Awakening Day were exemplary of localisations of globalised popular music from Britain and the USA, including both mimetic and parodic renditions of the oppositional posturing of the bands they covered.

The event promoted unity, including the unity of nation, but more so that of the street, the city, and the region. Signage and inter-song banter reflected identification with the Malioboro community, but to my knowledge the various performances did not call special attention to the state as either obstacle or vehicle to their requests for unity. In the context of daily life around Malioboro Street, the place where most people at the event spent a lot of their time, the theme of local unity was clearly an effort to promote harmonious and inclusive social relations at street level, including with westerners. Notably however, organizers and performers did not especially promote connections with other groups such as *becak* drivers and overtly conservative Muslims. In other words, they were using the theme of unity and re-applying it for local purposes among social groups around the *jalanan* scene, and drew on both the history of the nation and western-rock forms of expression to do so.

INDEPENDENCE DAY *WAYANG KULIT*

The final Regional Parliament performance addressed here was a shadow puppet (*wayang kulit*) show held to commemorate Indonesian Independence Day. As with the Awakening Day event, the stage was set on the roadway inside the grounds. It took place on the Saturday night following Independence Day, when many sections of the inner city were alive with activity: at the west end of nearby Pajeksan, 12 bands played to a largely local audience; four bands played in the Sosrowijayan commons; a fashion show took place in Hotel Garuda next door to the parliament; and, soon after midnight, a brief but heated clash broke out between the supporters of the Partai Demokrasi Indonesia-Perjuangan (PDI-P, Indonesian Democratic Party of Struggle) and the Partai Persatuan Pembangunan (PPP, United Development Party). In contrast to the semi-private and/or fleeting nature of such activities, *wayang kulit* in the DPRD grounds was public and drew in a large and diverse audience from eight pm until dawn.

The puppeteer (*dalang*) narrated and enacted numerous 'hero versus bandit' episodes from the Mahabharata Hindu epic that expound the philosophy for which Yogyakarta and Central Java are renowned (Keeler 1987; Hatley 2008). As usual, a large gamelan orchestra accompanied the wayang, along with five female singers (*pesinden*) along one side of the stage. But the performance on this occasion also incorporated new developments. The orchestra, which included several Indonesian Arts Institute members, combined the gamelan format with experimental features such as standard rock drums and circus-like rhythms. Such alterations were more like the 'ethnic' experiments of student groups than *campursari*, the latter of which invariably included keyboards and diatonic scales.

One of the Sriwisata street guides, who often sang the praises of Javanese culture, told me that these kinds of mergers began around a decade ago, whereas previous combinations included farmers' instruments and the Islamic *melayu rebana* frame drum. He also told me that the *dalang* for this event was paid a phenomenal Rp five million, compared with previous payments of around Rp 750,000, adding that this reflected the commodification of the traditional arts. The *wayang kulit* played its traditional role as a central medium for public entertainment, but holding a performance of a Javanese art form at a state institution for Indonesia's most important national day was a statement of ethnic identity. Performers added contemporary musical innovations by introducing overtly outside influences into a quintessentially Javanist performance.

By one am, around 500 audience members were sitting in rows of chairs set up in front of the stage, while many others spread across the grounds and onto the street, in all totalling over 2,000 people. Although more than 90% were male and presumably Javanese, in occupational or class terms there was extraordinary diversity; there were *becak* drivers, petty traders, street children, students and artists, along with office workers, teachers and other professionals. Indicative of the extent to which *wayang kulit* maintained importance for a great many Javanese, a few street children with brightly dyed hair and severely torn clothes expressed their admiration of the performance to me. By two am, a few hundred among those present, including some of the performers on stage, were dozing off. Yet their presence lent symbolic legitimacy to the wayang, and to the continued use of the gamelan as a vehicle for selectively incorporating outside influences while maintaining a sense of regional identity and history. The gamelan echoed into the nearby kampung through the remainder of the night, a phenomenon more common a decade ago.

Wayang kulit at the Regional Parliament for
Indonesian Independence Day, 2001

The wayang performance brought Javanism and Indonesian nationalism onto the same ground. If grounded cosmopolitanism at the Awakening Day performances could be reduced to imitations of the West, and the Awards Night saw *campursari* deployed at least in part to convert the capital of physical force into statist capital, the Independence Day *wayang kulit* performance was neither 'westernised' nor especially party political. At the same time, it was not simply an expression of an unchanging Yogyakarta tradition and Javanese views of the cosmos. The performance of and philosophy behind the wayang was witnessed by perhaps the widest array of occupational types of the several dozen large-scale performances that I attended during my research. The *wayang kulit* carried particularly Javanese rather than Indonesian messages, especially in the language of delivery; yet the *wayang kulit* was also tied to the nation through the official theme of national independence and by being held at the Regional Parliament.

Finally, the event showed expressions of grounded cosmopolitanism in three related ways: first, the word base 'cosmos', meaning broadly 'order of the world and universe', here brought wayang cosmology and Malioboro cosmopolitanism into the same arena; second, audience members displayed a great diversity of style choices and occupational orientations; and third, many of these same people were keen to introduce the form to outsiders, conveying both indigenist pride and signalling a reciprocal interest in other art forms.

The Awakening and Independence Day musical events were both inextricably associated with the nation-state, at the very least because of the setting, and also because historical themes of the Indonesian nation officially shaped each event. The Awards Night organizers and performers did not present *campursari* in terms of the nation but, more than the other events, this one succeeded in presenting political promotions in the guise of musical entertainment to over a thousand street workers and their associates. *Campursari* in this case was an important item in a package designed to gain the political support of rural-based street workers, which in turn proved to be an effective means of converting the capital of physical force into symbolic capital.

All three events were to some degree shaped by public debates over regional autonomy, presidential succession, and related current affairs of the time. The bureaucratic field concept thereby enables us to consider connections between contests over statist capital and entertaining performances that may otherwise seem incidental. At the same time, a focus on grounded cosmopolitanism compels us to consider the extent to which the various agendas and behaviours at these events were central or largely peripheral to contests for statist capital. The official themes of the events – community service, anti-colonial resistance, and national independence – were sometimes reflected in the performances, but at other times they were modified or absent altogether. Western style pop/rock, Javanist *campursari* and gamelan were all to some extent used to promote local-based unity and to incorporate outside influences. While most events at the Regional Parliament were shaped by nationalist intent, concurrent concerns with local-level unity, musical expression, humour and general entertainment demonstrate that none could be understood exclusively as either expressions of, or resistance to, Indonesian nationalism. These performances give rise to a number of questions. When is popular entertainment at state institutions separate from the state? Were representatives of the state promoting the appreciation of diversity for its own sake, or using the taste for popular music for their own specific ends? In order to pursue answers to these questions, I return to a number of the Malioboro-based groups and the *campursari* and *jalanan* musical worlds in the context of Armed Forces events.

7

Armed Forces

A key feature of the modern state is its monopoly of the legitimate use of violence, with its military and police forces the main instruments (Pierson 1996; Cohen and Service 1978). Military institutions are therefore central to the constitution of the bureaucratic field. On the other hand, the idea of a 'cosmopolitan soldier' is more difficult to entertain. Their careers are premised on being prepared to violently defend or expand the ideals or strategic interests of particular states. Yet military personnel in many states undertake humanities studies, travel the world, and in leisure time may gain a broad appreciation of cultural diversity.

With the rise of the Indonesian nation-state, its Tentara Nasional Indonesia (TNI, Indonesian Armed Forces) has played an important but often controversial role in Indonesian politics. The heroes of the anti-colonial revolution established and built up TNI. During the period from 1959 to 1965 however, TNI extended its political influence to the point of becoming what Munir (2003:71) called an 'octopus institution'. Through the New Order period, TNI further extended its direct involvement in politics, through guaranteed seats in parliament and positions in local political structures, often abusing human rights in the process.[1]

Militarism on Java itself is not a new phenomenon, a fact illustrated by the role of violence in 'traditional' Javanese culture. The dagger (*kris*) stored, ever ready, behind the back, as well as the prevalence of violent episodes in the wayang, demonstrate that 'Javanese culture' is not just about politeness (Boon 1990). Central Java also has longstanding links with TNI, and in the early post-Soeharto years the rise of militant youth and 'terror' wings of groups such as Laskar Jihad and Gerakan Pemuda Ka'bah (GPK) threatened and sometimes carried out violence both locally and in regions such as Maluku. TNI was implicated in these events, with various army and

---

1 Jun Honna (2003) provides an important analysis of shifts in civil-military relations in 1990s Indonesia.

ex-army officers suspected of coordinating provocateurs (*Violence in Ambon* 1999; Hefner 2001).

At the same time, calm and goodwill also presided in the city of Yogyakarta. Many groups were ambivalent towards TNI, and student and street-arts groups were active in anti-violence campaigns. By many accounts, the Sultan had successfully banned on-duty armed forces from entering the city centre. I rarely saw individuals or groups in official military or even police uniform, despite the regular presence of roving party political campaigners, some of whom were themselves led by men in quasi-military fatigues.

In the midst of changes in which the Reformasi movement had brought to a head attempts to expose and discredit large sections of TNI, Central Java remained home to a number of Jakarta-controlled military bases and training institutions. I will discuss music performances that took place at two of these. While musical dimensions of a modern nation-state's armed forces often consist of formal marching bands and high-precision processions (Bannister 2002), the examples in this chapter featured *campursari* and *musik jalanan* respectively.

CAMPURSARI AT AN ARMY BATTALION

A Tombo Sutris *campursari* performance was held to commemorate the thirty-sixth year of an Army Battalion. Over the research period, the orchestra performed on average three times a fortnight, always with a specific theme. I had first met the orchestra and its leader Yanto the previous year, and had on occasion performed with them. Regarding the event under discussion, I ran into some of the musicians at the Sultan's Palace for Yogya Heritage Week, when they invited me to perform with them the following evening. During the following afternoon the orchestra members gathered at their usual rehearsal space. After the Azan call to prayer, an army bus took us five kilometres north to the Army Battalion Base, although I did not know anything about our destination or the event theme until we reached the venue. The bus entered the army grounds from a side road, and the orchestra gathered in a spacious tent behind a large stage. A few of the eight young women singers were given final touches to their make-up and sat ready to perform. Tombo Sutris' Imam and two army personnel hauled in bags containing full army fatigues for the musicians, and after trying out different sizes and combinations we were fully fitted. A quick sound-check followed, then after a meal back at the tent it was time to begin the show.

Glaring spotlights facing outwards from the edge of the grounds illuminated the stage. In the dark, crowd numbers steadily built outwards in three directions. The orchestra began unannounced, and then after two high-tempo instrumentals the Imam halted the music to begin the official speeches. Two army officers spoke briefly, each emphasising the commitment of the Battalion and TNI to the community. Then the Imam spoke passionately, his early words tinged with criticism of army behaviour, but finally concluding by shouting 'Hidup TNI! Hidup Indonesia!' (Long live the Indonesian Army! Long live Indonesia!) a half-dozen times in an attempt to rouse the crowd.

The orchestra resumed with a few instrumental pieces, after which the two MCs stepped to the microphones and began introducing orchestra members, in the process imparting humorous takes on topical issues. First to be announced was Visnu, who sat back in dark sunglasses with his saxophone as the MC stated that he was a member of Gerakan Aceh Merdeka (GAM, Free Aceh Movement), soon adding that GAM actually stood for Gerakan Anak Mahasiswa (Junior Student Movement). Coincidentally the nametag on my fatigues read 'Japan', which the other MC called attention to but then turned back to the audience and announced that 'There is a spy among us tonight'. He added that I was a member of Interfet, calling attention to the Australian military involvement in the recent crisis in East Timor.

After telling a few more politically loaded jokes, the MCs introduced the female singers. Each was immaculately dressed and made-up, resembling high-class nightclub performers more than Javanists in traditionalist *kain* and *kebaya*. With the young women singing and acting out their parts, the songs became progressively more up-tempo and *dangdut*-inflected. Sections of the orchestra inserted syncopated and precise instrumental passages between vocals, such as that from the keyboardist who swung and swayed passionately as he swept through a series of synthesised flute refrains. By ten pm, the audience numbered over 5,000, with young men crowding toward centre stage, women and children off to the sides, and a smoky haze of others toward Kaliurang Road in the distance. As a girl of around nine years began singing at centre stage, a few and then more and more young children climbed from the side-supports, stomping their feet and filling the stage. Eventually an army authority, evidently feeling awkward at being called upon to control young children, was forced to shoo them down.

| *Musical worlds in Yogyakarta*

Tombo Sutris perform at an army battalion

Numerous guest appearances added variety to the evening. Three army officers sang *dangdut* and *campursari*-ised 1970s Indonesian pop songs. A comedy duo caused shrieks and hoots to ring across the audience. And the orchestra and singers inserted experimental sections into a number of their songs. The guest singers, comedians and MCs all enlivened the crowd, but the female singers produced the most animated response, especially among the younger men. The singers carefully gauged the sensuality of their actions and personas. Nevertheless, many older boys yelled out in the warbling tones of pubescent males, and a number of men in their mid-twenties rose to the stage. One shuffled slowly across the stage, smirking continuously in a self-contained 'other worlds' trance, deriving pleasure simply from being near the singers. Later in the evening, two other men rose from the audience and engaged in a kind of comedy caper, dancing slowly and sensually in front of the female singers but running out of reach when an army officer went to throw them off, only to move back to the middle of the stage each time the officer settled back.

After a song with a heavy rock beat, the show finished at midnight without speech or announcement. The crowd quickly dispersed, and backstage the musicians began changing back into their normal wear while Yanto, *preman* owner of the orchestra, talked with one of the main organizers, a soft-spoken commander of four battalions. The musicians were soon loaded back on to the bus and returned to their rehearsal space, where they sat about by the roadside for over an hour until Yanto returned with their pay.

This anniversary event for an army battalion in Yogyakarta exemplifies a military institution putting on a display of goodwill to the wider public. The audience included many residents from nearby neighbourhoods, army personnel and their associates and also, because the event took place near a main road, passers-by. As at the Tombo Sutris event at the Regional Parliament, the group (along with comedians and other entertainers) played a central role in fulfilling the organizers' aims of drawing a large audience and subjecting them to both entertainment and speeches. However, the two events differed in terms of the 'species of capital' involved. At the Regional Parliament, an underlying theme was the upcoming mayoral selections and the gathering of support among labour-based street workers. Power brokers at the Army Battalion performance, on the other hand, were concerned with displaying the cooperation of the Military and wider Indonesian society through the popular Javanist *campursari*. In terms of music and other performative aspects such as clothing and the overall program, there were some quite subtle differences between the two events. Most notable was the greater Islamic content at the Regional Parliament event, with the Army Battalion performance focussing more on secular endorsements of the state.

In addition to several people contesting various species of capital at such events, there was also some degree of grounded cosmopolitanism – an openness to and appreciation of otherness as viewed from home. As I have suggested, at one level military institutions and events might be seen as anathema to such an ethos. The main thrust on this occasion, it seems fair to say, was Javanist music and Islamic promotions with the aim of helping to restore the Military's reputation in wider society. Even the humour arguably did not lend itself to openness, with comedians and MCs making light of sensitive issues in Aceh, East Timor, and elsewhere. However, jokes at least gave air time to issues that would probably have been considered beyond discussion under the New Order government. And musically, the group's combinations of Javanist features with Islamic, western and other ornamentations could be said to be a model for cooperative relations between the centralised Armed Forces and the regions. Overall however, the military theme and setting meant that state interests dominated this performance.

| *Musical worlds in Yogyakarta*

MUSIC JALANAN AT THE AIR FORCE ACADEMY

The National Air Force Academy ran a five-day 'Arts and Sports Festival' in their grounds on the outskirts of Yogyakarta. While commemorating the fifty-fourth anniversary of the Indonesian Armed Forces, such events also became contested terrain for statist capital, all the more so in the Reformasi period. Of interest on this occasion was the involvement of Malioboro street-arts leaders and street music groups. As mentioned earlier, while much of the music played on Yogyakarta's streets is of genres that underpin *campursari* (*karawitan, langgam, kroncong, dangdut*), *musik jalanan* is generally western-influenced folk-rock music with social and political commentary. TNI's incorporation of Yogyakartan street musicians for this event was, in other words, a meeting between the nation-state's prime bearer of the capital of physical force and local representatives of the underclass who were outspoken and influential on public opinion at street-level.

Amidst all the turmoil and change in state-society relations during this period, this festival promoted an image of stability and celebration through glossy flyers, public signs, and an opening parade that traversed the densely crowded Malioboro Street. The event was therefore brought to the attention of thousands, even if numbers that actually attended were barely in the hundreds. A number of street-arts leaders and Air Force cadets concurred that the festival was an attempt by the Air Force to help restore TNI's damaged reputation. A couple of Air Force officers, despite having access to state-legitimised forms of violence, were in competition over which of them had initiated the involvement of street musicians. And yet the greatest initiative arguably came from the street musicians themselves. In other words, both officers sought to be recognised as grounded cosmopolitans who could relate to the downtrodden on Yogyakarta's bustling, multicultural street. At the same time, the inclusion of street musicians was an admission that the latter wielded some influence over public opinion and, by extension, the bureaucratic field.

On the first morning, I arrived with a small group for whom the event and locale was something of a mystery. To enter the grounds from the northern side by the city's airport involved a several hundred metre drive along an isolated high-security road to a sentry gate. As we were to learn by the second day, a quiet back road entrance by a residential complex provided a much more relaxed route into the Academy. The festival took place just inside this low-key, southern entrance. A row of temporary stalls was set up, leading to another part of the Academy, which during the festival was a site for Air Force and skateboarding displays. Overwhelmingly however, activities centred on the elevated performance stage overlooking two basketball courts.

By seeking to promote TNI's status, and therefore its statist capital, the festival site, theme and agenda were clearly part of the bureaucratic field. While I often socialised with Tyas and other Malioboro Arts Community musicians, seeing them in the Academy grounds struck me as unusual, especially given their antiviolent stance. However, at least outwardly, their appearance and behaviour was quite relaxed. On the Air Force side, the air of rigid formality was something I had not seen outside of courtly rituals. A young officer named Rudi clearly had authority over the dozens of 18 to 21 year old cadets identifiable by their orange tracksuits. As he ambled along, each passing cadet would stop bolt upright and salute him with an intense rigidity. Rudi's unusually good command of English, and his culturally sensitive general knowledge was, I found, hard to reconcile with his position as a trainee fighter pilot. He represented state-legitimised violence but also demonstrated his reflexive and broad-ranging knowledge.

Clothing and hairstyles presented striking visual contrasts between the cadets and street musicians, which also extended to differences of posture, physique and even motor skills. One late morning before the start of the basketball games, a group of street musicians in ragged clothes and long and/or rarely tended hair played basketball at one end of the court. While their musicianship reflected their artistic facility, on the court they stumbled about, clumsily bouncing the ball with both hands, then hurling the ball toward the ring, often missing the backboard altogether. A team of cadets meanwhile stood on the sideline, struggling to contain their restlessness while awaiting the opportunity to warm up on the court. The cadets were not only all dressed the same; they all had virtually identical haircuts and were each around six feet tall with very upright postures. Music at the festival was to bring out a more animated side of the cadets, and friends and other attendees blurred the group boundaries, but overall these cadet/street musician distinctions were especially stark.

Holding the music competition on a stage overlooking the basketball games allowed spectators to simultaneously watch the games and the performances. But cheers and applause for the basketball players often drowned out the music, such that the musicians at these times commanded very little attention. At other times music took centre stage, especially when Academy members became involved toward the end of each day. On stage, eight *musik jalanan* groups played on each of the first three days, and these were then narrowed down to a half-dozen finalists. Put another way, a total of 24 groups played, six of them twice each. Malioboro Arts Community leaders selected the *jalanan* groups and, apart from some informal Air Force input, were the principal judges. The *jalanan* groups played two songs each. Their first on each occasion was a choice between an Ambonese song titled 'Sio mama' (My loving mum) and 'Kebyar-kebyar' (Glittering fireworks) by the late Indonesian country artist Gombloh. Each band was free to choose their second song.

The music carried many trademark *jalanan* features, including multiple acoustic guitars, vocal harmonies, snare drums played with brushes, *kroncong* ukuleles, and mellow saxophone. However, there was considerable variation both between bands and within them over time. An Ambonese commander newly appointed at the Academy had chosen 'Sio mama' as one of the street musician's prescribed choices. This directive reflected an exercise of state power, but was nonetheless astute in that it encouraged Yogyakartan street musicians to sympathise with a group that had become the enemy of some local youth groups.

The other option for *musik jalanan* groups, Gombloh's (Lockard 1998:89-90) 'Kebyar-kebyar', begins with the following lyric: 'Indonesia, the red of my blood, the white of my bones / United in your spirit / Indonesia, the beating of my heart, the throb of my pulse / United in your dreams'.[2] This song, which received a number of treatments, promoted a sense of nationalism. On the early days, street groups played passionate but standard renditions, while by the finals they included extended Javanese-style atmospheric introductions with bells and shakers.

Songs of the groups' own choosing varied, especially in terms of their political messages. At the less obviously political end, groups played jazzed-up versions of songs such as Koes Plus' 'Buat apa susah' (What's the use of worrying?). Marthin, a young man from Flores, led the band that eventually won the competition. His group performed their original composition, 'Pesta dansa' (Dance party), which blended Indonesian and Pacific rhythms and harmonies. Other songs contained overt political commentary related to New Order-era contests over statist capital. One group played Bram Kampungan's 'Bung Karno', the original of which features a recorded speech delivered in 1964 by the then President Soekarno on Remembrance Day for the prophet Muhammad. Jimi Do-Re-Mi

---

2 Indonesia, merah darahku, putih tulangku / Bersatu dalam semangatmu / Indonesia, debar jantungku, getar nadiku / Berbaur dalam angan-anganmu.

played an original composition in which he both referred to well-known Japanese popular-culture characters and implored listeners to avoid conflict during the economic crisis. Another group built on a children's nursery rhyme to sing, in harmony, of the greediest children of the 'fat, deceitful king', this being Soeharto (Richter 2006).

Along with the street musicians' performances of popular, ethnic, and political songs, some days finished with a jam session. On the first day for example, the dozen musicians included Malioboro Streetside Singers, street group contestants and me. The jam finished with 'Bento', a *jalanan* anthem by Swami that criticises the greed of ex-Defence Minister Benny Moerdani and President Soeharto, and means 'stupid' in Javanese. But despite the many protest songs, the line between oppositional street musicians and obedient members of a violent arm of the state was not always sharp. For example, some street bands, including those who sang songs with anti-government messages, prefaced their performances with polite well wishes for TNI.

On the Air Force side, many of the cadets danced in *joged* style to the *jalanan* songs, thereby to some extent endorsing the performers' attitudes and messages. And at the close of the jam-session group's version of 'Bento', a senior Air Force fighter rose to the stage to sing. Dressed in full fatigues, red beret, and with weapons at his belt, the fighter motioned for the band to play the evergreen *dangdut* hit 'Kopi dangdut'. Cadets hooted with delight, a number of them stepping to the foot of the stage to dance in the *joged* style.

Non-*jalanan* associates of the street musicians, such as a newly formed funk band, also performed over the course of the festival. And Air Force members also gave a number of performances. A group of paratroopers enacted a coordinated gymnastic dance to

The author performs with KPJM and friends at the Air Force Academy

the recorded music of American boy band NSYNC. In contrast to their deadly function, the paratroopers' movements were nimble and delicate, and their uniforms were shiny and immaculately pressed. The Academy also had their own rock bands, one of which pounced and growled around the stage performing songs by US metal-rap group Limp Bizkit. These bands won the approval of many *jalanan* musicians.

A ten-member all-female Gadjah Mada-based dance troupe gave the only female performance in the five days, and thus brought out notable gender and class differences between the university students, street musicians and Air Force cadets. Performances analysed throughout this book provide one means of mapping out female/male interactions in this context. Street musicians may for the most part have lacked formal education, but they also tended not to become outwardly sexualised around performances involving women. At the other end of the scale, many rural-oriented (*kampungan*) youth became highly animated when viewing female performers, although as discussed earlier the extent to which such dancing was sexually driven was often difficult to gauge. In terms of sexualised engagement, the cadets seemed to fall in between the street musicians and the kampung youth: even in their slight movements, the cadets visibly engaged with the dancers, yet discipline demanded that they act with decorum.

Related variations were evident in the case of females. The university dance troupe performed sensually, but kept this within limits, whereas the *dangdut* singers who became salacious were largely 'kampung' girls. Professional performers such as Yayi and Vivin discussed in relation to musical sexualisation, whose performance skills could not only rouse males but also to a considerable extent control their behaviours, fell somewhere between the two. Interestingly, female/male audience ratios tended to be most even in neighbourhoods, where animated and often sexualised physicalisations were greatest. However, male street musicians and female university students were most adept at performing in arenas associated with the Armed Forces. This, I suggest, demonstrates the tensions between bureaucratic and cosmopolitan practices that street musicians and university students straddled in such public activities.

Promoting street musicians gave the Air Force some credibility in its relations with 'the people', and conversely the Air Force Academy to some extent endorsed the street musicians. But audience numbers at the festival rarely reached a hundred in a city of half a million. On the Malioboro Community side, the venture succeeded in securing the assistance of the Air Force in removing accumulated litter and debris from Malioboro Street the following weekend. To some degree, this public display of cooperation must also have helped to legitimise TNI as capable of playing a positive role in the community beyond the exercise of physical force. Musically there was considerable cooperation between the two groups, but there were also underlying tensions. This is particularly evident given that any arm of the military is legitimate to the extent that it has a monopoly on violence, and because many of the street musicians' songs had anti-New Order/TNI themes. In this context, cadets playing Limp Bizkit and the street musicians singing protest songs arguably masked over tensions and reflected the pragmatics of their relationship.

These two military institution events demonstrate the roles of popular music in the bureaucratic field in early post-Soeharto Yogyakarta. First, organizers and performers treated the musical component of the army battalion event as an attempt to present an image of a centralised military in harmony with Javanism, and to an extent Islam, through the use of *campursari* music, comedians, and sexualised female singers. The longer, and in a sense, more complicated Air Force *musik jalanan* event requires some reflection. Here much of the music was openly oppositional and ethnically diverse, but the event was nonetheless a tool for an agent of the centralised state to gain local-level acceptance. Again, official bearers of the capital of physical force sought public cooperation with street workers to gain symbolic capital. In these ways, Bourdieu's conception of bureaucratic field helps to explain how power brokers use music to build public support and negotiate conversions of different species of state-related capital.

While Bourdieu's theory therefore helps us to identify forms of political contestation that may otherwise be hidden, taking music rather than power as a starting point broadens the analytical parameters. Throughout the festival, and especially at the end of each day, the formality of the cadets and the surrounds did not intimidate the street musicians, who lounged about much as they do in their everyday environs. Their attitudes and presentations ranged from offering deferential good wishes to TNI to performing protest songs from the Soeharto and early post-Soeharto periods. But in all cases this anti-militant group were being broadly supportive of TNI. On the other hand, the cadets were highly disciplined, far more so than the junior soldiers at the Battalion event, even though they also danced and cheered with apparent abandon, especially when Air Force members were performing on stage. The main activity linking the groups was the performance of culturally diverse Indonesian musics.

It would nonetheless be problematic to assert that TNI members were imbued with an ethos of being at ease with cultural diversity. While a focus on power and political contestation cannot entirely explain the more light-hearted elements of the event, the congenial reception of ethnically diverse and often anti-military performances cannot supplant the past practices of this state institution. These cast a long shadow over possibilities for a genuinely cosmopolitan openness to cultural difference. The capital of physical force at both TNI-organized events therefore renders problematic the idea that cosmopolitan practice can flourish in such contexts. Indeed, power brokers in both cases were able to attract people with cosmopolitan, culturally diverse musics, and to then use these as a smokescreen for their capital-gathering agendas. Yanto's localised understanding of music was spectacularly successful in this regard, in the Army Battalion as elsewhere. In the context of the TNI military commemorations, therefore, even apparently cosmopolitan behaviours were largely subsumed as species of capital within the bureaucratic field. In contrast to this, the following chapter considers music performance at universities, sites of the production of homogenising national ideologies, critiques of state power, and artistic and intellectual creativity.

8

Universities

Universities and education systems more broadly are key sites for the struggles to control and reproduce statist capital (Bourdieu and Wacquant 1992:114-5). Entrance to the game of cultural capital accumulation is determined in the first instance through competitive recruitment examinations. These examinations 'institute an essential difference between the officially recognised, guaranteed competence and simple cultural capital, which is constantly required to prove itself' (Bourdieu 1986:248). At the same time, universities and anthropology departments in particular have become central to debates over cosmopolitanism. Pnina Werbner (2004:11) contends that Hannerz's definition of a cosmopolitan is 'really an anthropologist!'. Kahn (2003:409) too suggests that 'anthropological practice is best thought of (and assessed, for better or worse) as cosmopolitan'. In this sense, we can expect university scholars and students, especially those in the humanities and social sciences, to be concerned with inter-cultural tolerance and appreciation.

Indonesia's tertiary education sector has contributed to the codification and standardisation of the national language, and to formulating the meaning of Indonesia as a nation. As such, it has long been embroiled in relations of power (Hadiz and Dhakidae 2005) and is a part of the bureaucratic field. Intellectuals more generally have played important roles throughout the history of Indonesia, firstly through 'educational and administrative pilgrimages' (Anderson 1983:140) in the nation's formative period, and second, in recent decades as sites of engagement between student activism, journalism and nation building.[1] But while many student groups have been lauded as central to social and political change, in my experience many circles have often criticised students for being idealistic but altogether unrealistic.

1 *Press closures* 1995; Aspinall 1999; Aspinall, Van Klinken and Feith 1999.

| *Musical worlds in Yogyakarta*

Apart from being a centre of government and cultural tourism, Yogyakarta is for good reason renowned as a student city. With an urban population of a mere half million, in 2000 it was home to most of the province's estimated 70 tertiary institutions (*Yogya dalam angka* 2000). Most large education institutions in Yogyakarta were not associated primarily with musical performance, the notable exceptions being the Indonesian Arts Institute and the Middle-level Music School. However, as I want to show here, productive synergies often operated between higher education and the performing arts. It is not possible to document all musical and social life across Yogyakarta's many education institutions, but I do seek to identify relations between cosmopolitan and bureaucratic practice around musical activities at two significant ones: the State Institute of Islamic Studies and Gadjah Mada University.

A great deal of (predominantly western-funded) research and reportage following September 11 has scrutinised Islamic education in Indonesia by calling attention to preacher/student relationships and rising militancy at religious schools (*pesantren, pondokan, madrasah*) (for example, Luckens-Bull 2001; Perlez 2003). By contrast, an analysis of music at the State Institute of Islamic Studies in the same period offers other perspectives on activities of Islamic education, in this case among young, relatively independent adult students. The second institution, Gadjah Mada University, is a logical choice due to its sheer size and stature. In much of this book I have concentrated on musical practices and orientations by building outwards from observations of and interactions with street workers. This chapter relates these to university students and their musical tastes and practices over the same period.

THE STATE INSTITUTE OF ISLAMIC STUDIES

Of Yogyakarta's several Islamic organizations that link education and music, two major tertiary state institutions in 2001 were: firstly, the Islamic University of Indonesia, its main Yogyakarta campus being an opulent gold-domed building recently relocated to the foot of Mount Merapi north of the city; and second, the Institut Agama Islam Negeri (IAIN, State Institute of Islamic Studies). IAIN was to change its name to Universitas Islam Negeri (UIN, State Islamic University) in 2003, and has since then undergone a major transformation with grand new buildings and grounds. In 2001, Yogyakarta's IAIN (hereafter referred to as the Islamic Institute) was a medium-sized campus with around 7,000 students, including

8 Universities

a number from Malaysia, Singapore, South Korea and Nigeria. Its orientation toward Islamic teachings was evident in its five faculties: Adab (Humanities); Dakwah (Islamic predication and outreach); Syari'ah (Islamic law); Tarbiah (Islamic education); and Ushuluddin (a branch of Islamic philosophy) (*Yogya dalam angka* 1998:125). Analysing music performance here offers a sense of the roles of music making in contests over Islam and the nation, but it also calls attention to other interests, attitudes, and practices.

I learned of activities at the Islamic Institute through a couple of *musik jalanan* community leaders. Kenyeot, who was also Kubro Glow's singer/lyricist, had been travelling to various *pesantren* (Islamic boarding schools) around the region to record an album titled *Hadrah Gugat* (mystical prayer gatherings that include social criticism). A'at by contrast worked in the Culture Department at the government offices on Malioboro Street. Both Kenyeot and A'at were what I would consider to be grounded cosmopolitans, in that they had not travelled beyond Indonesia but were at home with the ethnic, religious, and international diversity of Malioboro Street. They were also involved in planning and performing music at the Islamic Institute.

A third contact, Yoyok, who I met when he MC'd at the Air Force *jalanan* festival, introduced me to a number of Islamic Institute musicians. He studied at the Islamic Institute's Dakwah Faculty, majoring in Islamic Communications and Broadcasting (Penyiaran dan Komunikasi Islam), or (he smirked as he told me) 'PKI', the acronym also of the Indonesian Communist Party. Given Yoyok's stylish urban wear and body piercing, as well as his clownish antics as MC, he appeared aligned less with Islamism or Communism than the capitalist vestiges of MTV-Asia. He also imparted the humour and mannerisms of the 'Jakarta chic' with ease by regularly inserting effeminate 'sentence sweeteners' such as '*bok*'. These and others with links to the Islamic Institute were typical of the variety of cultural orientations and musical performances there.

The Islamic Institute flanked a busy arterial road on the outskirts of the city, with its eastern entrance leading into a concrete quadrangle lined by a number of rooms where groups of students regularly gathered. Two rooms in the quadrangle had 'Gambus' and 'ESKA' scrawled artistically on their doors. The Gambus room was a place for rehearsals, discussion, prayer, and general relaxation. Musical instruments including a few *rebana* (Islamic *melayu* frame drums) and electronic keyboards were stored here, along with sporting and prayer equipment placed along the walls. I interviewed a group of musicians (three men and a woman) in the central floor space of this room. A student named Mulyadi began by explaining that, while there are significant overlaps in terms of membership, each of the two rooms serve as a centre for a band – Orkes Gambus Al Jamiah (Gambus Orchestra Association) and ESKA respectively.

A group of students founded Orkes Gambus in 1981. Nowadays it apparently continued to function well, but had lost much of its recordings and documentation when an important songwriter/arranger moved to another city. According to Hamdi, another member, Orkes Gambus performed *qasidah* (religious chants) and some *dangdut*. At Hamdi's mention of *dangdut*, another member promptly pointed out that they only played well-mannered *dangdut* songs; this perhaps reflecting some sensitivity over associating the genre with Islam. Both *gambus* and *qasidah* could be seen as forms of entertainment, Hamdi continued. 'However', he then added, patting his chest with conviction, *qasidah* is 'deeper, a little like the difference between pop and rock'.

ESKA derives from Sunan Kalijaga, one of the nine saints or *wali* credited with spreading a syncretic form of Islam in Java, and part of the full name of the Islamic Institute (IAIN Sunan Kalijaga; see also Geertz 1960:123). ESKA was an 'ethnic group', Mulyadi explained, that combined theatre and rock:

> A defining characteristic is that, unlike genres such as *campursari*, where audience requests dominate performances, ESKA's music is not entertainment but rather explores sounds in order to induce transcendental contemplation.

Their music drew from 'classic rock' such as The Beatles and Iwan Fals, with additional sounds ranging from machine noise to standard gamelan instruments played in unconventional ways. ESKA's influences included ska, underground, and rap, while their performance format had grown out of the *hadrah* (communal mystical gathering).

Adding religious themes to popular songs, Mulyadi told me, could be said to 'ESKA-ise' music. 'Moving the emotions', Hamdi added, 'could also be used to call attention to other causes such as environmental sustainability and non-violence'. In this way, members of the group voiced what could be called a political agenda, although none of the members spoke directly about the nation-state or party political ideology. Moreover, unlike most secular nationalists or those who advocate an Islamic state, the members emphasised the importance of aesthetic means of influencing opinion.

The students I interviewed subsequently performed during celebrations for the anniversary of the Islamic Institute. A series of bands played in the large indoor hall throughout much of the afternoon, and well over a thousand people attended, most being male and female students. An MC introduced the group on stage as members of the '*gambus* orchestra mixed with Sunan Kalijaga'. Musically, the group combined gamelan instruments, *dangdut* sounds on synthesised flute and distorted guitar, and Arabic-*melayu* vocal styles and chord progressions. Most of the players on stage kept their faces downcast, thoroughly immersed in their playing. Lead performers entered at ground level and, singing from the dance floor, were visually obscured from most of the audience. It was nonetheless evident that each time a female singer emerged from backstage and began to sing and move to the music, large sections of the audience would hoot and shriek with delight, often breaking into a *joged* dance at the same time.

One female singer interspersed romantic/sexual themes with calls to Allah, a combination that I, like many westerners, have found somewhat confusing (Strong 2004). These connections between Islam and popular musical entertainment in Indonesia call attention to what appear to be diverging symbols of women's status. Most notably, these symbols include the female headscarf (*jilbab*) or even the full burqa on the one hand, and on the other the eroticism of *dangdut* with its associated costumes and sexualised dance moves. There was certainly a celebratory atmosphere at this Islamic Institute birthday performance, with female students playing an important role in setting the tone of the event.

Viewed within Bourdieu's schema, music making at the Islamic Institute was political to the extent that it was able to influence the flow of statist capital. The two musical groups based at the campus combined entertainment and eclectic influences into a kind of syncretic mysticism. The musicians were passionate about music's transcendental qualities, which they consciously sought to use for social and political ends such as disseminating views on social issues ranging from corruption to violence. Even when not articulated in a language of nationalism or religion, such activities and sensibilities engaged participants in debates over national, religious and, to an extent, ethnic aspects of their identities.

At the same time, a sense of openness, acceptance and tolerance was also generated through these same musicians, associates, audiences, and the music itself. This was evident in the influences ESKA drew from, as well as the numerous causes to which they put their music. At the Institute's anniversary event moreover, light-hearted themes of love and romance roused and entertained fellow students and their friends. Actions such as these cannot easily be associated with missionising efforts; instead, music making at the Islamic Institute was foremost characterised by transcendental spiritualism, Islam, engagement with social issues, and pleasure and entertainment. The Institute and its musical activities was in many senses an inclusive environment, with Islam and Javanism in general influencing the musicians more than western-style popular culture.

GADJAH MADA UNIVERSITY

Gadjah Mada University is among Indonesia's top centres for tertiary education and scholarly research. It is virtually synonymous with higher education in Yogyakarta for tens of thousands of current and former domestic and foreign students, and for millions outside the education system. The University was built in 1946 and in 2001 had around 55,000 students and over 2,000 lecturers. Despite minimal facilities, Gadjah Mada staff produced large volumes of publications ranging from books to independent journals, reflecting the institution's significance as a centre of intellectual culture. All this suggests that we would expect activities around the Gadjah Mada grounds to have considerable influence in Yogyakarta and beyond.

Gadjah Mada's role as a site where both cosmopolitanism and bureaucratic forces conflict and harmonise was clearly observable during my research. Education institutions are primary sites for national standardisation and ideological indoctrination (Bourdieu 1986). At Gadjah Mada, official billboards around the campus displayed messages invoking patriotic feelings and compliance with national regulations. And the many ethnic-based boarding houses around the campus served to reinforce state-sanctioned ethnic group separations. At the same time, arts projects by separate ethnic groups with loose membership requirements can enrich the idea of Indonesia; and more generally, academic life fosters intellectually oriented social connections across and beyond the nation. While many graduates end up in positions in Indonesia's bureaucracy, to the extent that open and critical thinking is encouraged in a multi-ethnic, internationalist setting, students and graduates learn to balance appreciations of diversity against the homogenising imperatives of state power.

In tandem with these kinds of state-building functions at Gadjah Mada, anthropology and sociology postgraduates I met there kept libraries of photocopied books. These included a team that translated the Theory, Culture & Society series. It is this intellectual environment, whether supportive of, critical of, or ambivalent towards the state, that musical performance at Gadjah Mada must also be situated. Music making was prominent in daily life in numerous settings on and around the campus. As will become evident, the dozens of independently organized student groups – formed through ethnic/regional affiliations or, in the case of many popular music groups, study discipline – constituted distinct education-based versions of musical life in Yogyakarta.

SUNDAY MORNINGS ON THE BOULEVARD

Pancasila Street is a major thoroughfare connecting the Gadjah Mada campus to residential areas and the city more widely. 'Pancasila' is a nationalist slogan describing the five principles of being Indonesian as enshrined in the national constitution. The state also dominated in concrete form on Pancasila Street, housing as it did the Demography and Village Studies buildings, as well as the large Gelanggang Mahasiswa student forum. The Graha Sabha Pramana building commanded a view to the north. Beyond that, and visible on a clear day, the volcanic Mount Merapi maintained the mountain-Kraton-ocean presence, the source of Yogyakarta's symbolic power. Clashes between students and the military occurred on the roundabout at Pancasila Street's southern end during the dramatic period of Soeharto's downfall (Hatley 1999:274). These brought to a head the conflict between intellectual and military forces over what could be termed the composition of the bureaucratic field. Students and others knew Jalan Pancasila colloquially as 'the Boulevard', and music making there was diverse in its range and intentions. The Boulevard/Pancasila area was therefore a place for the expression of inter-cultural sensibilities, as well as a site of conflict with, and machinations within, the state.

On weekdays, only a handful of roadside eateries operated along the Boulevard, since the sweltering midday hours precluded 'hanging out'. However, early each Sunday morning students and others transformed the strip into a popular socialising area. Already by daylight, Yogyakarta's main and arterial roads were busy and polluted; by contrast, the flow of motorised traffic along the Boulevard remained at a trickle. Of the vehicles that did pass through – from restored Holdens to vintage motorcycles – many were on parade with their proud owner/drivers. The Boulevard at this time was most of all a gathering place for the health conscious who arrived in stylish joggers and track wear, many of whom, according to the cynics, were merely walking from their cars parked around the corner. University staff and students and their friends and families made up the majority of customers who settled at one of the 30 or so *lesehan* eateries along both sides of the road, each equipped with portable cookers, straw mats, and awnings.

Amidst the breakfasting and general socialising, *pengamen* played from one *lesehan* to the next. They would usually stop to entertain eatery customers that agreed to patronise them, sometimes circulating among the eateries a couple of times before moving on elsewhere. One Sunday morning I documented the broad pattern of their music between seven-fifteen and nine-forty-five am. Members of a four-piece and a nine-piece group, both of which played acoustic guitars, double bass and conga-cymbal arrangements, sang requests mostly in the *dangdut* and Latin genres. An elderly zither player crouched and sang verses of early Javanese poetry; a vocal duo with guitar and mandolin played in the *kroncong* style. Another zither player with two female singers (*pesinden*) played *karawitan* and sang in the *langgam* style, as did a solo woman with her tambourine. And a couple of *icik-icik* (bottle-tops nailed to a piece of wood) players sang various melodies over their percussion.

While most of these *pengamen* also played around Malioboro Street and at various public transportation terminals, a number of other musical ensembles also played on the Boulevard. These in turn created both competition over the soundscape, and opportunities for inter-group cooperation or exchange. On the same morning for example, a seven-piece jazz-funk combo, comprising three brass instruments, drums, bass, electric guitar, and keys, set up at an intersection midway along the street. Most players were lecturers and senior students from the Indonesian Arts Institute, with many of the 50 or so spectators being friends aged in their late twenties or older. The group's repertoire, while full of improvised solos, consisted entirely of African-American jazz, funk, and blues standards, with no discernible signs of nationalism or regionalist inflection except during their banter between songs.

The jazz-blues group's highly proficient performance could be seen as expressive of xenocentrism, this being 'the belief […] that a foreign culture is superior to all others, including one's own', that Wallach (2002:82) has identified in Indonesia. However, given that the players were university lecturers and students in the stronghold of the Javanese arts, their performances could equally be seen as manifestations of a cosmopolitan openness to outside influences, and a desire to learn alternative styles from foreign visitors and/or recordings. In turn, they presented what many who were passing by evidently saw as new and exciting music.

Other musical groups performed in and around buildings lining the Boulevard on the same morning. At the steps of the Student Forum, a four-piece student group played UK rock group Radiohead's 'High and dry' as a dozen spectators looked on with the preoccupied earnestness of youth. In a reception area on the other side of the street, a woman sang *kroncong* accompanied by an electone player who, having the latest technology, sounded almost like a full orchestra. As on other Sundays, by lunchtime the Boulevard was again a stream of traffic beneath the searing midday sun.

8 Universities

Sunday morning on the Boulevard

All of the above musicians can to an extent be categorised according to musical style as well as motivation and socio-economic position, age, and gender. The sedentary middle-class musicians performed mostly for entertainment, and perhaps also to put their cultural capital on display while at the same time identifying with 'the people'. The mobile *pengamen*, by contrast, were performing mainly out of a need for money. Middle- to lower-class young men generally played *dangdut*, Latin, and occasionally *campursari*. Middle-aged women and older men played *langgam* and *campursari*; the very poor, of both genders and all ages, played *langgam* songs and, at times, contemporary popular songs in the *langgam* style.

Mobile *pengamen* combos were the largest in number; and yet the amplified middle-class performers playing on a fixed site overshadowed them. Musicians generally stuck to their own genres and groups, reflecting clear separations between the groups and a lack of interest in collaborating, but also an ability to coexist. For eatery clientele, the numerous buildings along Pancasila Street were a constant reminder that they were at a state institution, but the entertainment ranged from regionalist *karawitan* and *langgam* to nationalist *dangdut*, Latin American songs, and western-style funk and rock.

HANGOUTS, CAPITAL CONVERSIONS, ACTIVITIES UNITS

At universities, high levels of mental activity often take place in classrooms behind semi-deserted corridors, and among seemingly idle social groups elsewhere. The Graha Sabha Pramana building, whose lonely grandeur was compounded by its generally deserted grounds, was Gadjah Mada's centrepiece. By contrast, students 'hung out' and socialised in large numbers around the older and more modest buildings and their rubbly surrounds. Organized groups also gathered at various places in the nearby tree-lined and tranquil neighbourhoods. On the campus itself, these smaller buildings offered shelter from the harsh sun and streaming traffic. Cultural Sciences students tended to congregate by the corner of the Cultural Sciences building (known simply as *gedung baru*; the 'new building'). Some sat outside the small Anthropology library, some at the nearby international student office by the entrance to the 'new building', others in the shaded areas against classroom walls, or in the open-air canteen by the parking lot. As well as being places to chat, read, or rest, these areas were also sites of informal musical activities ranging from solo musings on a guitar to quiet sing-alongs.

The capital accumulation and conversion themes discussed in Part One can also be applied to university students. Outside the Gadjah Mada grounds, music along with other social activities played a key role in social hierarchies involving university students around the streets of Yogyakarta. This helps to explain some of the shifting levels and kinds of influence among individuals from different groups, which itself underpins much of the organization behind public performances held at state institutions. The result is a set of groupings distinguished largely by their access to different capitals: university students; *jalanan* figures with downtown 'street-cred'; and the 'kampungan' associated with lower-class neighbourhoods.

Rather than constituting fixed entities, many in these groups would undergo processes of capital conversion (Bourdieu 1986:252-5). A poignant example of this was evident among young adults newly arrived to begin tertiary studies in the city. According to a former street guide, there were 'thief seasons', such as Idul Fitri (the feast celebrating the end of the fasting period of Ramadan), New Year, and the weeks leading up to a new university semester. In relation to the latter case, new students arrived in Yogyakarta with money in search of accommodation while simultaneously aiming to make new friends and build and consolidate their 'street cred'. The streetwise meanwhile had little or no money but sought to 'befriend' the students in order to cheat them of their savings, somewhat like the earlier-discussed phenomenon of the foreign backpacker being deceived into parting with money through 'sales at so-called 'batik art exhibitions'.

Alternatively, if the student had the wherewithal, the *jalanan* increasingly accepted him or her without them having to part with all of their money, and they could join forces, the student thereby gaining social credibility and the streetwise economic security. At the same time, many street guide 'hustlers' on Malioboro Street exaggerated their connections to Gadjah Mada and other prestigious institutions in an effort to bolster their status and credibility, especially among foreigners. More specifically, these were efforts on the guides' part to associate themselves with Yogyakarta's prestigious north-side universities, middle-class eateries, and campus radio stations, as opposed to Sosrowijayan and tourism to the south. In both cases, musical knowledge and/or skills often underpinned the formation of sub-cultural affiliations between groups that would otherwise have remained largely separate. In turn, these newly formed groups sometimes collaborated to produce public statements through performance.

Similar processes of economic and social capital conversion were also apparent on the university performance circuit. Street guide members of the Sosrowijayan-based Shower Band aspired to enter the university circuit, sponsorship being the main obstacle. Much the same was true of some motor mechanics I met who lived out of town and were proficient musicians with their own band, but found themselves unable to enter the university circuit without sponsorship and a manager. They were marked by a kind of rural shyness in unfamiliar social situations, and lacked what I earlier called globalist cultural capital and *habitus* plasticity.

By contrast, established 'street groups' often held equal or even superior status to university bands, as demonstrated by their headlining position at many musical events. As a rule, then, musicians with money were generally able to gain access to the university performing circuit. By contrast, *jalanan* figures generally possessed greater social capital because of their local connections to groups, government workers and community leaders. Finally, the rural- or neighbourhood-oriented actors, known generally as '*orang kampungan*', lacked both money and social connections and therefore had difficulty entering the university music scene altogether.

There were also many people who stayed on in Yogyakarta long after graduating because of their preference for the 'Yogya lifestyle'. Many of these lived with declining financial security but over time increased their social connections, often through musical activities. As examples, Lui of the Dayak Etniks continued to live near the Arts Institute eight years after graduating; and, discussed below, Udi long ago graduated from Gadjah Mada but stayed on at the campus largely through the musical wing of its Philosophy Faculty. In Bourdieu's terms, we find various processes of capital conversion and struggles within sub-strata of the bureaucratic field. But again the following performances also show that such processes and interactions among these groups can also foster a general appreciation of cultural diversity, in this case through the accumulated intellectual knowledge of former students and *jalanan* multicultural street-based interactions, and particularly through their collaborative musical expressions.

Tied in with these collaborations, extracurricular Student Activities Units (UKM) were to varying degrees integral to student life at universities. At the official University level, in 2001 Gadjah Mada had four forms of units – sport, art (ranging from theatre to marching bands), spirituality, and 'special'. The prominent musical forms in the art unit were associated with regional traditional dances, especially those of Java and Bali, as well as gamelan performance and vocal groups, rehearsals of which often took place at the Boulevard's Student Forum. Importantly, the less formally organized pop bands seemed to generate at least as much interest. Members of the Philosophy Faculty's 'Sunday Morning' group explained the evolution of pop music around the campus to me as follows:

> Each faculty at Gadjah Mada has at least one group of musicians. Some years ago, a small group in Philosophy started out playing among themselves and found that others around them enjoyed it. In order to extend their reach they held a small concert, which in turn grew to performances held every Sunday morning. The Arts Faculty has thousands of enrolled students, and its activity units include performance groups ranging from dance and *ketoprak* (Javanese comedy/drama) to music groups playing *dangdut, campursari* and reggae, each of which has in common a focus on entertainment. Performance groups in the smaller faculties tend to be more specialised, with Natural Sciences for example playing mostly alternative pop and ska, and Philosophy playing hard rock and funk. Despite these differing performance attitudes and styles, the faculties often work together and help each other out. And the networks extend to other universities, most notably Yogyakarta State University, and Sabtu Sontan at the Islamic University of Indonesia.

Evidently, a whole series of group-based extracurricular student activities were geared toward some form of public cultural expression, which often included capital conversions and exercises in cosmopolitan practice between students and other groups. For example, a young woman with dreadlocks named Suci was a regular at the alternative Bima Books in Sosrowijayan. Suci claimed that she and some friends in the Social and Political Sciences Faculty were the first to secure an Activities Unit from the Gadjah Mada authorities. While in that period she was in a Gadjah Mada-based student performance group, more recently her increasingly Sosrowijayan-based social life put her in contact with older and more experienced street guides and travellers. In 2002 she was to become lead singer in the Shower Band. By then, her intermediary position between university and the street produced some leverage for the Shower Band to enter the university circuit. Capital conversion also flowed from *jalanan* musicians to students, with the former taking university students in new directions through collaborative performance. One example here was Sigma Dance, a ten-member all-female Gadjah Mada dance troupe that, through a street-arts leader, performed at events ranging from a military celebration to the PAN political party's third birthday.

LARGE-SCALE MUSICAL PERFORMANCE

Large-scale performances around Gadjah Mada generally displayed some consistency across venue, musical genre and the social status of participants. Classical orchestras and famous jazz bands performed at the grandiose Graha Sabha Permana, a building that also housed weddings and graduation ceremonies. Smaller-scale classical ensembles performed at the Doctorate Building, while the nearby Lembaga Indonesia-Perancis (LIP, Indonesia France Institute) often held arts events ranging from films and exhibitions to theatrical and music performances, and rock groups sometimes played on a nearby sports oval. As domains within the bureaucratic field, these ranged from high-stature events with (or with potential access to) powerful individual wielders of statist capital, to those with larger audiences and greater scope for directly influencing public opinion. Viewed in this way, contests for statist capital in these settings were ultimately fought between powerful elite individuals and the resistance of popular groups. However, the following cases reflect the often porous nature of both participant/performer and elite/popular boundaries at university music performances.

| *Musical worlds in Yogyakarta*

Most public performances in the study period took place at the northern end of the Boulevard, either on the road itself or at Purnabudaya, a large pavilion located only metres away. Audiences were comprised mostly of students, but this varied depending on the theme of the event and the actual performers. Musical performances ranged from epic-style theatre and avant-garde comedy to a major concert to honour the life of renowned scholar and activist Herb Feith. A benefit concert for farmers held at the Boulevard included a Regional Literature group, who played upbeat American pop with regular insertions of humorous commentary, followed by Philosophy's extended cover versions of Deep Purple classics. Another concert, co-organized by a number of education institutions and the Malioboro Arts Community, featured music ranging from *gambus* to *kroncong* to, finally, *jalanan* percussion and vocal groups.

Finally, a 'moonlight concert' by renowned Islamic culturalist Emha Ainun Nadjib and his Kyai Kanjeng Orchestra brought together religious and national themes before over 5,000 spectators on the Boulevard. Visual signs of support for Islam were evident throughout the audience, with many women wearing white headscarves and men sporting colourful and ornate fez caps. An elaborate stage backdrop featured the slogan Musik dan Ilmu: Perajurit Bangsa (Music and Knowledge: Warrior Nation). Around 40 performers filled the large stage, these being separated into *bedug* (large drums used for calls to prayer at mosques) players; a university viola section; a rock-style ensemble; a large all-female choir; and a row of clerics (*ulama*). The group performed their intricately arranged songs with great professionalism, at times drawing gasps of pleasure and appreciation from across the audience.

Between songs, Emha (known colloquially as Cak Nun) inserted topical narratives on national party-politics, regionalism, and religion, and emphasised that Islam should transcend divisions across parties. At another point, he introduced a medley through an extensive narration on contemporary concerns with national integration. He told the at times humorous story about how he and friends in the orchestra had recently travelled to numerous provinces and then composed a medley containing melodies from Irian Jaya (which was to become Papua in 2002), Madura, Riau, and Aceh.

These regions, Emha added, 'are in fact those that according to [the then President] Gus Dur will break away from Indonesia if he ceases leading the nation', which received supportive applause from the large audience. While visiting Banda Aceh, Emha continued, he asked for 'help with the concept for June 1 at Gadjah

Mada University, to make songs from our friends' cultures, because all of them are already part of our heart and love for the nation'. After more applause the orchestra began their medley, consciously displaying in the music a number of cultural associations with the regions he had outlined in his story, in particular Islamic *melayu* and Mandarin-style flute and percussion sticks. This served to bring Kyai Kanjeng's musical version of Indonesia's 'unity in diversity' (Bhinneka Tunggal Ika) to the attention of thousands.

As a Gadjah Mada sociologist remarked to me during the show, Emha's concert was an effective means of spreading news and opinions to a large audience, many of whom rarely read or listened to the news. This event was clearly intended to influence public opinion through combining entertainment with education and religion. Emha's ability to draw such a large audience to this prestigious state institution served to legitimise the relationship between Islam and state education, in turn exercising influence on the bureaucratic field. At the same time, Emha, himself extremely well travelled, was also fostering a cosmopolitan appreciation of nationwide diversity beyond that of the dominant Javanism, and doing so to a predominantly 'grounded' audience.

At first glance, the above performances may appear to hold little in common beyond taking place at state-owned tertiary education institutions. But the relations between musical performance, nationalist discourse and the state tertiary sector are evident in the thematic, organizational, and performative features of the events. Most of the large-scale performances were, with varying degrees of directness, nationalistic and part of the wider bureaucratic field. Even those not premised directly on the nation used specifically Indonesian props and/or banners and catchphrases in order to draw attention to issues such as the plights of specifically Indonesian farmers and street children. Other events addressed matters of national concern more directly. Emha for example orchestrated an evening of musical and spoken statements all but exclusively concerned with the role of regions and religion within the Indonesian nation-state.

Musical events at both the Islamic Institute and Gadjah Mada University also displayed certain cosmopolitan features. Many Gadjah Mada music groups, such as the Regional Literature and Philosophy bands, were formed because of intellectual rather than ethnic (sub-national) or religious affinity. The Islamic Institute and Gadjah Mada groups performed at events with themes and locations linked to the nation, but the agendas of the groups and their audiences were to a considerable extent fuelled by youth and romance. Around these institutions, in other words, music performances often brought national issues to the fore, yet there were also both cosmopolitan/intellectual associations and less high-minded social and romantic interests typical of youth everywhere. The plethora of musical activities around these tertiary institutions in Yogyakarta thereby gave rise to unique combinations of nationalist impositions or promotions, critiques of these, and at the same time encouraged an appreciation of the pleasures of diversity.

Conclusion

Public events involving musical performance at Yogyakarta's state institutions in 2001 tended to produce discernible combinations of struggles for statist capital with practices I have described as grounded and cosmopolitan. At the Regional Parliament on Malioboro Street, cosmopolitanism and political practice were manifest in articulations of themes of nation and unity on the one hand, and the localisation of outside influence on the other. The capital of physical force dominated the Armed Forces examples that incorporated, respectively, *campursari* and *jalanan* musics. By contrast, musical performances at universities produced unique combinations of national ideals and standardisations on one hand, and playful experimentation on the other.

The realities of the bureaucratic field were never far removed. Political, business, and religious leaders used the music and associated promotions and speeches to curry favour with those who came to listen, and music enthusiasts in turn exercised influence in Yogyakarta's bureaucratic field. In some cases, such as the street musicians' ethnically diverse and politically oppositional performance at the Air Force Academy, performers were to some degree able to steer the agenda away from an exclusivist, homogenising, Javacentric, and nationalist one. I have also suggested that viewing music performance and social relations at state institutions solely in terms of a contest for statist capital is insufficient. A major domain in which scholars and others have long sought meaning beyond quests for power is 'the sacred' (Shils 1982): the above chapters have offered grounded cosmopolitanism as an alternative domain, a consideration to be further discussed below, in the Conclusion to this monograph.

In the midst of the intense political, economic and religio-ethnic quests for dominance in Indonesia over this period, it is easy to overlook or dismiss how street-level grounded cosmopolitan practices could help to temper intergroup enmities. A good example of this was the interactions between people of diverse occupation, religion, and cultural orientation at *angkringan* snack stalls along Malioboro Street. It is more difficult to assess whether state policies and practices assist, impede, or are largely irrelevant to appreciations of diversity and openness to otherness. Appiah (1997:629) cautions against state-enforced cultural values, but at the same time endorses the need for political institutions when he argues that '[w]hat we need is not citizens centring on a common culture but citizens committed to common institutions'. Kahn (2003:409) highlights the existence of diverse groups living 'side by side in relative harmony', and suggests that impositions of nation-states and international organizations may have actually exacerbated rather than alleviated conflict in areas of Indonesia such as Maluku, Aceh, West Papua, and Kalimantan.

To what extent, then, can it be said that grounded cosmopolitanism characterised musical performances at Yogyakarta's state institutions in the early post-Soeharto years? Many performances saw participants engaged in socially enriching activities such as romance, self-expression or humour, regardless of the statist agenda of organizers. In the same way, while the Regional Parliament is a major centre of political contestation, this does not mean that the multi-ethnic and international, cosmopolitan nature of Malioboro Street and its cultural events exist only within the bureaucratic field.

Similarly, the *campursari* entertainment of the Tombo Sutris orchestra cannot be reduced merely to a desire to dupe the masses. Rather than being part of a New Order-style depoliticised public (Pemberton 1994), a number of the participants conveyed their awareness of the underlying agendas to me. Furthermore, a number of Tombo Sutris members in other contexts played an extremely diverse range of musical genres. However, while Tombo Sutris were by no means representative of *campursari* orchestras across the region, it remains the case that their large public performances were chiefly the products of a *preman* attempting to transform financial and religious resources into political gain through the threat, and occasional enacting, of physical force.

Musical events held at universities tended to bring together students and their friends, often with little sign of authority over the proceedings. Many of the student groups performing here formulated musical genres and styles of presentation according to their intellectual and aesthetic interests rather than by predetermined markers of ethnicity or religion. In this way, student activity units and their concerts at Gadjah Mada conveyed a western pop-influenced form of grounded cosmopolitanism, even though such university events were very much part of the bureaucratic field. The cases of the Islamic Institute music groups and the Emha Ainun Nadjib and Kyai Kanjeng performance demonstrate the combinations of political activism, pleasure seeking, and social inclusiveness that characterised the activities of many educated Muslim artists in Yogyakarta. Finally, as will be addressed next, members of the Malioboro Arts Community were central to many musical events with state-based themes and involving diverse musical genres and performers across the state institutions.

Conclusion
Campursari and *jalanan* at the Sultan's Palace

In this monograph I have sought to construct a framework through which to analyse musical performance and social relations as I observed them in early post-Soeharto Yogyakarta. To achieve this, I drew on Bourdieu's concepts of capital, *habitus* and field, and counterpoised these with the alternative perspectives of inter-group social capital, musical physicalisation and grounded cosmopolitanism respectively. My wider aim has been to produce a nuanced account of social relations and cultural influences that highlights the roles of music in peaceful inter-group relations in Yogyakarta in the early post-Soeharto period. I now wish to conclude by discussing events at the Sultan's Palace (Kraton), as these serve to bring together the main social groups, musical genres and concepts already addressed.

The Kraton and its Sultan, Hamengku Buwono X, continued to wield great symbolic power following President Soeharto's downfall. This was evident to me in that virtually everyone on the street, from visiting villager to radical democracy activist, spoke positively of Kraton culture and its importance for the stability and progress of the nation. The Kraton is deservedly renowned for its Javanese arts and traditions, with gamelan and *wayang kulit* being cases in point. At the same time, less widely advertised performances featuring musical genres such as *campursari* and *jalanan* characterised several events held in the Kraton grounds. Collectively these involved hundreds of organizers and performers and tens of thousands of spectators, and highlight connections and separations between the social worlds of street workers, community leaders, and other social and political networks.

A central hypothesis running through this book is that the enormous popularity of *campursari* music was largely confined to certain social groups and contexts. I have identified *campursari* with lower class *becak* drivers who plied the inner city seeking fares while maintaining permanent residence in villages, and discussed examples of the genre as performed in settings ranging from kampung to state institution. By contrast, *jalanan* music for the most part referred to a localised version of folk/rock supported and played by tourist

| *Conclusion*

street guides and street musicians, among others. In the remaining sections, I reflect on earlier discussions and attempt to clarify the musical identities of *becak* driver and street-guide groups in light of Kraton events featuring the *campursari* and *jalanan* musical genres respectively.

Campursari performances were integral to a number of Kraton events, which in turn brought one major disenfranchised group into Yogyakarta's epicentre of symbolic capital through music. The *sekaten* rituals at Yogyakarta's Kraton, long central to Java's cultural and religious calendar, feature a month-long carnival leading into a week of formal rituals. The final week of *sekaten* in 2001 did not include any *campursari*, but some of the music contained elements underpinning the Javanese side of the genre while being distant from folk-rock *jalanan*. Furthermore, attitudes I encountered regarding *sekaten* week were revealing of differences between street worker groups.

To my knowledge, relatively few *jalanan* street musicians, and even fewer Sosrowijayan-based street guides, attended *sekaten*.

Gamelan performance in the Sultan's Palace during *sekaten* week

Although many enjoyed *wayang kulit* shows and, unlike most *becak* drivers, argued that *wayang kulit* was far superior to any *campursari* performance, some made a point of not going along to *sekaten*. While few street musicians of western-rock orientation attended *sekaten*, several *becak* drivers ventured down to the grounds at some point during the week. These diverging levels of support for *sekaten* map broadly onto the street workers' musical tastes and practices discussed earlier. The rural-based *becak* drivers favoured *campursari* and, in many cases, attended *sekaten*, while street guides did not attend any Kraton events involving *campursari*. By contrast, the *jalanan* leader and Kubro Glow guitarist Tyas did attend, reflecting his unusual ability to straddle various musical and social worlds.

The first evening of the carnival leading up to *sekaten* week featured performances by Sosrowijayan-based groups. These began around seven pm with six primary school dance groups, *karawitan* and *qasidah*, all in the first hour. The first of the final two acts was an enlarged version of the *kroncong* orchestra based in Sosrowijayan's Gang One, including lead female singers Bu Meni and Bu Ina from the backpacker-frequented Woodpecker Restaurant. For the final song, the seven women and five men who had sung earlier now lined up in gender-divided rows and sang a patriotic *kroncong* song in unison. I found it interesting to view the restaurant staff on stage supporting the Sultan within the nation-state, and at the same time recall their daily 'grounded cosmopolitan' interactions with backpackers from many parts of the world. The final act was Sekar Wuyung, a group discussed at length in Part One. The group themselves often called their music *dangdut Jawa*: for this event the organizing government department classified them as *campursari*; but they were introduced on stage as *pop Jawa*, all of which reflects the importance of context on how the band was described. In any case, the MC introduced Sekar Wuyung by their district rather than the name of the band, suggesting that the community took precedence over group names and musical definitions.

Sekar Wuyung, dressed in matching Javanese *blankon* headwear and other symbolic markers of the Kraton, began with an instrumental piece, as did many *campursari* groups. On this occasion they played 'Ojo diperoki', a *campursari* favourite about intercultural sensitivities involving a Javanese couple and outside, especially western, influences. The MC then introduced the first singer, Mbak Ira, who had many years ago been a *dangdut* performer at Purawisata's Taman Ria. She greeted the audience with the seductive tones of *dangdut* singers, after which the group launched into the full version of 'Ojo diperoki', some in the audience dancing to the *dangdut* sounds and the singer's movements. Overall, the eroticism of *dangdut* performances, so dominant in earlier years (on neighbouring Surakarta, see Pioquinto, 1995), had been toned down, with the more conservative, Java- and/or Islam-oriented features now dominating. Here Sekar Wuyung nonetheless managed to introduce *dangdut* and its associated sexualisation, thereby exercising resistance to these conservative constraints. This is not to suggest that the Kraton hierarchy was always prudish; the following case shows that the Sultan himself witnessed and evidently did not always oppose displays of sexuality and ribald humour at Kraton performances.

The Sultan and his entourage attended a Tombo Sutris orchestra performance in the Kraton's Northern Square one evening. The theme, as displayed on banners at each end of Malioboro Street, read 'A night of solidarity for *becak* drivers and pavement-sellers'. Over a thousand people attended, most in fact male *becak* drivers and pavement sellers between 18 and 40 years of age. Around 30 men danced on a dirt patch behind the rows of royalty seated before the stage. Behind and around these groups were several layers of people, separated by steps and other permanent and temporary fixtures, while trailing back into the Square a few hundred curious passers-by sat on their motorcycles.

On stage, one of the MCs stood dressed in traditional court attire. The other MC suddenly re-emerged from nowhere, this time dressed as a transvestite (see Peacock 1968). In a combination of Javanese and Indonesian, the transvestite cracked lewd jokes along the lines that 'I service both men and women' and, moving the microphone close to his lips, 'We're alike, you and I, an MC and I both work with our mouths'. Such jokes, along with the transvestite's camp mannerisms, provoked riotous hoots and looks of mischievous pleasure. As at the Awards Night at the Regional Parliament, the Tombo Sutris MCs ran mock competitions, on this occasion offering prizes for the shortest person in the audience as well as for the oldest.

Apart from these interludes, music was the focus of the evening. The musicians blended *campursari* with an intricate variety of other styles including *dangdut* and James Bond themes. Front of stage was largely the domain of the young and glamorous female singers, who would emerge from backstage to sing a song, and then, sometimes after a brief innuendo-filled dialogue with the MCs, recede to be followed by another. This Tombo Sutris performance demonstrates the role of musical entertainment in drawing in large numbers of people while facilitating connections among the powerful, here the Sultan and *preman* Yanto. Musical gatherings between these leaders and large groups of people highlight tensions between, on the one hand, feudalism, hereditary leadership and patron/client networks involving the capital of physical force, and on the other efforts to influence the democratic process in such a way as to ensure equality for the underprivileged.

A number of non-*campursari* events at the Kraton were far more likely to involve street guides and *jalanan* affiliates, at least as spectators. These projects featured an urban-oriented variant of regional musical identity, and involved collaborations between *jalanan* groups and a stratum of intellectuals with high levels of cultural capital. On Indonesian Independence Day for example, the annual daytime street parade was followed by a symbolically rich evening event involving multiple musical genres, an unusually mixed audience, and *jalanan* and university-based leadership. The first evening performance, scheduled to start at eight pm, was delayed because, a number of people told me, one of the nearby banyan trees had yet to grant permission for the use of electricity in the area (see also Pigeaud 2003:6).

The audience meanwhile continued to build up, with most people chatting contentedly in circles on the ground in the dark and expanding outwards from the stage. The audience was mostly young adults who seemed to fall into two broad groups. The first were urban youth, or more specifically members of the loose-knit Malioboro community along with student associates, most of whom wore denim jeans and black tops. The second group, sitting on the large concrete slab at the front of the stage, was the 'village folk' (*orang desa*) that appear at festivals and carnivals such as the *sekaten* carnival, though in this case most were noticeably younger. Such co-presence of street and village groups thereby represented an unusually broad cross-section of the community – this did not occur at the *sekaten* or at university-based events.

Performances began at ten-thirty pm, and included the witty and skilled role-parody group Kelompok Swara Ratan (The Stringy-voiced Family), including members of Emha's Kyai Kanjeng Orchestra. The evening also featured the *jalanan* band of local legend status Kelompok Penyanyi Jalanan Malioboro (KPJM, Malioboro Streetside Singers). As on other occasions, they played time-honoured original songs such as 'Geger' (Tumult) among others, which the audience received with lengthy and appreciative applause. As discussed in the Introduction, many KPJM songs contain prominent signifiers of both western rock and Javanese culture, in particular through combinations of blues riffs on acoustic guitar, Javanese scales on flute, and various drums and rhythms. As well as performing creative street music, the band members were also known for providing support for street children. The penultimate act was the legendary local *pengamen* Pak Sujud Sutrisno, who

| *Conclusion*

was also well received, while the final performance, *wayang kulit*, commenced at around one am and continued to a large audience through until after dawn.

The audience for this event was especially diverse, and the acts included Islamic *qasidah* and the nineteenth-century Javanese *angguk* dance, through to current popular music and comedy. Housing such varieties of musical act was a unifying force for one of the broad groups of inner-city oriented people I have sought to identify in this monograph. The music on this occasion was on the one hand benignly nationalistic, a matter of some importance given the climate of political, economic, ethnic and religious tension; on the other, collectively the performances were exceptionally varied. As at the State Institute of Islamic Studies, performers and audience alike were keen to share their cultural performances with anyone interested, and evidently did not feel threatened by outside influences. Moreover, the setting of the Kraton promoted a sense of place and of humility in the face of the powers of nature. But the event was of course not magically removed from power struggles: not only did the various acts present versions of urban renewal, traditionalist Java, Islam and the like to a diverse audience, the involvement of the Perhimpunan Indonesia Baru (New Indonesia Association) was made prominent through signage.

Angguk dance at the Northern Square

Conclusion

Kubro Glow headline for the Yogyakarta Arts Festival finale in the Kraton pavilion, 2001

The last event I wish to mention in relation to the *jalanan* musical world is a seven-act performance that was held inside the Kraton pavilion for the Yogyakarta Arts Festival. Acts ranged from 'hip metal' to *jalanan* folk guitarists and the Jagongan street percussion and Gila Gong ethnic groups. The headline act was Kubro Glow, whose members included Tyas and Kenyeot, two key figures in my research. As at the Indonesian Arts Institute some months earlier, here they began with a 40-member Islamic choir, who chanted a Javanese-sounding melody apparently composed by Sunan Kalijaga, the sixteenth century *wali* (saint) after whom the State Institute of Islamic Studies in Yogyakarta was named. After the choir's five-minute introduction, the group launched into their epic-style songs combining, in one member's words, Jesus Christ Superstar-inspired rock with Javanese scales and chords. Viewed in relation to the Independence Day event above, along with a number of events that took place at state institutions such as Gadjah Mada University, I suggest that discernible lines of influence interconnected the Malioboro Arts Community, student groups and street guides that did not, in the main, involve the *campursari* worlds of *becak* drivers and others.

Musical events at the Palace did not unite all groups in Yogyakarta, and to varying degrees they exercised symbolic influence to the benefit of some political groups and causes over others. However, they also helped to maintain groundedness through respect for the powers of nature, and promoted or reflected openness to cultural difference in the world. Additionally, mysticism and Islam were more important here than at events at other state institutions, such that notions of the sacred and the cosmopolitan were indeed often hard to disentangle. More generally, many examples of what I earlier sought to define as cosmopolitan practice were also versions of contemporary Javanese musical identity based primarily on combinations of Java/Indonesia, Islam and the West. Following Thomas Turino (2000), these combinations can also be seen as cosmopolitan in that they include deeply internalised foreign ideas and practices.

Tombo Sutris' performances politicised the rural-oriented Javanist modernism represented by *campursari*. By contrast, another loose group discussed in the previous chapters was more representative of street-intellectualism and urban politics. This second group, the Malioboro Arts Community, centred on the Pajeksan area south of Sosrowijayan, and included the KPJM, Jagongan and Kubro Glow groups and their related projects. These groups consciously displayed some combination of Javanism, Islam, and the West, and they did so at all state institutions discussed above and often in leading/headlining roles.

Notwithstanding Tombo Sutris' connections to criminal activities, the Tombo Sutris/Pajeksan division had a lot in common with that between the *becak* driver/*campursari* and street guide/*jalanan* typology discussed at the outset. Pajeksan-based street musicians could more readily be identified by their sub-cultural and/or cosmopolitan markers than was the case with Tombo Sutris members. As examples, Imam Rasta by his very name fused Islam and reggae; Kenyeot managed a *pesantren*-based Islamic musical project and sang of modern romance to funk/rock accompaniment; and Tyas taught a Sufi-influenced form of yoga and managed a jazz café out of town.

Of significance to the individuals and groups I came to know, the Tombo Sutris *campursari* orchestra included members with friends and/or siblings in the militant youth group GPK, while members of Kubro Glow were connected with the radical arts group, Taring Padi. Despite open clashes between GPK and Taring Padi (Nicolai and Hillsmith, 2002), mutual and long-term friends crossed the Tombo Sutris/Kubro Glow divide, particularly through music. This highlights how difficult it is to classify people into social groups, and furthermore that divisions such as violent/peaceful, rural/urban and conservative/progressive need to be treated with great caution. Related to this, political and economic considerations alone cannot fully explain the presence of several hundred *becak* drivers, and of the Sultan himself, at the Tombo Sutris performance. Neither can religion, even though it certainly played a role. In light of the above, I would argue that musical pleasure is an important motivation for attending and/or performing at public events.

On a return visit in 2005, I discovered that Tombo Sutris was no longer active: members had needed to find alternative employment, while the owner, Yanto, was now studying Law. Kubro Glow's core members, Tyas and Kenyeot, continued to manage the band along with other projects such as the Indonesian Musical Poetry Festival that took place while I was there. Kubro Glow's new drummer was the son of senior figures in the Malioboro Arts Community. He played in five other groups, including a reformed version of the hip-metal group that played at the Yogyakarta Arts Festival performance at the Kraton in 2001. A Tombo Sutris member had joined Kubro Glow for a time, but the merger failed, apparently due to creative differences. Kubro Glow's ex-drummer now played with former Tombo Sutris members to a predominantly foreign audience at the former Resto in Sosrowijayan. In other words, older siblings and friends of the violently opposed GPK and Taring Padi groups continued to shift between musical groups, genres, and settings. All of this reinforces the argument that music both influences and reflects the fluidity of social groups, political agendas, and musical genres in Yogyakarta.

The musical setting for Part One of this monograph was the roadsides and alleyways of the inner-city Sosrowijayan kampung and backpacker area. The demarcations of these spaces were less defined than those of formal establishments and institutions, and thereby called attention to connections between music and everyday sociality. In Part Two, musical performances in the two settings of kampung and commercial entertainment venues provided a means through which to analyse gender relations in the Sosrowijayan area, and to consider generational and class/international dimensions of gender more broadly. Finally, music performances at state institutions were logical sites to focus on state/society relations. Because the performances analysed took place on the street and in commercial zones, neighbourhoods and state institutions, most public spaces have been considered. In light of this, the study has gone at least some way toward producing a broad representation of popular musical activities in early post-Soeharto Yogyakarta.

Musical genres have very fluid, generally subjective, boundaries. In Yogyakarta this porousness often served to facilitate inter-group harmony, or at least manageability. For example, hybridizations of

| *Conclusion*

campursari and *dangdut* in kampung events catered to the tastes of older and younger participants. Musicians often mixed elements of several genres, and organizers arranged a diversity of musical performances for one event. These processes encouraged different voices and sensibilities to work together for common themes and causes. At other times, musical genres kept people apart. This was notable between followers of *campursari* and *jalanan* musics, as evident in Sosrowijayan and at the Sultan's Palace. I also identified related divisions in kampung and commercial venues.

The two genres I most often heard about, *campursari* and *jalanan*, turned out on closer inspection to be as much sub-cultural sensibilities as anything verifiable through the objective analysis of sound. Paradoxically, again, many street buskers played the individual components behind *campursari*; and yet, while *musik jalanan* was in theory any music played on the street, most people used the term to refer to oppositional, western-influenced musics, and to their connotations of street cred and specifically urban sensibilities. These factors highlight how considerations of taste and context are necessary in discussions of musical genres in living social situations.

In turn, different aspects of social identity were influenced by, and expressed through, musical performances and their contexts. Class or occupational groups around the inner-city streets tended to associate foremost with one broad genre: *becak* driver and *campursari*; street guide and *jalanan*; cigarette seller and *dangdut*; upwardly-aspiring urbanite and 'hip' (for those up to 25 years old) or jazz (for those over 25). Bourdieu's formulations helped to identify contestation involving economic and other forms of capital among social, work and musical groups such as these. But alternative perspectives of social capital enabled phenomena of in-group and inter-group cooperation to be included in the discussion. The gendered *habitus* often transformed into one of three kinds of musical physicalisation at musical events – detachment engagement, other worlds or sexualisation. These physicalisations affected social relations within the performance setting, and in turn the music itself. Increased physical animation sometimes signified greater dominance and exploitation by authorities and patrons, at others a measure of actors' agency.

The nexus between national and ethnic identity, whether subjectively felt or engineered by authorities, was at the centre of most musical events at state institutions. At many state-held events, grounded cosmopolitanism helped to foster a more tolerant, inclusive atmosphere, for example at universities. By contrast, Tombo Sutris at the Regional Parliament was a clear case of the influential roles musical entertainment can play in contests for statist capital.

Conclusion |

Performances by *jalanan* and other groups at a National Air Force Academy festival highlighted difficulties associated with drawing clear lines between streetwise, politically oppositional groups and agents of the state wielding the capital of physical force. In Yogyakarta, cosmopolitan practices often manifested as variations of regional identity. These were especially apparent at musical performances at the Kraton.

The focus on *jalanan* and *campursari* musical worlds revealed divergent social identities based primarily on occupation and, especially, urban/rural orientations. Identifying these kinds of divisions is not in itself new, but I have focused on how music helped the two groups to coexist peacefully, a matter of great importance in the early post-Soeharto years. Research on the complexity, or 'melange', of social and cultural influences in Indonesia also has a long history. I have drawn on Bourdieu as a corrective to the overly celebratory nature of some of these accounts. At the same time, I have argued that musical research that restricts its focus to power dimensions cannot account for the cooperation, pleasure, and intercultural appreciation that also occur at musical events. Furthermore, excessive emphasis on contestation risks adding to the already burgeoning literature on conflict in Indonesia.

The concepts of inter-group social capital, musical physicalisation, and grounded cosmopolitanism were proposed as means of identifying aspects of social life that cannot be reduced solely to quests for power. Perhaps these perspectives can extend Bourdieu's concepts to better account for social and musical practices and forms in culturally diverse, inner-city settings. I hope that this study of musical worlds in Yogyakarta can help toward identifying some of the social factors and cultural influences that promote peaceful social interaction in times of political upheaval and change. By demonstrating the presence of both contestation and harmony at public musical performances through this monograph, my overarching conclusions are that ethnographic research on musical performance can help to conceptualise political and other dimensions of social and cultural life in dense urban settings and, more specifically, that music in Yogyakarta plays a crucial role in the cultural expression and inter-group appreciation for which the city is renowned.

Bibliography

Adorno, Theodor W. and Max Horkheimer
1999 'The culture industry: Enlightenment as mass deception', in: Simon During (ed.), *The cultural studies reader*. Second edition, pp. 31-41. London: Routledge. [First edition 1993.]

Anderson, Benedict R.O'G.
1983 *Imagined communities: Reflections on the origin and spread of nationalism.* London: Verso.
1990 *Language and power: Exploring political cultures in Indonesia.* Ithaca, NY: Cornell University Press. [Wilder House Series in Politics, History and Culture.]

Antariksa
2001 'Rulers of the streets', *Latitudes* 7:18-23.

Appiah, Kwame Anthony
1997 'Cosmopolitan patriots', *Critical Inquiry* 23:617-39.

Arta, Arwan Tuti
2001 *Yogyakarta tempoe doeloe: Sepanjang catatan pariwisata.* Yogyakarta: BIGRAF.
2002 'Sosrowijayan wetan dan Prawirotaman: Kampung internasional di Yogya', *Kedaulatan Rakyat*, 16 March.

Aspinall, Edward
1999 'The Indonesian student uprisings of 1998', in: Arief Budiman, Barbara Hatley, Damien Kingsbury (eds), *Reformasi: Crisis and change in Indonesia*, pp. 212-38. Clayton, VIC: Monash Asia Institute. [Monash Papers on Southeast Asia 50.]

Aspinall, Edward, Herb Feith and Gerry van Klinken (eds)
1999 *The last days of President Suharto.* Clayton, VIC: Monash Asia Institute. [Monash Papers on Southeast Asia 49.]

Attali, Jacques
1985 *Noise: The political economy of music.* Manchester: Manchester University Press. [Theory and History of Literature 16.] [Originally published as *Bruits: Essai sur l'économie politique de la musique.* Paris: Presses Universitaires de France, 1977.]

Bibliography

Bader, Sandra
2011 'Dancing bodies on stage: Negotiating *nyawer* encounters at *dangdut* and *tarling dangdut* performances in West Java', *Indonesia and the Malay World* 39:333-55.

Bannister, Roland
2002 'How are we to write our music history?: Perspectives on the historiography of military music', *Musicology Australia* 25:1-21.

Barendregt, Bart and Wim van Zanten
2002 'Popular music in Indonesia since 1998: In particular fusion, Indie and Islamic music on video compact discs and the internet', *Yearbook for Traditional Music* 34:67-113.

Baulch, Emma
2007 *Making scenes: Reggae, punk and death metal in 1990s Bali.* Durham, NC: Duke University Press.

Bauman, Zygmunt
1998 'On glocalisation: Or globalisation for some, localisation for some others', *Thesis Eleven* 54:37-49.

Beatty, Andrew
1999 *Varieties of Javanese religion: An anthropological account.* Cambridge: Cambridge University Press. [Cambridge Studies in Social and Cultural Anthropology 111.]

Beazley, Harriot
2000 'Street boys in Yogyakarta: Social and spatial exclusion in the public spaces of the city', in: Gary Bridge and Sophie Watson (eds), *A companion to the city*, pp. 472-88. London: Blackwell.

Becker, Howard
1982 *Art worlds.* Berkeley, CA: University of California Press.

Becker, Judith
1975 'Kroncong: Indonesian popular music', *Asian Music* 7:14-9.

Berman, Laine
1994 'The family of GIRLI: The homeless children of Yogyakarta', *Inside Indonesia* 38:18-21.
2000 'Surviving on the streets of Java: homeless children's narratives of violence', *Discourse & Society* 11:149-74.

Bhabha, Homi K.
1994 *The location of culture.* London: Routledge.

Bodden, Michael
2005 'Rap in Indonesian youth music of the 1990s: "Globalization", "outlaw genres", and social protest', *Asian Music* 36:1-26.

Body, John
1982 *Music for sale: Street musicians of Yogyakarta* (cassette liner notes). Wellington: Kiwi/Pacific Records.

Boon, James A.
1990 *Affinities and extremes: Crisscrossing the bittersweet ethnology of East Indies history, Hindu-Balinese culture, and Indo-European allure.* Chicago: University of Chicago Press.

Bourdieu, Pierre
1977 *Outline of a theory of practice.* Translated by Richard Nice. Cambridge: Cambridge University Press. [Cambridge Studies in Social Anthropology 16.] [Originally published as *Esquisse d'une théorie de la pratique: Précédé de trois études d'ethnologie kabyle.* Geneva: Librairie Droz, 1972.]
1984 *Distinction: A social critique of the judgement of taste.* Translated by Richard Nice. London: Routledge. [Originally published as *La distinction: Critique sociale du jugement.* Paris: Minuit, 1979.]
1986 'The forms of capital', in: John G. Richardson (ed.), *Handbook of theory and research for the sociology of education*, pp. 241-58. New York: Greenwood.
1994 'Rethinking the state: Genesis and structure of the bureaucratic field', *Sociological theory* 12:1-18.
2001 *Masculine domination.* Translated by Richard Nice. Cambridge: Polity Press. [Originally published as *La domination masculine.* Paris: Seuil, 1998.]

Bourdieu, Pierre and Loïc J.D. Wacquant
1992 *An invitation to reflexive sociology.* Chicago: University of Chicago.

Brata, Nugroho Trisno
1997 'Kekerasan kampanye di Kota Jogja: Studi etnofotografi peristiwa kampanye PPP 1997'. MA thesis, Gadjah Mada University, Yogyakarta.

Bubandt, Nils
2004 'Menuju sebuah politik tradisi yang baru? Desentralisasi, konflik, dan adat di wilayah Indonesia Timur', *Antropologi Indonesia* 74:12-32.

Budiman, Arief, Barbara Hatley, Damien Kingsbury (eds)
1999 *Reformasi: Crisis and change in Indonesia*, pp. 212-38. Clayton, VIC: Monash Asia Institute. [Monash Papers on Southeast Asia 50.]

Bull, Michael and Les Back (eds)
2003   *The auditory culture reader.* Oxford/New York: Berg. [Sensory Formations.]
Calhoun, Craig (ed.)
2002   *Reader in contemporary sociological theory.* Oxford: Blackwell.
Cassell, Phillip (ed.)
1993   *The Giddens reader.* Stanford, CA: Stanford University Press.
Clara van Groenendael, Victoria M.
2008   *Jaranan: The horse dance and trance in East Java.* Translated by Maria J.L. van Yperen. Leiden: KITLV Press. [Verhandelingen 252.]
Clark, Marshall
2010   *Maskulinitas: Culture, gender and politics in Indonesia.* Caulfield: Monash University Press. [Monash Papers on Southeast Asia 71.]
Cleaver, Frances
2005   'The inequality of social capital and the reproduction of chronic poverty', *World Development* 33:893-906.
Clifford, James and George E. Marcus (eds)
1986   *Writing culture: The poetics and politics of ethnography.* Berkeley, CA: University of California Press.
Cohen, Matthew Isaac
2006   *Komedie stamboel: Popular theatre in colonial Indonesia, 1891-1903.* Athens, OH: Center for International Studies. [Ohio University Research in International Studies, Southeast Asia Series 112.]
Cohen, Ronald and Elman R. Service (eds)
1978   *Origins of the state: The anthropology of political evolution.* Philadelphia: Institute for the Study of Human Issues.
Colombijn, Freek
2007   'Toooot! Vroooom! The urban soundscape in Indonesia', *SOJOURN: Journal of Social Issues in Indonesia* 22:255-72.
Coppel, Charles A. (ed.)
2006   *Violent conflicts in Indonesia: Analysis, representation, resolution.* London: Routledge. [Contemporary Southeast Asia Series 7.]
Couldry, Nick
2004   'Media meta-capital: Extending the range of Bourdieu's field theory', in: David Swartz and Vera L. Zolberg (eds), *After Bourdieu: Influence, critique, elaboration*, pp. 165-89. New York: Kluwer.

Cowan, Jane K.
1990   *Dance and the body politic in northern Greece.* Princeton, NJ: Princeton University Press. [Princeton Modern Greek Studies.]

Craig, Timothy J. and Richard King (eds)
2002   *Global goes local: Popular culture in Asia.* Vancouver, BC: University of British Columbia Press.

Curtis, Richard
1997   *People, poets, puppets: Popular performance and the wong cilik in contemporary Java.* PhD thesis, Curtin University of Technology, Perth.

Dahles, Heidi
2001   *Tourism, heritage and national culture in Java: Dilemmas of a local community.* Richmond: Curzon Press, Leiden: IIAS. [Curzon-IIAS Asian Studies Series.]

Dahles, Heidi and Karin Bras
1999   'Entrepreneurs in romance: Tourism in Indonesia', *Annals of Tourism Research* 26:267-93.

Damage earthquake
2006   'Damage from Indonesian earthquake much greater than earlier thought', *Worldbank.* http://web.worldbank.org/WBSITE/EXTERNAL/NEWS/0,,contentMDK:20949343~pagePK:64257043~piPK:437376~theSitePK:4607,00.html (accessed 5-1-2012).

Dawe, Kevin and Andy Bennett
2001   'Introduction: Guitars, cultures, people and places', in: Andy Bennett and Kevin Dawe (eds), *Guitar cultures*, pp. 1-10. Oxford/New York: Berg.

DeNora, Tia
2000   *Music in everyday life.* Cambridge: Cambridge University Press.

Dick, Howard
1990   'Further reflections on the middle class', in: Richard Tanter and Kenneth Young (eds), *The politics of middle class Indonesia*, pp. 63-70. Clayton, VIC: Centre of Southeast Asian Studies, Monash University. [Monash Papers on Southeast Asia 19.]

Diehl, Keila
2002   *Echoes from Dharamsala: Music in the life of a Tibetan refugee community.* Berkeley, CA: University of California.

Bibliography

DINAS
2001   *Statistik Pariwisata tahun 2000 Daerah Istimewa Yogyakarta.* Dinas Pariwisata Daerah Istimewa Yogyakarta.

Doidge, Norman
2007   *The brain that changes itself: Stories of personal triumph from the frontiers of brain science.* New York: Viking.

Echols, John M. and Hassan Shadily
1982   *Kamus Indonesia-Inggris: An Indonesian-English dictionary.* Jakarta: Gramedia.

Emerson, Robert M., Rachel I. Fretz and Linda L. Shaw
1995   *Writing ethnographic fieldnotes.* Chicago: University of Chicago Press.

Epstein, Stephen J.
2000   'Anarchy in the UK, solidarity in the rok: Punk rock comes to Korea', *Acta Koreana* 3:1-34.

Erb, Maribeth, Priyambudi Sulistiyanto and Carole Faucher (eds)
2005   *Regionalism in post-Suharto Indonesia.* London/New York: RoutledgeCurzon. [Contemporary Southeast Asia Series.]

Erlmann, Veit (ed.)
2004   *Hearing cultures: Essays on sound, listening, and modernity.* Oxford: Berg. [Wenner-Gren International Symposium Series.]

Errington, Shelly
1990   'Recasting sex, gender, and power: A theoretical and regional overview', in: Jane Monnig Atkinson and Shelly Errington (eds), *Power and difference: Gender in island Southeast Asia*, pp. 1-58. Stanford, CA: Stanford University Press.

Eyerman, Ron and Andrew Jamison
1998   *Music and social movements: Mobilizing traditions in the twentieth century.* Cambridge: University of Cambridge. [Cambridge Cultural Social Studies.]

Feld, Steven
2003   'A rainforest acoustemology', in: Michael Bull and Les Back (eds), *The auditory culture reader*, pp. 223-39. Oxford/New York: Berg. [Sensory Formations.]

Field, John
2003   *Social capital.* London: Routledge.

Finnegan, Ruth
1989   *The hidden musicians: Music-making in an English town.* Cambridge: Cambridge University Press.

Foulcher, Keith
1990 'The construction of an Indonesian national culture: Patterns of hegemony and resistance', in: Arief Budiman (ed.), *State and civil society in Indonesia*, pp. 301-20. Clayton, VIC: Centre of Southeast Asian Studies, Monash University. [Monash Papers on Southeast Asia 22.]
2004 'Community and the Metropolis: *Lenong, Nyai Dasima* and the new New Order'. Asia Research Institute, National University of Singapore. [Working Paper 20.] http://www.ari.nus.edu.sg/docs/wps/wps04_020.pdf (accessed 12-6-2012).

Frederick, William H.
1982 'Rhoma Irama and the dangdut style: Aspects of contemporary Indonesian popular culture', *Indonesia* 34:103-130.

Frith, Simon
1987 'Towards an aesthetic of popular music', in: Richard Leppert and Susan McClary (eds), *Music and society: The politics of composition, performance and reception*, pp. 133-50. Cambridge: Cambridge University Press.

Geertz, Clifford
1960 *The religion of Java*. Glencoe: Free Press of Glencoe.
1973 *The interpretation of cultures: Selected essays*. New York: Basic Books.

Gemert, Hanneke van, Esther van Genugten and Heidi Dahles
1999 'Tukang becak: The pedicab men of Yogyakarta', in: Heidi Dahles and Karin Bras (eds), *Tourism & small entrepreneurs: Development, national policy and entrepreneurial culture: Indonesian cases*, pp. 97-111. New York: Cognizant Communication Corporation. [Tourism Dynamics.]

Giddens, Anthony
1984 *The constitution of society: Outline of the theory of structuration*. Cambridge: Polity Press, Oxford: Blackwell.

Gomes, Alberto
2007 *Modernity and Malaysia: Settling the Menraq forest nomads*. London: Routledge. [The Modern Anthropology of South-East Asia.]

Guinness, Patrick
1986 *Harmony and hierarchy in a Javanese kampung*. Singapore: Oxford University Press. [Asian Studies Association of Australia, Southeast Asia Publications Series 11.].

Hadiz, Vedi R. and Daniel Dhakidae (eds)
2005 *Social science and power in Indonesia*. Singapore: Institute of Southeast Asian Studies, Jakarta: Equinox. [Celebrating Indonesia.]

Hanan, David and Basoeki Koesasi
2011 'Betawi modern: Songs and films of Benyamin S from Jakarta in the 1970s: Further dimensions of Indonesian popular culture', *Indonesia* 91:35-76.

Hannerz, Ulf
1996 *Transnational connections: Culture, people, places.* London/ New York: Routledge.

Harmunah, S. Mus
1987 *Musik keroncong: Sejarah, gaya dan perkembangan.* Yogyakarta: Pusat Musik Liturgi.

Hatley, Barbara
1999 'Cultural expression and social transformation in Indonesia', in: Arief Budiman, Barbara Hatley, Damien Kingsbury (eds), *Reformasi: Crisis and change in Indonesia*, pp. 267-86. Clayton, VIC: Monash Asia Institute. [Monash Papers on Southeast Asia 50.]
2008 *Javanese performances on an Indonesian stage.* Singapore: NUS Press.

Hefner, Robert W. (ed.)
2001 *The politics of multiculturalism: Pluralism and citizenship in Malaysia, Singapore, and Indonesia.* Honolulu: University of Hawai'i Press.

Heryanto, Ariel
1996 'Bahasa dan kuasa: Tatapan postmodernisme', in: Yudi Latif and Idi Subandy Ibrahim (eds), *Bahasa dan kekuasaan: Politik wacana di panggung Orde Baru*, pp. 94-103. Bandung: Mizan.
2008 'Pop culture and competing identities', in: Ariel Heryanto (ed.), *Popular culture in Indonesia: Fluid identities in post-authoritarian politics*, pp. 1-36. London/New York: Routledge. [Media, Culture and Social Change in Asia 15.]

Hill, David T. and Krishna Sen
2000 *Media, culture and politics in Indonesia.* Melbourne: Oxford University Press.
2005 *The Internet in Indonesia's new democracy.* London/New York: Routledge. [Asia's Transformations.]

Honna, Jun
2003 *Military politics and democratization in Indonesia.* London/ New York: RoutledgeCurzon. [Research on Southeast Asia, Rethinking Southeast Asia 4.]

Howes, David (ed.)
1990   *The varieties of sensory experience: A sourcebook in the anthropology of the senses.* Toronto: University of Toronto Press. [Anthropological Horizons 1.]

Inda, Jonathon X. and Renato Rosaldo
2002   'Introduction: A world in motion', in: Jonathan Xavier Inda and Renato Rosaldo (eds), *The anthropology of globalization: A reader,* pp. 1-34. Malden, MA: Blackwell. [Blackwell Readers in Anthropology 1.]

Jurriëns, Edwin and Jeroen de Kloet (eds)
2007   *Cosmopatriots: On distant belongings and close encounters.* Amsterdam/New York: Rodopi. [Thamyris Intersecting: Place, Sex, and Race 16.]

Kahn, Joel S.
1988   'Ideology and social structure in Indonesia', in: John G. Taylor and Andrew Turton (eds), *Sociology of 'developing societies': Southeast Asia,* pp. 181-90. New York: Monthly Review Press. [First published 1978.]
1995   *Culture, multiculture, postculture.* London: Sage.
2003   'Anthropology as cosmopolitan practice?', *Anthropological Theory* 3:403-15.

Kartomi, Margaret J.
1973   'Music and trance in Central Java', *Ethnomusicology* 17:163-208.
1998   'From kroncong to dangdut: The development of the popular music in Indonesia', in: Franz Foedermayr and Ladislav Burlas (eds), *Ethnologische, historische und systematische Musikwissenschaft,* pp. 145-66. Bratislava: Institut für Musikwissenschaft der Slowakischen Akademie der Wissenschaften.

Keeler, Ward
1987   *Javanese shadow plays, Javanese selves.* Princeton, NJ: Princeton University Press.
1990   'Speaking of gender in Java', in: Jane Monnig Atkinson and Shelly Errington (eds), *Power and difference: Gender in island Southeast Asia,* pp. 127-52. Stanford, CA: Stanford University Press.

Kristiansen, Stein
2003   'Violent youth groups in Indonesia: The cases of Yogyakarta and Nusa Tenggara Barat', *SOJOURN: Journal of Social Issues in Southeast Asia* 8:110-38.

| Bibliography

Kunst, Jaap
1968 *Hindu-Javanese musical instruments.* The Hague: Nijhoff. [KITLV, Translation Series 12.] [Originally published as *Hindoe-Javaansche muziek-instrumenten, speciaal die van Oost-Java.* Bandoeng: Koninklijk Bataviaasch Genootschap van Kunsten en Wetenschappen, 1927.]

Lane, Jeremy F.
2000 *Pierre Bourdieu: A critical introduction.* London: Pluto Press. [Modern European Thinkers.]

Lash, Scott and John Urry
1987 *The end of organised capitalism.* Cambridge: Polity Press.

Latour, Bruno and Steve Woolgar
1979 *Laboratory life: The social construction of scientific facts.* Beverly Hills: Sage. [Sage Library of Social Research 80.]

Leeuwen, Lizzy van
2011 *Lost in mall: An ethnography of middle-class Jakarta in the 1990s.* Leiden: KITLV Press. [Verhandelingen 255.]

Lindsay, Jennifer
1992 *Javanese gamelan: Traditional orchestra of Indonesia.* Second edition. Singapore: Oxford University Press. [First edition 1979.]

Lockard, Craig A.
1998 *Dance of life: Popular music and politics in Southeast Asia.* Honolulu: University of Hawai'i Press.

Luckens-Bull, Ronald A.
2001 'Two sides of the same coin: Modernity and tradition in Islamic education in Indonesia', *Anthropology and Education Quarterly* 32:305-72.

MacClancy, Jeremy and Chris McDonough (eds)
1996 *Popularizing anthropology.* London/New York: Routledge.

McIntosh, Jonathan
2010 'Dancing to a disco beat?: Children, teenagers, and the localizing of popular music in Bali', *Asian Music* 41:1-35.

Mandal, Sumit
2003 'Creativity in protest: Arts workers and the recasting of politics and society in Indonesia and Malaysia', in: Ariel Heryanto and Sumit K. Mandal (eds), *Challenging authoritarianism in Southeast Asia: Comparing Indonesia and Malaysia,* pp. 177-208. New York/London: RoutledgeCurzon.

Manuel, Peter
1988 *Popular musics of the non-Western world: An introductory survey.* New York: Oxford University Press.

Marianto, M. Dwi
2001 *Surrealisme Yogyakarta*. Yogyakarta: Merapi.
Martin, Daniel
1999 'Power play and party politics: The significance of raving', *Journal of Popular Culture* 32:77-99.
Meintjes, Louise
2003 *Sound of Africa!: Making music Zulu in a South African studio*. Durham, NC/London: Duke University Press.
Mrázek, Jan
1999 'Javanese wayang kulit in the times of comedy: Clown scenes, innovation, and the performance's being in the present world. Part One', *Indonesia* 68:38-128.
Mujiyano
1985 'Pelacuran di Pasarkembang'. MA thesis, Gadjah Mada University, Yogyakarta.
Mulder, Niels
1996 *Inside Southeast Asia: Religion, everyday life, cultural change*. Amsterdam/Kuala Lumpur: Pepin Press.
Mundayat, Aris Arif
2005 *Ritual and politics in New Order Indonesia: A study of discourse and counter-discourse in Indonesia*. PhD thesis, Swinburne University of Technology, Melbourne.
Munir
2003 'The future of the civil-military relationship in Indonesia', in: Arief Budiman and Damien Kingsbury (eds), *Indonesia: The uncertain transition*, pp. 70-96. Adelaide: Crawford House Publishing.
Murray, Alison J.
1991 *No money, no honey: A study of street traders and prostitutes in Jakarta*. Singapore: Oxford University Press.
Nakagawa, Shin
2000 *Musik dan kosmos: Sebuah pengantar etnomusikologi*. Jakarta: Yayasan Obor Indonesia.
Nayak, Anoop
2003 *Race, place and globalization: Youth cultures in a changing world*. Oxford: Berg.
Nederveen Pieterse, Jan
2004 *Globalization and culture: Global mélange*. Lanham, MD: Rowman and Littlefield.
Newland, Lynda
2000 'Under the banner of Islam: Mobilising religious identities in West Java', *The Australian Journal of Anthropology* 11:199-223.

Ng, Stephanie Sook-Ling
2005 'Performing the "Filipino" at the crossroads: Filipino bands in five-star hotels throughout Asia', *Modern Drama* 48:272-96.

Nicolai, Jamie and Charlie Hillsmith
2002 *Indonesia – Art, activism and rock'n'roll.* Documentary Film. Australia: SBS/The House of Red Monkey.

Pachet, François, Pierre Roy and Daniel Cazaly
2000 'A combinatorial approach to content-based music selection', *Sony Computer Science Laboratory*. http://www.csl.sony.fr/downloads/papers/1999/pachet99c.pdf (accessed 5-1-2012)

Palumbo-Liu, David
1997 'Introduction: Unhabituated habituses', in: David Palumbo-Liu and Hans Ulrich Gumbrecht (eds), *Streams of cultural capital: Transnational cultural studies*, pp. 1-21. Stanford, CA: Stanford University Press. [First edition 1993.]

Palumbo-Liu, David and Hans Ulrich Gumbrecht (eds)
1997 *Streams of cultural capital: Transnational cultural studies.* Stanford, CA: Stanford University Press. [Originally published in *Stanford Literature Review* 10, 1993.]

Peacock, James L.
1968 *Rites of modernization: Symbolic and social aspects of Indonesian proletarian drama.* Chicago: University of Chicago Press. [Symbolic Anthropology.]

Pemberton, John
1994 *On the subject of 'Java'.* Ithaca, NY: Cornell University Press.

Perlez, Jane
2003 'Saudis quietly promote strict Islam in Indonesia', *New York Times*, 5 July.

Perlman, Marc
1999 'The traditional Javanese performing arts in the twilight of the New Order: Two letters from Solo', *Indonesia* 68:1-37.

Pierson, Christopher
1996 *The modern state.* London: Routledge. [Key Ideas.]

Pigeaud, Th.
2003 'The northern palace square in Yogyakarta', in: Stuart Robson (ed.), *The Kraton: Selected essays on Javanese courts.* Translated by Rosemary Robson-McKillop, pp. 1-11. Leiden: KITLV Press. [Translation Series 28.] [Originally published as 'De noorder aloen-aloen te Jogjakarta', *Djåwå* 20, 1940, pp. 176-84.]

Pioquinto, Ceres
1995 'Dangdut at Sekaten: Female representations in live performance', *Review of Indonesian and Malaysian Affairs* (*RIMA*) 29:59-89.

Piper, Suzan and Sawung Jabo
1987 'Indonesian music from the 50s to the 80s', *Prisma* 43:25-37.

Press closures
1995 'Indonesia: Press closures one year later', *Human Rights Watch*. http://www.hrw.org/reports/1995/Indonesi2.htm (accessed 7-12-2011).

Putnam, Robert D.
2000 *Bowling alone: The collapse and revival of American community.* New York: Simon and Shuster.

Richter, Max M.
2004 'Race, place and globalization: Youth cultures in a changing world' (Book Review), *Thesis Eleven* 78:135-8.
2006 'Grounded cosmopolitans and the bureaucratic field: Musical performance at two Yogyakarta state institutions', *SOJOURN: Journal of Social Issues in Southeast Asia* 21:178-203.
2008a 'Other worlds in Yogyakarta: From jatilan to electronic music', in: Ariel Heryanto (ed.), *Popular culture in Indonesia: Fluid identities in post-authoritarian politics*, pp. 164-81. London/New York: Routledge. [Media, Culture and Social Change in Asia 15.]
2008b 'Musical sexualisation and the gendered habitus', *Indonesia and the Malay World* 36:21-45.

Ricklefs, M.C.
2001 *A history of modern Indonesia since c.1200.* Third edition. Basingstoke: Palgrave. [First edition 1981.]

Riley, Pamela
1988 'Road culture of international long-term budget travelers', *Annals of Tourism Research* 15:313-328.

Robertson, Roland
1995 'Glocalization: Time-space and homogeneity-heterogeneity: An introduction', in: Mike Featherstone, Scott Lash and Roland Robertson (eds), *Global modernities*, pp. 1-24. London: Sage. [Theory, Culture and Society.]

Robinson, Kathryn May
1986 *Stepchildren of progress: The political economy of development in an Indonesian mining town.* Albany, NY: State University of New York Press. [SUNY Series in the Anthropology of Works.]

Robson, Stuart (ed.)
2003 *The Kraton: Selected essays on Javanese courts*. Translated by Rosemary Robson-McKillop. Leiden: KITLV Press. [Translation Series 28.]

Ryaas Rasyid, M.
2003 'Regional autonomy and local politics in Indonesia', in: Edward Aspinall and Greg Fealy (eds), *Local power and politics in Indonesia: Decentralisation & democratisation*, pp. 63-71. Singapore: Institute of Southeast Asian Studies. [Indonesia Update Series.]

Sahlins, Marshall
1972 *Stone-age economics*. Chicago: Aldine.

Sasongko, Haryo
2001 'Visi, misi dan strategi pembangunan kota Yogyakarta'. [Manuscript.]

Scanlon, Christopher
2004 'What's wrong with social capital?', *Arena Journal* 8:1-12. [Blue Book Supplement.]

Sedyawati, Edi (ed.)
1998 *Indonesian heritage: Performing arts*. Singapore: Archipelago Press.

Shafer, R. Murray (ed.)
1977 *Five village soundscapes*. Vancouver: ARC Publications. [The Music of the Environment Series 4.]

Shils, Edward
1982 *The constitution of society*. With a new introduction by the author. Chicago: University of Chicago Press. [The Heritage of Sociology.]

Siegel, James T.
1986 *Solo in the New Order: Language and hierarchy in an Indonesian city*. Princeton, NJ: Princeton University Press.

Simatupang, Lono L.
1996 '"Dangdut is very... very... very Indonesia": The search for cultural nationalism in Indonesian modern popular music', *Bulletin Antropologi* 11:55-74.

Simpson, Timothy A.
2000 'Streets, sidewalks, stores, and stories', *Journal of Contemporary Ethnography* 29:682-716.

Slone, Thomas H.
2003 *Prokem: An analysis of a Jakartan slang*. Oakland, CA: Masalai Press.

Solvang, Ingvild
2002 '"Migrants cannot have success": Street youth as cultural agents in Jogjakarta, Java'. MA Thesis, University of Oslo.
Stokes, Martin
1994 'Introduction', in: Martin Stokes (ed.), *Ethnicity, identity and music: The musical construction of place*, pp. 1-27. Oxford: Berg. [Ethnic Identity Series.]
Straw, Will
1991 'Systems of articulation, logics of change: Communities and scenes in popular music', *Cultural Studies* 5:368-88.
Street children
2005 'Promotion of improved learning opportunities for street children in Indonesia', *UNESCO*. http://unesdoc.unesco.org/images/0013/001395/139562eo.pdf (accessed 7-12-2011).
Strong, Geoff
2004 'Under the veil', *The Age*, 18 September.
Sullivan, John
1992 *Local government and community in Java: An urban case-study*. Singapore: Oxford University Press. [South-East Asian Social Science Monographs.]
Sullivan, Norma
1994 *Masters and managers: A study of gender relations in urban Java*. St Leonards, NSW: Allen and Unwin. [Asian Studies Association of Australia, Women in Asia Publication Series.]
Supanggah, Rahayu
2003 'Campur sari: A reflection', *Asian Music* 34:1-20.
Sutton, R. Anderson
1996 'Interpreting electronic sound technology in the contemporary Javanese soundscape', *Ethnomusicology* 40:249-68.
2009 'Asia/Indonesia', in: Jeff Todd Titon (ed.), *Worlds of music: An introduction to the music of the world's peoples*. Fifth edition, pp. 213-40. New York: Schirmer Books. [First edition 1984.]
Swartz, David
1997 *Culture and power: The sociology of Pierre Bourdieu*. Chicago: University of Chicago Press.
Tajfel, Henri and John Turner
1979 'An integrative theory of intergroup conflict', in: William G. Austin and Stephen Worchel (eds), *The social psychology of intergroup relations*, pp. 33-47. Monterey, CA: Brooks-Cole.

Thung, Ju Lan, Yekti Maunati and Peter Mulok Kedit
2004 *The (re)construction of the 'Pan Dayak' identity in Kalimantan and Sarawak: A study on minority's identity, ethnicity and nationality.* Jakarta: Pusat Penelitian (Puslit) Kemasyarakatan dan Kebudayaan, Lembaga Ilmu Pengetahuan Indonesia (PMB-LIPI).

Turino, Thomas
2000 *Nationalists, cosmopolitans, and popular music in Zimbabwe.* Chicago: University of Chicago Press. [Chicago Studies in Ethnomusicology.]

Turner, Victor
1982 *From ritual to theatre: The human seriousness of play.* New York: PAJ Publications.

Violence in Ambon
1999 'Indonesia/East Timor: The violence in Ambon', *Human Rights Watch.* http://www.hrw.org/reports/1999/03/01/indonesiaeasttimor-violence-ambon (accessed 7-12-2011).

Wallach, Jeremy
2002 'Exploring class, nation and xenocentrism in Indonesian cassette retail outlets', *Indonesia* 74:79-102.
2004 'Dangdut trendy', *Inside Indonesia* 78:30.
2008 *Modern noise, fluid genres: Popular music in Indonesia, 1997-2001.* Madison, WI: University of Wisconsin Press. [New Perspectives in Southeast Asian Studies.]

Weintraub, Andrew N.
2010 *Dangdut stories: A social and musical history of Indonesia's most popular music.* New York: Oxford University Press.

Werbner, Pnina
1999 'Global pathways, working-class cosmopolitans and the creation of transnational ethnic worlds', *Social Anthropology* 7:17-35.
2004 'Cosmopolitans, anthropologists and labour migrants: Deconstructing transnational cultural promiscuity', in: *Ethnicities, diasporas and 'grounded' cosmopolitanisms in Asia*, pp. 10-25. N.p.: Asia Research Institute. [Proceedings of the Asia Research Institute Workshop on Identities, Nations and Cosmopolitan Practice: Interrogating the Work of Pnina and Richard Werbner, Singapore, 29 April 2004.]

Werbner, Richard
2002 'Cosmopolitan ethnicity, entrepreneurship and the nation: Minority elites in Botswana', *Journal of Southern African Studies* 28:731-53.

White, Benjamin
1976 'Population, involution and employment in rural Java', *Development and Change* 7:267-90.
Whyte, William Foote
1943 *Street corner society: The social structure of an Italian slum.* Chicago: University of Chicago Press.
Wibawanta, Budi
1998 *Dari shopping centre ke civic centre (Studi tentang perubahan perilaku berbelanja masyarakat kota: Kasus Malioboro Mall dan Ramai Mall Yogyakarta).* Undergraduate thesis, Gadjah Mada University, Yogyakarta.
Wienarti, M.
1968 'Pertundjukan djatilan di Sentolo'. MA thesis, Gadjah Mada University, Yogyakarta.
Williams, J. Patrick
2006 'Authentic identities: Straightedge subculture, music, and the internet', *Journal of Contemporary Ethnography* 35:173-200.
Willis, Paul E.
1978 *Profane culture.* London: Routledge and Kegan Paul.
Wilson, Ian
2010 'The biggest cock: Territoriality, invulnerability and honour amongst Jakarta's gangsters', *Indonesian Studies Working Papers* 13:1-19.
Wong, Kean
1995 'Metallic gleam', in: Hanif Kureishi and Jon Savage (eds), *The Faber book of pop*, pp. 761-66. London: Faber and Faber. [First published 1993.]
Yampolsky, Philip
1989 'Hati yang luka: An Indonesian hit', *Indonesia* 47:1-17.
2001 'Can the traditional arts survive, and should they?', *Indonesia* 71:175-86.
Yogya dalam angka
1998 *Daerah Istimewa Yogyakarta dalam angka 1998.* Yogyakarta: Badan Pusat Statistik Provinsi DI Yogyakarta.
2000 *Daerah Istimewa Yogyakarta dalam angka 2000.* Yogyakarta: Badan Pusat Statistik Provinsi DI Yogyakarta.
Young, Ken
1999 'Consumption, social differentiation and self-definition of the new rich in industrialising Southeast Asia', in: Michael

Pinches (ed.), *Culture and privilege in capitalist Asia*, pp. 56-85. London/New York: Routledge. [The New Rich in Asia Series.]

Zainu'ddin, Ailsa
1968 *A short history of Indonesia*. Melbourne: Cassell.

Zorbaugh, Harvey W.
1929 *Gold coast and slum: A sociological study of Chicago's near North Side*. Chicago: University of Chicago Press.

Zorn, John (ed.)
1999 *Arcana: Musicians on music*. New York: Granary Books.

Zurbuchen, Mary S. (ed.)
2005 *Beginning to remember: The past in the Indonesian present*. Singapore: Singapore University Press, Seattle, WA: University of Washington Press. [Critical Dialogues in Southeast Asian Studies.]

Index

abangan 4, 33
Aceh 147, 168, 172
Ade, Ebiet G. 67
Adorno, Theodor W. 34
Alaska Band 115
Algeria 84, 125
aliran 4, 33, 135 *see also abangan, santri, priyayi*
Ambon 150
Anderson, Benedict R.O'G. 123
angkringan 4, 65, 92, 171
Aniesenchu 92
Appiah, Kwame Anthony 127, 172
Arabic musical influence *see dangdut, gambus, nasyid, qasidah*
Arena, Tina 14
Astro Band 1, 58-60, 78, 90, 97
Attali, Jacques 34

Bambu Resto 98
bangsa 136
Bar Borobudur 51, 74, 98-9, 113-6, 118
barongsai 10
Basuki, Untung 24, 92
Batak 9, 37, 75, 97
Beatles, The 58, 98, 158
Beatty, Andrew 33
becak drivers 7, 9, 16, 31-5, 43-9, 56-7, 60-1, 68-9, 77-80, 135, 175-8, 182-4

Becker, Howard 11
bedug 168
Bee Gees 31
black metal 105
blues 62, 66, 91, 97, 162, 179
Boomerang 41
Bourdieu, Pierre 12, 21-3, 26-8, 34-7, 77, 84-6, 124-6, 131, 134, 137, 153, 159, 166, 175, 184-5 *see also* capital, field, *habitus*
Britpop 63, 72
Brown, James 112-3
Budi Utomo 135
bureaucratic field 124-6, 131, 137, 141, 143, 148-9, 155, 161, 167, 169

Calhoun, Craig 22
Calypso 95
campursari 12-7, 19-20, 26, 33-5, 41-2, 47-8, 50-1, 54-5, 57-8, 60-1, 66-9, 71, 77-9, 83-4, 91, 93, 97, 108-13, 118-9, 125, 132-5, 139-41, 144, 146-8, 153, 158, 163, 166, 171-2, 175-9, 181-2, 184-5
capital 33
– conversion 34, 63, 153, 164-6
– cultural 34-5, 37, 52, 54, 66, 78, 155, 163 *see also* spatial identification
– economic 22, 36-7, 39-40, 74, 78, 96, 117, 134

Index

–social 23, 28, 36-7, 44, 50-2, 67-8, 127, 164-6
–statist *see* bureaucratic field
celumpung see zither
Chicago (band) 14
Clapton, Eric 62
Clifford, James 23
congdut 48
congrock 56
Corea, Chick 14
cosmopolitanism 22-3, 27-8, 32, 119, 124-8, 135, 140-1, 147, 155, 160, 162, 171-2, 175, 181-2, 184-5
country music 71, 150
Cowan, Jane K. 88, 109
cultural globalisation 22, 126

Dahles, Heidi 41, 49-50
dance 10, 13-4, 57, 60-1, 117-8, 134, 137, 146, 151-2, 177, 178, 180 *see also joged*, musical physicalisation
dangdut 10, 12-4, 16, 21, 33, 35, 48, 54, 57, 59-60, 69-70, 78-9, 84, 90-3, 108-11, 113-8, 132, 135, 145-6, 148, 151-2, 158-9, 162-3, 166, 177-8, 184
Daratista, Inul 13
Dayak 74-5, 166
Deep Purple 59, 168
DeNora, Tia 11
Dewa 41, 63, 110
Dick, Howard 41
D'Lloyd 40
Doors, The 63, 66
dukun 105

East Timor 123, 145, 147
electone 89, 91, 162

electronic 103, 106, 118
Emerson, Robert M. 26
Emha Ainun Nadjib (Cak Nun) 168-9, 172, 179
Errington, Shelly 86-7
ethnography 3, 11, 23

Fadholi, Sukri 133-4
Fals, Iwan 16-8, 24, 54, 66, 91, 99, 158
Feith, Herb 168
Field, John 36
Finnegan, Ruth 11
folk/rock 16-7, 33, 54, 92, 98-9, 148, 175-6
Foster, David 14
Foulcher, Keith 123
Fretz, Rachel I. 26
funk 63, 113, 115, 151, 162-3, 166

gambus 12, 19, 157-8, 168 *see also* Orkes Gambus, Jagongan
gamelan 4, 10, 12-4, 16, 26, 33, 50, 54-6, 60, 67, 70, 93-4, 96-7, 113, 132, 134, 139, 141, 158-9, 166, 175-6 *see also wayang kulit, karawitan*
Geertz, Clifford 3-4, 20, 23, 33, 43, 113 *see also aliran*
gender 86-7, 105, 107, 112-3, 115, 119, 152, 184
genre (*also* jenis) 10-3, 16-7, 20-1, 25, 27, 33, 53-4, 60, 68-9, 73-4, 78-9, 83-4, 90-1, 93, 95, 98, 105-10, 112-3, 117-9, 148, 158, 162-3, 167, 172-3, 175-6, 179, 183-4
Gerakan Pemuda Ka'bah (GPK) 9, 65, 143, 182-3

Giddens, Anthony 21
Gombloh 10, 150
grounded cosmopolitanism *see* cosmopolitanism
Guinness, Patrick 39, 41, 43
guitar(s) 1, 13-4, 16-7, 19, 24-5, 31, 33, 50, 53, 55-8, 60, 62-3, 66-8, 72, 74-5, 90-3, 95, 97, 132, 150, 159, 162, 164, 179

habitus 21-3, 26-8, 84-8, 95, 100-1, 103, 113, 117-8, 125, 165, 175, 184
Hamengku Buwono X, Sultan 8, 131, 136, 144, 175, 177-8, 182-3
Hannerz, Ulf 155
hard rock *see* rock
Harno 33, 108
Hawai'i 13
hangout 4-5, 31, 37, 41-3, 45-6, 53-4, 60-1, 64-7, 75, 77-8, 115, 164
heavy metal (British) 13, 17, 40, 97, 136
hip-metal 98, 110, 183
homogenisation 12, 126, 154, 160, 171
Horkheimer, Max 34
Howes, David 23, 86

icik-icik 162
Inda, Jonathon X. 22
Indonesian National Armed Forces 2, 123, 143-54, 161
Institut Agama Islam Negeri (IAIN) *see* Islamic Insitute
inter-generational relations 19, 84-6, 90-1, 98, 104-10, 169-70
Islamic Institute 134, 156-9, 169, 172

Jabo, Sawung 16, 19, 24, 40, 66, 92-3
Jagongan 19, 135, 181-2
Jakarta 1, 5, 8, 10, 19, 40-1, 50, 63, 67, 75, 92, 106, 114, 128, 131, 144, 157
jalanan scene *see musik jalanan*
jam session 65, 74, 91, 97, 151
Japan 14, 39, 59, 62, 95, 135, 151
Jasmati 20
jatilan 12, 87, 103-5, 107, 113, 117-8
Java Tattoo Club
Javanism 4, 19, 33, 35, 84, 110, 113, 128, 133, 139-41, 145, 147, 153, 159, 169, 182
jazz 14, 63, 95, 135, 150, 162, 167, 182, 184
joged 61, 91, 109, 118, 151, 159

Kahn, Joel S. vii, 11, 32, 127, 155, 172
Kamil, Amien 24
Kant, Immanunel 32
karawitan 12, 17, 21, 54-6, 79, 148, 162-3, 177
Kartomi, Margaret 104
Keating, Ronan 41
kejawen see Javanism
Kelompok Penyanyi Jalanan Malioboro (KPJM) 18-20, 24, 92, 110, 136, 151, 179, 182
Kelompok Swara Ratan 179
kendang 13, 19, 55
Kenyeot 20, 157, 181-3
ketoprak 166
Khan, Chaka 14
Kidjo, Angelique 115
Koes Ploes 40, 150
Koesbini, Nowo Ksvara 24

Index

Kravitz, Lenny 62
Kridosono 87, 103, 106-7, 110, 117
Kristiansen, Stein 32
kroncong 10, 12-4, 16-7, 21, 33, 48, 54-8, 60, 69-70, 79, 92-3, 96, 132, 135, 148, 150, 162, 168, 177
Kubro Glow 24, 157, 177, 181, 182-3
Kuda lumping 71, 113
Kyai Kanjeng Orchestra 168-9, 172, 179

langgam Jawa 12-4, 16-7, 54-5, 60, 66, 92, 148, 162-3
Laskar Jihad 9, 143
Latin American music 37, 58-9, 75, 95, 135, 162-3
lesehan 4, 58-9, 161-2
lesung 4
Limp Bizkit 152-3
Lockard, Craig A. 17
Log Zhelebour 106
love, romance (lyrical themes) 13, 16, 63, 66, 90-3, 159, 182

Madura 9, 75, 168
Makahekum, Bram 24
Maluku 143, 172
Manthous 14-6, 24, 91
Marcus, George E. 23
Marley, Bob 67, 137
melayu 93, 139, 158-9, 169
Moby 92
Moerdani, Benny 151
Mulder, Niels 44
Munir 143
Murray, Alison J. 41
musical physicalisation 86-8, 93, 98, 101, 103, 112, 117, 175, 184-5

– detachment engagement 87, 89-101, 107
– other worlds 87, 103-7, 112, 118, 146
– sexualisation 16, 87, 106, 108-17, 134, 159, 177-8
musik jalanan 12, 16-20, 26, 33, 51, 54, 66, 72, 78, 83, 91-2, 110, 144, 148-53, 157, 164-7, 175-6, 179, 181-2, 184-5
mysticism 103, 159, 182

Nadjib, Emma Ainun 115, 168, 172
nasyid 10
nationalism 10, 13, 113, 140-1, 150, 159, 162
neuroplasticity 85
New Order 2-4, 66, 123, 131, 143, 147, 150, 153, 172
North American folk and popular music 17-9, 58, 67, 72-3, 75, 168
NSYNC 152

Oasis 63
Opposite Resto 64-8, 76, 78, 115
Orkes Gambus 158
orkes melayu 13

Pacific musical influence 12-3, 150
Padi 41, 91, 110
Pajeksan 20, 39, 110, 138, 182
Palumbo-Liu, David 34
Papua 168
West Papua 172
Partai Amanat Nasional (PAN) 134
Partai Demokrasi Indonesia-Perjuangan (PDI-P) 138
Partai Indonesia Raya (Parindra) 135

Partai Persatuan Pembangunan (PPP) 138
Pemberton, John 32
pengamen 17, 53-8, 60, 68-9, 78-9, 136, 161-3, 179
perek 51, 62, 83-4, 91, 93, 95-7, 100-1, 115-9, 127
Perhimpunan Indonesia Baru 180
pesinden 12, 108, 139, 162
pesantren 156-7, 182
Pink Floyd 17, 66
Pioquinto, Ceres 13
plesetan 59, 67, 133
Police, The 136
pop lama 56-8, 90-1, 146
pop melayu 93
pop nostalgia see pop lama
power *see* capital
Prada 1, 25, 43, 59, 78, 115
preman 20, 132, 146, 172, 178
Presley, Elvis 98
priyayi 4, 33, 135
punk 10, 104-5
Purawisata 112, 114, 116, 118, 177
Putnam, Robert D. 37

qasidah 19, 135, 158, 177, 180 *see also gambus*, Jagongan

Radikal Corps 106
Radiohead 162
rakyat 10
rebana 139, 157
Red Hot Chilli Peppers 62
Reformasi 2-3, 32, 41, 44, 98, 123, 144, 148
reggae 33, 40, 74, 79, 92, 135-7, 166, 182

regional autonomy 124, 131, 141
religion 25, 33, 125, 159, 168-9, 171-2, 183
Resto 31, 43, 51, 56-7, 60, 65-6, 72, 74-5, 183
Riau 168
RiF 41
rock 1, 11, 17, 34-5, 40, 48, 57, 64, 77, 79, 84, 106, 108, 110-1, 113-5, 118, 135-6, 138-9, 146, 152, 158, 162-3, 166-8, 177, 179, 181 *see also congrock*, folk/rock
rock and roll *see* rock
Roem 132
Rosaldo, Renato 22

Sahlins, Marshall 37
santri 4, 33
Sekar Wuyung 42, 48, 69-72, 177-8
sekaten 3, 13, 176-7, 179
senggok 93
senses, sensuality 3, 23, 92, 100, 134-5, 146, 152 *see also habitus*
September 11 2, 9, 96
Shaw, Linda L. 26
Sheila on 7 41, 66
Shower Band 31, 42, 69, 72-7, 165, 167
Sigma Dance 167
singing 1, 31, 59-60, 62, 74-5, 91, 93, 96-7, 106, 111-2, 118, 146, 151, 159, 164, 178
Slank 41, 106
Soeharto 2-4, 32, 40-1, 66, 115, 123, 131, 143, 147, 150-1, 161, 172
Sosro Boys 43, 51, 60, 62, 64, 66, 74, 78, 91, 116 *see also* street guides

Sosrowijayan 25, 31-2, 35, 39-45, 48-51, 53, 55-60, 62, 64, 67-70, 72, 74, 77, 79-80, 83-5, 90, 100, 110-1, 114-5, 117-9, 135-6, 138, 165, 167, 176-7, 182-4
soul 110-1, 113
spatial identification 34-5, 41, 55-6, 60, 64, 67, 79, 103, 128, 162, 165
see also nationalism
Sting 99
street guides 16-7, 25-6, 31-5, 37, 40-3, 45, 48-54, 57, 60, 62, 64, 66-9, 71-3, 77-8, 80, 83, 90-1, 115, 119, 128, 136, 139, 167, 176-7, 179, 181-2
street music *see musik jalanan*
Sugiyanto, Suharso 92-3
Sukarnoputri, Megawati 2, 31, 134
Sullivan, Norma 86-7, 105
Sultan's Palace (*kraton*) 5, 61, 124-7, 161, 175-82, 185
Sunda 13, 57
Surakarta (Solo) 13, 96, 178
Sutrisno, Sujud 19, 179

Tajfel, Henri 21
Taman Ria 113-4, 116, 177
techno 98, 106
Tentara Nasional Indonesia (TNI) *see* Indonesian National Armed Forces
Tombo Sutris 24, 111, 132-5, 144, 146-7, 172, 178, 182-4
tongkrongan see hangout

TransWeb 42, 60-6, 68, 74, 78, 115
Turino, Thomas 182
Turner, John 21
Turner, Victor 87
Tyas 20, 24, 67-8, 92, 132, 137, 149, 177, 181-3

U2 66, 136
underground 105, 158
Universitas Gadjah Mada (UGM) 24, 152, 156, 160-1, 164-7, 169, 172, 181

violence, non-violence 2, 3, 12, 28, 32, 36, 65-6, 80, 124, 126-7, 134, 137, 143, 158-9, 182-3, 185
– militant youth groups 9, 32, 143-4, 150, 182-3
Visnu 20, 70-1, 111, 113, 145

Wacquant, Loïc 21
Wahid, Abdurrahman (Gus Dur) 2, 31, 123, 134, 168
Wallach, Jeremy 67, 93, 162
wayang kulit 16, 138-40, 175, 177, 180
Williams, Robbie 115

Yampolsky, Philip 13
Yanto 20, 132-5, 144, 146-7, 154, 178, 183
Yayi 95, 97, 111-4, 118, 152

zither 55, 60, 162

www.ingramcontent.com/pod-product-compliance
Lightning Source LLC
Chambersburg PA
CBHW051522230426
43668CB00012B/1706